C000095487

THE AGE OF SPECTACI

This book explores death in contemporary society – or more precisely, in the 'spectacular age' – by moving beyond classic studies of death that emphasised the importance of the death taboo and death denial to examine how we now 'do' death. Unfolding the notion of 'spectacular death' as characteristic of our modern approach to death and dying, it considers the new mediation or mediatisation of death and dying; the commercialisation of death as a 'marketable commodity' used to sell products, advance artistic expression or provoke curiosity; the re-ritualisation of death and the growth of new ways of finding meaning through commemorating the dead; the revolution of palliative care; and the specialisation surrounding death, particularly in relation to scholarship. Presenting a range of case studies that shed light on this new understanding of death in contemporary culture, *The Age of Spectacular Death* will appeal to scholars of sociology, cultural and media studies, psychology and anthropology with interests in death and dying.

Michael Hviid Jacobsen is Professor of Sociology at Aalborg University, Denmark. He is the editor of *The Poetics of Crime, Nostalgia Now, Postmortal Society, The Contemporary Goffman* and *Critical and Cultural Interactionism*, and co-editor of *The Sociology of Zygmunt Bauman, Encountering the Everyday, The Transformation of Modernity, Utopia: Social Theory and the Future, Liquid Criminology, Imaginative Methodologies: The Poetic Imagination in the Social Sciences, Towards a Criminology of Emotions, Exploring Grief: Towards a Sociology of Sorrow* and *Death in Contemporary Popular Culture*.

THE AGE OF
SPECTACULAR DEATH

Edited by Michael Hviid Jacobsen

Routledge
Taylor & Francis Group

LONDON AND NEW YORK

First published 2021
by Routledge
2 Park Square, Milton Park, Abingdon, Oxon OX14 4RN

and by Routledge
52 Vanderbilt Avenue, New York, NY 10017

Routledge is an imprint of the Taylor & Francis Group, an informa business

© 2021 selection and editorial matter, Michael Hviid Jacobsen; individual chapters, the contributors

British Library Cataloguing-in-Publication Data
A catalogue record for this book is available from the British Library

Library of Congress Cataloging-in-Publication Data
A catalog record has been requested for this book

ISBN: 978-0-367-36826-5 (hbk)
ISBN: 978-0-367-36827-2 (pbk)
ISBN: 978-0-429-35155-6 (ebk)

Typeset in Bembo
by Deanta Global Publishing Services, Chennai, India

CONTENTS

PREFACE AND ACKNOWLEDGEMENTS

In the beginning was death ...

Life is from the very outset marked by mortality. Although the specific time and date of our individual death is always until further notice (unless a doctor starts explaining to us how little time is in fact left), everything brought into life will at some point in time pass on into the world of death. This is the way of all flesh. Ever since I was a young man thinking about the meaning and purpose of life, and even well before I had obtained the academic training to find the right words to express my thoughts, I have subscribed to what Ernest Becker once in his classic book *The Denial of Death* (1973) called 'the morbidly-minded argument'. According to this argument, our fear of death is natural and is present in everyone; it is the basic fear that influences all other fears, and it is, in Becker's perspective, a fear from which no-one is immune, no matter how disguised or denied it may be. Besides being a thorn in the side of human beings, to Becker this natural and ever-present fear of death was, however, also the wellspring of human ingenuity, creativity and attempts at trying to make life lived in the shadow of death meaningful. So, to subscribers of the 'morbidly-minded argument', death is a natural occurrence to be expected in life, and although we try to avoid thinking about it, it is our very fear of death that provides life with its depth and direction. Death is indeed an indelible part of life, and we are all just anxiously waiting for it to happen.

* * *

In the end awaits death ...

Life is one long process of gradual deprivation throughout which we lose people with whom we have shared time, smiles, handshakes, caresses, thoughts, arguments, food and drink. This book is dedicated to the living and loving memory of three good colleagues and dear friends who have all passed away within the past few years: Zygmunt Bauman (1925–2017), Michael C. Kearl (1949–2015) and Keith Tester (1960–2019). It was my privilege and luck to have known them, and each in their way passed on so much knowledge and wisdom to me, for which I am forever grateful. It is indeed strange to think that they are no more. It feels as if it were only yesterday that we enjoyed each other's company, discussing matters of sociology, football, poetry, popular culture, politics, life and death. It is also strange to think that one day within the no longer so distant future, these very words will have been written by a 'recently deceased person' and that in a lifetime most of what has been written here was written in 'the past'. Life is indeed short and precious, and precious because short. Life is in this way a learning process that mercilessly teaches us that death is part and parcel of it.

I would like to take this opportunity to extend my gratitude to the many contributors to this book who have here shared their insightful ideas and experiences of death and for engaging with my notion of 'spectacular death'. Moreover, I wish to thank my two usual collaborators at Routledge, Senior Commissioning Editor Neil Jordan and Senior Editorial Assistant Alice Salt. It has, as always, been a pleasure working with you and seeing what was initially only scattered words turning into a completed book and thereby bringing life into the world.

Michael Hviid Jacobsen
Aalborg University, Winter 2020

NOTES ON CONTRIBUTORS

Arnar Árnason is Senior Lecturer in Social Anthropology in the Department of Anthropology, University of Aberdeen, Scotland. His research focuses on the topics of death, grief, emotions, memorialisation, subjectivity and power.

Jacque Lynn Foltyn is Professor of Sociology, COLS, National University, La Jolla, California, United States. A social theorist and media expert, her research focuses on popular culture, death and culture, celebrity deaths, grief and fashion. She has appeared on *NBC Today*, *CNN*, *BBC* and *NPR* and has been interviewed by *The New York Times*.

Michael Hviid Jacobsen is Professor of Sociology at the Department of Sociology and Social Work, Aalborg University, Denmark. His research is concerned with topics such as: crime, deviance, utopia, ethics, emotions, death and dying, immortality, palliative care and social theory.

Elaine Kasket is a psychotherapeutic practitioner, independent scholar, keynote speaker and author. Her research is concerned with death and dying in the online sphere, digital ethics and privacy.

Michael C. Kearl was Professor of Sociology at Trinity University, San Antonio, Texas, United States. His research focused on collective memory, the social observances given to last survivors and the rise of political apologies for past injustices. He passed away in 2015.

Dina Khapaeva is Professor of Russian at the School of Modern Languages, Georgia Institute of Technology, United States. Her research comprises death studies, historical memory and Slavic Studies.

Carlo Leget is Professor of Care Ethics at the University of Humanistic Studies in Utrecht, the Netherlands. At the same university, he holds an Endowed Chair in Palliative Care, established by the Netherlands Comprehensive Cancer Organisation (IKNL) and the Association Hospice Care Netherlands (AHZN). His research focuses on care ethics, palliative care, spirituality and the contemporary art of dying.

Peter Clement Lund is a PhD fellow at the Department of Psychology and Communication, Aalborg University, Denmark. His research is concerned with topics such as: grief, death, psychiatric diagnoses, emotions, critical theory and social theory.

Tal Morse teaches at the Department of Photographic Communication at Hadassah Academic College in Jerusalem, Israel. His research is concerned with topics such as: media ethics, representations of suffering, death studies, digital remains, and discourse analysis and visual culture.

Ruth Penfold-Mounce is Senior Lecturer of Criminology at the Department of Sociology, University of York, United Kingdom. Her research is concerned with topics such as: celebrity, popular culture, death, corpses and crime.

Anders Petersen is Associate Professor of Sociology in the Department of Sociology and Social Work at the Aalborg University, Denmark. His research is concerned with topics such as: social theory, diagnostic culture, grief and emotional aspects of the climate crisis.

Rosie Smith is Lecturer in Sociology and Criminology at the Department of Social Sciences, York St John University, United Kingdom. Her research is concerned with topics such as: criminal justice, media, crime, death and social theory.

Daniel William Mackenzie Wright is Lecturer in Tourism Management in the Lancashire School of Business and Enterprise at the University of Central Lancashire, Preston, United Kingdom. His research focuses on the study of society and tourism, presenting scenario narratives for the future of the travel industry and tourists and applying trend analysis methods.

INTRODUCTION

The whole world is watching – death in a spectacular age

Michael Hviid Jacobsen

Death in life

This book starts out with the bold suggestion that death is the most important thing in life. As once expressed by Belgian author and playwright Maurice
Maeterlinck in his booklet *La mort*: 'Death and death alone is what we must
consult about life ... For us, death is the one event that counts in our life and
in our universe' (Maeterlinck 1911/2015:4–5). To many, this will undoubtedly
read not only as an eerie and unpleasant suggestion, but also as a gross exaggeration – because to them life is the most important thing, and life is what matters.
Avoiding any lengthy and, for our purposes, unnecessary philosophical discussion of the relative importance of life versus death, one may suggest that death is
indeed *one* of the most important things in life – alongside all the other elements
and experiences making life meaningful, rich and precious. The reason why
death matters in life is not only the simple fact that we all will and must eventually die, but also that death – the knowledge of and experience with it – unavoid-
ably leaves a mark on the way we decide to live our lives. Even when we are alive,
death is in an odd way still there – something which has puzzled philosophers
and poets throughout thousands of years. We *live with* death, we *think about* death,
we – even when we do not know it – *prepare for* death, and we thus constantly live
our lives towards death and in the valley of the shadow of death. This, however,
is not something we only do individually. Our thoughts, feelings, actions and
plans regarding death are after not all *that* idiosyncratic. Billions of people have
lived and died before us (and at the moment, billions of people, like you and
I, live with the knowledge of the inevitability of their own deaths) – and they
have also thought about and prepared for death. However, there is no doubt that
the historical, cultural and societal context in which we live our lives impacts
the way we understand and relate to death. Thus, what scholars and researchers

call our 'death culture' or 'death mentality' is indeed a collective phenomenon, shared by thousands, if not millions, of people. This does not mean that we as individuals cannot entertain original or peculiar ideas about death and dying – in fact, most often we may tend to think that the way we contemplate death (our fears, worries, wishes and decisions) is something unique and private – something others will not be able to understand. The reason for this is perhaps the fact that we nowadays only seldom confess or share our innermost feelings and thoughts about death with others. There seems to be something shameful and embarrassing about being afraid of death. Even though each death is unique, death as such, however, is not. Besides being born, having to die is the only universal certainty in human life. In this way, despite all of our uniquenesses, individualities and singularities, we are all just puppets in the theatre of death.

Death is a historical constant in human life. It has been there all along and it will, in all likelihood, also in the future continue to constitute an irremovable cornerstone of human existence. Everybody who has ever lived has also at some point – and within a rather predictable and limited time horizon – died again. Of all those billions of people who have lived and died throughout human history, no-one (at least in the end) has ever returned in order to live on. Death is, and therefore continues to be, an incontrovertible fact of life. Even though death (or at least, actual death) is in many ways perhaps more invisible in contemporary society as compared to prehistoric cultures, it is indeed still there, most often submerged, but sometimes – often unexpectedly, violently and painfully – breaking through the thin water surface and spreading like ripples throughout our individual and collective consciousness and life experience. Despite its absolute normality and naturalness (after all, what is more normal and natural than that we are all born and that we will all die?), death is often seen as something deviant, alien and unfamiliar that we would prefer to expel once and for all from the world of the living. Despite its ubiquity, death thus remains a conundrum to human beings – the only creatures on this earth capable of contemplating their own death (Bauman 1992). After all, what is more unimaginable to the human being than the unthinkable thought of the irrevocable disappearance of his/her physical body, his/her cognitive capacity or his/her experiences and memories from the face of the earth? Therefore, we find it difficult, if not downright impossible, to fathom a world in which we – or those whom we love – are no longer there. This is also the reason why grief is nowadays so painful and why the prospect of one's own death can be so tormenting. People throughout history have struggled with this conundrum of death and found, culturally and individually, their own useful and meaningful devices and strategies with which to make such a life with death liveable.

Death has always been there since time immemorial. There is thus no known human culture that has not mourned, performed rites for its dead and that has not in one way or the other had to develop distinctive ways of taking the sting out of death. Death is therefore of incomparable significance when trying to understand the human condition. It is one of the very few things that we all share: the fact

that we will, and must, die. As mentioned above, although this may sound exces-
sively bleak and discouraging, the idea that death – the inevitability of death,
the inescapability of death, the tormenting knowledge of death – forms the very
backbone of all our living endeavours is perhaps, after all, a correct observation,
as the so-called 'Terror Management Theory' has also persuasively argued (see,
e.g. Solomon, Greenberg and Pyszczynski 2015). Humans simply cannot avoid
thinking about death – the mind that throughout an entire lifetime is capable of
steering clear of thoughts of death and dying is nothing but fancy fiction. Even
when people are seemingly successful in avoiding thinking about death, death is
still in the end the event that triggers this avoidance. Because humans are born,
mature, grow older and feebler, the thought and reality of death gradually and
forcefully enters our consciousness (Becker 1973/1997). This does not mean that
we have not been able to develop an impressive inventory of more or less effective defensive mechanisms and survival strategies intended to avoid being either
obsessed with, or haunted by, the constant knowledge and fear of death, but it
does mean that death is always there somewhere beneath the surface of our everyday consciousness. In this way, humans are hard-wired to live with death at
the same time as this forced cohabitation seldom develops into a loving embrace.

The ambivalence of death

Just as individuals must try to juggle dexterously with the knowledge and reality of death, all societies as a collection of individuals must also be able to perform the difficult balancing act of simultaneously denying and accepting death
(Dumont and Foss 1972). They must, on the one hand, recognise that all of its
members at any moment in time find themselves at various stages in the process
of dying, and that they will all, each in their due time, eventually and necessarily
die. But, on the other hand, they must also encourage people to continue living meaningful lives and to attend to all the activities, routines and obligations
that such lives require – getting an education, working, procreating, founding
families, pursuing careers, paying taxes, participating in private and public life
and so on – even in the constant shadow of death. Societies simply cannot allow
their individual members to be constantly paralysed or stifled by the fear of
death. Hence, all societies develop different ways of talking about and dealing
with, displaying and hiding, organising and sequestrating, orchestrating and cir-
cumscribing, accepting and denying death, but most societies have their historically and comparatively rather unique ways of doing so. One might differentiate
between these different ways in which societies deal with death – just as all societies deal with birth, sexuality, illness, ageing, deviance and many other natural
phenomena in human life differently – through the use of a so-called 'scripting'
perspective (Macdonald 2005). Three overall, and admittedly ideal-typical and
tentative, scripts may then be proposed. Firstly, *death-denying/death-tabooing societies* that do their utmost to keep death a secret and as far away from the living
as possible – from their thought, sight and touch. In such societies, the cultural

impact of death is minimised and experience with death is minimal. Secondly, *death-embracing/death-tolerating societies* that celebrate death and put it on public display through recurring collective rites and ceremonials. In such societies, the cultural importance of death is upgraded and death is, to varying degrees, visible and openly talked about. Finally, *death-ambivalent/death-tergiversating societies* that in ingenious ways try to strike the delicate balance between denying/tabooing and embracing/tolerating death. In such societies, the cultural presence of death is constantly negotiated, but is seen as problematic. Most societies will probably fall into the third and final category, as few societies in the long run will be successful in suppressing and hiding death from its members for long, and as few (at least modern) societies can function properly if death constantly constitutes the fulcrum of individual and collective life activity. The question is thus not about acceptance *or* denial of death (Dumont and Foss 1972), but rather of acceptance *and* denial (presence *and* absence, proximity *and* distance, celebration *and* taboo, communication *and* silence, and so on) and the always complex and context-specific mixture that this internal relationship takes on. As French sociologist Jean Baudrillard would once have had it, this inherent and probably unresolvable ambivalence becomes evident particularly if we regard 'our whole culture [as] just one huge effort to dissociate life and death, to ward off the ambivalence of death' (Baudrillard 1976/2017:168). Contemporary society under consideration in this book, and its relationship to death, as the book's contributions will all show, is indeed, in a deep-seated manner, ambivalent about the role, importance and proper place of death.

For a long time, the so-called 'tabooists' dominated the social scientific discourse on death and dying. For example, more than a hundred years ago in his reflections on war and death, Sigmund Freud believed that he at that time saw a 'disturbance that has taken place in the attitude which we have hitherto adopted towards death'. According to Freud, as a consequence of this disturbance, 'we have shown an unmistakable tendency to put death aside, to eliminate it from life' (Freud 1918/1963:109), thereby laying the foundation for the longstanding and almost unopposed claim within studies of death and dying that death was the last taboo in modern society, having thereby overtaken the role previously occupied by sexuality (Jacobsen 2020). Even though there is indeed a lot of evidence from the 20th century to support the view that death is and continues to be tabooed (at least as compared to previous historical periods), something new has also happened throughout the past century since Freud's observations that warrants our attention. On the one hand, two tendencies seem to point to an increasing estrangement and alienation towards death. For example, natural death is being relentlessly medicalised, institutionalised and professionalised, thereby making it some sort of anomaly or pathology requiring treatment until the dying person's very last breath. The same, it seems, is the case with grief being now incorporated into diagnostic manuals as a sort of psychological disorder. Simultaneously, we, in a heretofore unprecedented manner, seem to wallow in unnatural and violent death as part of the ever-present and ever-profiting entertainment industry. This latter tendency was already noted by English anthropologist Geoffrey Gorer in the mid-1950s when he, in his description of the so-called 'pornography of death', suggested that 'while natural death became more and more smothered in prudery, violent death has played an ever growing part in the fantasies offered to mass audiences' (Gorer 1955:51). This tendency, it seems, has only been exacerbated in recent years due to the increased popularity of the many murder story documentaries and horror genre productions depicting vampires, ghosts, robots, and inhuman and undead creatures in movies and television series now available 24/7 on global networks and streaming services. In this way, death has most certainly become a spectacle today, as also recently observed by Australian sociologist Anthony Elliott:

> Death is "on show" everywhere – it is the spectacle of our information age – and yet it functions as spectacle only to the extent that the proper distance is maintained. This is the distance of generalization, of repetition, and of objectivity, all of which are crucial to the trivialization of death.
>
> *(Elliott 2018:117)*

An opposing tendency – one more oriented towards the acceptance, recognition and contemplation of death – is evident in the spreading and consolidation of the hospice and palliative care initiatives, in the new 'death awareness movement' and in the many different attempts at re-domesticating death and dying through the development of new communal and personal rituals, traditions and ceremonies intended to make death more authentic and less alien (see, e.g. Stanley and Wise 2011). So, to claim that death is simply taboo is thus to miss out on something important that is going on in our contemporary culture of death (Jacobsen 2020). It is this curious coexistence of these different, seemingly mutually unconnected and unconnectable, tendencies that appears to characterise our contemporary society's awkward and ambivalent relationship with death rather than either 'taboo' or 'revival'.

This book is about death. Even though death, as mentioned, is indeed a constant in human life, it does not, however, stand still. Our individual and cultural conceptions of, approaches to and ways of dealing with death and dying change quite considerably over time as we continuously seek to negotiate, deconstruct and reinvent the meaning of death in life (Jacobsen 2013). No culture has ever been able to leave death to *itself* or just accept death *as it is* – all cultures have developed, for them, culturally specific ways of understanding and relating to this certainty of life. From historical epoch to epoch, from culture to culture, from one social group to another, from individual to individual, death is 'done' differently. Undoubtedly, there are many reasons why and how even seemingly comparable and historically coexisting contemporary societies 'do' or 'manage' death differently that relate to a variety of structural, cultural and individual factors (see, e.g. Walter 2012). Our approach to and understanding of death is in many ways a more or less direct reflection of life – the way we have organised our lives, the way we conceive of human life, the way life is being lived, the ideals and norms guiding our life purposes, hopes and dreams. The book is concerned with death in contemporary society – in what is here being called 'the spectacular age'. By invoking this particular notion, the book seeks to move beyond the confines of many by now classic studies of death and dying that were almost exclusively concerned with death taboo, death denial and the invisibility of death in modern society throughout the 20th century. Moreover, it also seeks to build on some of the more recent work claiming that we have witnessed a 'revival', 'renaissance' and 'de-tabooing' of death towards the end of the 20th and the beginning of the 21st century (see, e.g. Walter 1994; Berridge 2002; Noys 2005; Árnason and Hafsteinsson 2003; Zakowicz 2011). Although this book does not deny that this was indeed the case, it does, however, suggest that we nowadays, in the new millennium, think about and 'do' death differently than we did just a generation or two ago and that notions such as 'tabooed' or 'de-tabooed' are perhaps no longer suitable to capture the deep-seated complexity of our contemporary attitude towards death.

The age of 'spectacular death'

The underlying notion of 'spectacular death' of this book was proposed (in the meaning used in this volume) by me in an article from 2016. Here I suggested that we need a new and updated vocabulary in order to capture the most recent changes within the realm of death and dying in contemporary society. Even though the impressive, and in many ways immortal, ideas of such death scholars as Philippe Ariès, Geoffrey Gorer and Ernest Becker from the latter part of the 20th century still retain their relevance, we do need to look more closely at the present and at the way in which death unfolds in what – using typical abstract sociological lingo – is variably being called 'late-modern', 'post-modern', 'liquid-modern' or 'hyper-modern' society. Even though there are still remnants lingering from the near and far past in the way we think about and practically, emotionally and culturally deal with death, there is also a lot of evidence suggesting that we are indeed at the threshold of entering a new phase of historical development that cannot meaningfully be captured by Ariès's famous notion from the 1970s of 'forbidden death' (Ariès 1974a). According to the understanding of 'spectacular death' proposed by me, there are – at least – five important and identifiable dimensions involved. These are as follows: (1) *The new mediation/ mediatisation of death and dying* (that death today is for most no longer a familiar or first-hand experience, as it was for most people just a century or two ago, but it is now something increasingly filtered through media and social media screens); (2) *the commercialisation of death* (that death is today a marketable commodity used within different commercial branches and artistic forms of expression in order to attract attention, to sell products and to provoke our curiosity); (3) *the re-ritualisation of death* (that we in the wake of the 'de-tabooing' of death and grief have witnessed an intensified quest for inventing new ways and/or rediscovering old ones for memorialising and commemorating the dead as well as launching many new initiatives in trying to make death a meaningful, rather than an alien, aspect of life); (4) *the palliative care revolution* (that death is no longer the monopolised realm of modern medicine and that other professions have gradually gained a foothold in shaping the way we think about, handle and organise ourselves around death in society); and (5) *the specialisation of death* (that death has become the object of intense scientific scrutiny and interest, perhaps particularly within the humanities and social sciences over the past two to three decades). All in all, these five dimensions – each in their own way, and not least when combined – capture some important, but far from all, aspects of the age of spectacular death (Jacobsen 2016).

Let me here, in some detail, provide a few concrete examples and illustrations of each of these general dimensions of 'spectacular death' in order to show its empirical presence in contemporary society. Firstly, *the mediation/mediatisation of death* is evident in the way that death – real death as well as fictional death – is now an integral part of the expansive media landscape through television, social media, internet pages, movies, literature, popular culture and so on (see, e.g. Arnold et al. 2017; Han 2019; Hanusch 2010; Gibson 2007; Moreman and Lewis 2014; Morse 2017; Penfold-Mounce 2018; Sullivan and Greenberg 2016; Teodorescu and Jacobsen 2020). In this way, we frequently encounter and consume images or stories about death and dying from the news, movies or other forms of visual and/or written communication. Death is no longer as invisible as Ariès (1981) claimed to be the case throughout large parts of the 20th century. Death is now visible within many different mediated/mediatised contexts, and we seem to wallow in the way in which death is almost always depicted and described dramatically or sensationally in and by the media. As observed by British journalist Kate Berridge: 'A society which has for so long averted its gaze from death cannot stop staring at it' (Berridge 2002:255). This is perhaps particularly the case when celebrities suddenly or unexpectedly die and there is a flood of collective mourning and sympathy spreading throughout the media and social media (think of the much publicised cases of Princess Diana, Michael Jackson, David Bowie, George Michael, Prince, Robin Williams, Jade Goody and so on) (see, e.g. Walter 2010). A similar pattern can also be witnessed whenever disaster, terrorism or violence strikes, killing people indiscriminately – when death strikes under tragic, comprehensive or potentially avoidable circumstances or when it happens to people who due to fame and fortune are regarded as 'common property', it tends to become even more spectacular. Moreover, the number of movies or television series devoted to attracting audiences to dramatic deaths carried out by superheroes, zombies, monsters, goblins, ghosts, vampires and other categories of 'the undead' is at an all-time high. On the other hand, our experience with non-fictional death seems to have rapidly declined and is now replaced by mediated/mediatised death. American pastor and writer Matt McCullough captured this so-called 'new pornography of death' (with a reference to the classic notion by Geoffrey Gorer) spot on when recently stating:

> Think about it: the deaths shown in our most popular shows and mov-
> ies are violent deaths. They come to relatively young people who usu-
> ally aren't expecting to die. Characters aren't dying of old age and natural
> decay. They're dying because a psychopath, a mafia hit man, or a zombie
> killed them. You don't watch these shows for insight into genuine human
> experience. You watch them to escape from genuine human experience.
> Too often where death shows up in popular culture, it belongs to a fantasy
> world. It's newsworthy. It's tragic. It's psychopathic or maybe apocalyptic.
> But one way or another, death is exotic. It's something that happens to
> someone else.
>
> *(McCullough 2018)*

Just as the pornography of the conventional porn industry does not really depict
sexual reality as it is experienced by most people, but shows people having sex
because they are paid to do it, to pretend that they enjoy it and perform certain
roles and characters in often silly, one-dimensional and predictable plots, neither
does the pornography of death depict real and actual death as most of us will
eventually encounter it. Just as the male ejaculation has always constituted the
so-called 'money shot' in adult entertainment movies, so the dramatic moments
of death mark the culmination in the pornography of death in which the corpse
has become 'chic' and in which the new voyeurism does not stop short of the
sight or the exposition of dead bodies (Foltyn 2008, 2010). Despite its new and
widespread mediated/mediatised visibility, actual death, however, is seldom
encountered or confronted directly, and thus to most of us seeing a dead person
is far from a familiar sight as it was to people a century or two ago. In this way,
our previous direct exchange with the dead – in which the dead remained an
integral part of social life – has now been replaced with a new indirect type of
exchange with the dead, in which we wallow in simulations and simulacra of real
death (Baudrillard 1976/2017). So the familiarity and fascination with fictional,
celebrity, violent or dramatic deaths come at the price of having little to almost
no experience with how most people most of the time mostly die.

Secondly, *the commercialisation/commodification of death* highlights how death is
increasingly being regarded as a product or consumer item that may increase sales
or as a spectacle intended to create hype and attention from a paying audience.
According to some prominent sociological theories, in contemporary society
people are first and foremost behaving and being interpellated as consumers – they
are continuously seduced into consuming goods, activities and simulated experiences (Baudrillard 1970/1998; Bauman 2007). Death is no exception to this rule.
Even though each death is unique (at least for the dying and the bereaved), for
the professions that manage death in our society, death is a standardised event. It
is work to be done – and it is paid work. Death is therefore also necessarily commodified by those who process the dead body and provide ceremonial expertise and emotional support (e.g. from so-called 'grief therapists' or 'bereavement
counsellors'). Death has, ever since the establishment of the modern funeral trade

(and in a broader sense the so-called 'Death Care Industry'), been something that required a transaction between the bereaved relatives and professional service providers. One of the consequences of this development was the de-skilling of the family and local community in the preparation of the dead body and in the planning and execution of the funeral process (Walter 1996:95). However, it seems as if this transaction – not least with the ingeniously invented assortment of death symbolism and the cornucopia of funeral and burial paraphernalia growing by the year – has taken on new meanings in recent decades. Already, American journalist Jessica Mitford in her bestselling book from the 1960s *The American Way of Death* (1963) showed how death and grief were being thoroughly manipulated by the funeral industry in its profit-seeking business strategy. However, whereas the funeral during the increasingly secularised 20th century, as compared to the so-called 'beautiful death' (Tamm 1992) of the 19th century, was increasingly marked by a certain ritual restraint or recession, to which we return below, the 21st century with its celebration of the individual and of emotional expressionism has inaugurated a new era for personalised funerary rites and thus also for profiteering. Today, funerals need to be memorable and unique personal testimonies for the deceased and this opens up a market for product development and sales. Not only in connection to the funeral ceremony is death increasingly being commercialised and commodified. We also see it in the way in which death is put on display in many different artistic, cultural and popular cultural contexts. In her book *Vigor Mortis*, Kate Berridge provided many examples of how death was fast becoming fashionable among artists and art consumers, and she observed how 'we have more opportunity than ever before to experience death vicariously' (Berridge 2002:247). Also, others have insisted that death is now visible in many settings in which it has become the object of intense attention (see, e.g. Macho and Marek 2007; Aaron 2013). For instance, death is now the centrepiece of photographic exhibitions and art installations (just think of Gunther von Hagen's world-touring *Body Worlds*), spectacular artistic products (just think of Damien Hirst's diamond-covered cranium *For the Love of God*), advertising and marketing strategies, television dramas and movies, literary fiction and personal biographies, and indirectly in the way that especially medicine and functional foods are now being marketed in magazines and on television by promising dubious anti-ageing or life-extending effects (see, e.g. Foltyn 2010; Hirschauer 2006; Noonan, Little and Kerridge 2013; Walter 2004). Moreover, we have seen the return of the skull known as far back as in medieval death art but now re-appearing in a more commercialised and branded manner (Kearl 2015). We also witness the commercialisation of death in so-called 'dark tourism' that takes its participants on tours to famous murder sites, war zones, terrorist hideouts and scary and mythical graveyards (Kaul and Skinner 2018; Stone 2018) – and now also spreading to dark tourism on morbid and macabre internet sites (McDaniel 2018). In this way, death becomes a spectacle, something to be observed, marketed, consumed and discarded again after use, which makes death not all that different from other consumer items.

Thirdly, *the re-ritualisation of death* refers to the way in which seemingly de-ritualised, secularised and de-sacralised modern death today requires new forms of ritualised expression and the rediscovery of older ones in order for people, individually and collectively, to make sense of death. Throughout human history, death has always been ritualised and commemorated, but during the time of 'forbidden death' in the 20th century, the so-called 'reversal of death' (Ariès 1974b) meant that traditional death attitudes were turned 'inside out' (Ariès 1974c), resulting in a situation in which previously time-consuming, elaborate and public ritual practices, known particularly during the period of the 'death of the other' in the 19th century, in many places were increasingly starved off and replaced with less religiously grounded, less choreographed and less extensive alternatives. This was a time of increasingly minimalistic rituals that, perhaps particularly fuelled by the free-minded and anti-authority spirit of the 1960s, marked a showdown with established conventions, ingrained traditions and religious authorities. Baptisms, weddings, funerals and other rites of passage were no longer extended ritual spectacles, and more mundane, more informal and more secular variants were invented in order to provide alternatives for a less religious and more experimental generation. This was captured by Dutch sociologist Cas Wouters (2007) as a process of increasing 'informalisation' spreading throughout society. Today, rituals once again seem to return. They flourish in many different social contexts, some relating to life in general, others specifically pertaining to death and mourning. Our society is marked by a 'memorial mania' (Doss 2010), an obsession with celebrating the past, with mourning the dead and with creating cults surrounding that which society deems traumatic or intolerable. Moreover, the dividing line between commercialisation and ritualisation is perhaps becoming increasingly blurred in contemporary consumer capitalism. On the one hand, public rituals are to a large extent also staged events that attract consuming audiences and media attention and, on the other hand, different types of consumer items can be used specifically for ritual purposes in relation to death, as we saw above. There are also an increasing number of death-specific ritualisation and memorialisation initiatives such as 'Death Awareness Weeks', 'Children's Grief Awareness Weeks', 'Memorial Walks', 'Death with Dignity', 'Dining with Death', 'Death Cafés', 'Halloween', national re-inventions of the Mexican 'Day of the Dead' and so on. Many such concepts have been developed in order to cater for our curiosity, to increase awareness and to create a new sense of familiarity with death, while others seem to have been invented primarily as a way to market concepts or sell products. Alongside this, we also witness an interest in developing new mortuary practices, more personalised, authentic and inventive ways of memorialising the deceased during and after the funeral ceremony, the importance of burial ground and graveside beautification, the rise of 'quirky gravestones' (Höflinger 2013), the proliferation of forest and natural burial grounds, the scattering of ashes at personally significant sites, the popularity of 'last wills' and similar documents, as well as the invention of post-cremation rituals as new and emerging ways of re-ritualising death, not only in Western culture, but also beyond (see, e.g. Boret, Long and Kan 2017; Prothero 2001). In addition to this, televised memorial programs and memorial concerts for dead celebrities, live-streamed funerals, QR codes and video screens on gravestones, internet-based mourning and memorial sites and the like bear witness to a new interest in new rituals. All this also shows how technology increasingly facilities our ritual experiences with death. Finally, the intensified professional and public focus on the ethics and rituals of 'dying well' and the 'good death' (see, e.g. Dugdale 2015; Leget 2017) inaugurates a new and often ritualised way of approaching, re-appropriating and domesticating the death from which we have seemingly become alienated. Whereas the modern death mentality provided quickly prepared, pre-packaged, standardised and McDonaldised death and mourning rituals (Ritzer 1993), perhaps our contemporary time and age rather relies on more Disneyised ways of creating meaning, enchantment and emotional attachment in death and mourning rituals (Bryman 2004; Zornado 2017).

Fourthly, *the palliative care revolution* is a term used here to capture the many different trends and tendencies over the past 50 years within the domain of death that seek to refocus the way in which death, dying and bereavement is conceived, viewed, handled and processed within professional and non-professional contexts. The starting pistol, as it were, for the palliative care revolution was the opening of St Christopher's Hospice in London in 1967 as an alternative/supplement to a more conventional medical/curative orientation towards death and dying that dominated hospital settings at that time. It was, one might say, a revolt against what has been termed 'closed awareness contexts' (Glaser and Strauss 1965) in which the dying were denied control of their own deaths and in which the emotional pain and distress associated with death and dying remained largely unrecognised. Although prior to the establishment of this particular hospice there had been other hospice initiatives as far back as medieval times (Leming 2003), St Christopher's – not least due to the pioneering work of Dame Cicely Saunders – is normally regarded as the first modern hospice relying on a comprehensive philosophy of care and a commitment to dealing with 'total pain' (see, e.g. Clark 2018). The hospice alternative sought to create a new (or perhaps rather re-invent a forgotten) context for dying with dignity, for recognising the emotional and spiritual needs of the dying and bereaved, for a reconciliation of the dying with death, for a more holistic understanding of, and approach to, pain and pain relief, and for more humane and inclusive ways of dealing with end-of-life decisions. What was initially seen as a limited experiment later turned out to constitute nothing less than a landslide change, with the establishment of hospices and palliative care units throughout many countries in the Western world. Today, the palliative care perspective is thus institutionalised and recognised as a field of research and practice in its own right. We have palliative medicine, palliative care research centres, palliative care doctors, professors, nurses and researchers, palliative care journals, palliative care conferences, palliative care book series, palliative care teaching programmes and so on. All in all, what was not a well-known notion – 'palliative care' – just a few decades ago is now widely recognised as an integral part of the healthcare system. Alongside hospices and palliative care, during this period we have also witnessed the development of the so-called 'death awareness movement' that, especially during the 1960s and 1970s, aspired to making the, at the time, unspoken topic of death recognised as a natural and inevitable aspect of social life. The 'death awareness movement', although not a coherent or organised movement, was therefore an important source for a number of initiatives – writings, research, education, experiments, happenings etc. – that sought to reintroduce death into social discourse and clinical practice and familiarise people with the fact of death (Doka 2003). Even though today there is still some distance to be covered, these different, and in many ways mutually overlapping, early developments have greatly contributed to an increasing awareness and visibility of death and to the recognition – inside and outside of the healthcare system – of patient rights, patient-centred care, palliative support and not least of the necessity to address – institutionally and societally – the fact that patients and people in general die, that there must be dignity in death and that death must be recognised instead of denied.

Finally, we have *the specialisation of death*, which is also part of the aforementioned palliative care revolution but extends beyond this into other areas not specifically related to medical science or healthcare settings. In this way, death is now visible within many different quarters of the academic world as a topic of intense research interest. The death that was widely shunned when psychologist Herman Feifel in 1959 published his edited book *The Meaning of Death* has now come out of the closet and attracts scholarly interest, particularly within the social sciences and humanities, often appearing under the multi-disciplinary heading of 'thanatology' or 'death studies'. There is thus now a 'sociology of death', a 'psychology of death', an 'anthropology of death', a 'social history of death' and so on. Although this is not an entirely new development, the curve has been steadily rising throughout the past few decades, which is evident in numerous book publications devoted to the topic, the establishment of scientific journals dedicated specifically to the study of death, academic seminars and conferences on death, dying and grief, education modules and research programs designed to enhance and develop our knowledge of death and so on. Death now thrives in the academic world in a manner unimaginable half a century ago. Back in the late 1970s, death scholar Michael A. Simpson collected an annotated bibliography of death-related literature within the fields of thanatology and terminal care and paradoxically observed how 'there are over 750 books now in print asserting that we are ignoring the subject' (Simpson 1979:vii). Since then, the number of printed books – either asserting that we are ignoring the topic of death, embracing it, rediscovering it or exposing it – has increased drastically. This is not only a specialisation reserved to research settings – the educational system is also gradually beginning to grapple with the topics of death, dying and grief so unmentionable to young people (pupils and students) not so long ago. Back in the heydays of the academic interest in death and dying throughout the 1960s and 1970s, the idea of 'death education', which constituted one of the cornerstones of the aforementioned 'death awareness movement', was regarded as a provocative invention that tangled with a taboo topic (Jacobsen and Kearl 2013). Nowadays, death has gradually become part of many different sections and levels within both the general and the specialised educational system. Today, colleges and universities offer courses and modules in death and dying (e.g. within sociology, anthropology, psychology, social work, medical science, theology, media and literary studies), and prominent medical practitioners and writers such as Atul Gawande (2015), Seamus O'Mahony (2016) and Paul Kalanithi (2016) have recently encouraged a more explicit concern with, and acceptance of, death and dying when training healthcare personnel, in particular. Even though teaching and training in death, dying and bereavement have primarily been reserved for professional groups, there is also an increasing interest in the topic outside such specialised contexts (Moreman 2008:2–3). Despite its pedagogical, ethical and emotional challenges, when teaching children and young people, death can also be a relevant theme, and it seems as if death is now increasingly becoming a 'hot topic' within different parts of the primary and secondary school curriculum. For example, in a contemporary Danish context, in the autumn of 2019 the topic of the primary school's annual nationwide media competition for the pupils was death ('Death is something we talk about'). Moreover, numerous are the times when I have been contacted by pupils or students doing assignments or writing semester projects on death and who seek advice on thanatological literature or ask for 'expert interviews'. There is indeed life in death within research and education in the first decades of the 21st century.

Obviously, much more theoretical as well as empirical work is still needed (in general, as well as within each of the five dimensions mentioned) in filling out, specifying, nuancing, correcting, supplementing or further developing this basic and tentative understanding of 'spectacular death'. This is one of the main ambitions of this book, and all the chapters included each in their own way contribute to filling in holes, adding bricks or erecting new conceptual structures for enhancing our understanding of the current attitudes towards and practices relating to death, dying and grief.

About this book

This book is about death in contemporary society. The purpose of the book is to show – through many different angles and dimensions – how contemporary society understands, deals with, represents, mediates, manages and confronts the fact that humans die. The book is an attempt to capture the spirit of the times when it comes to our current death mentality – what I, as mentioned above, have called 'spectacular death'. Although the contributing authors have been encouraged to consult and relate to this idea of 'spectacular death' in their chapters, they have not been requested to use, accept or agree with this particular diagnosis of contemporary death culture. They do all, however, each in their way seek to provide examples of, and food for thought regarding, the way contemporary society deals with death based on many years of research on the topic. The book is thus intended to show some of the main changes that have occurred within our overall culture of death – some of the main transitions and transformations identifiable within contemporary Western death culture – as well as to present some more specific case studies that in and by themselves provide important pieces to the overall puzzle of understanding our age of 'spectacular death'.

In Chapter 1, *Elaine Kasket* investigates and critically examines big tech companies' role in making modern death truly 'spectacular', not least due to the impact of social media in contemporary social and individual life. The author argues that that big tech companies such as Facebook, Google and Apple have rapidly assumed a position as viewfinder, lens and frame for death, and they become important and powerful agencies in the way death is experienced, mediatised, commercialised, ritualised and memorialised in the 21st century, and big tech is thus seen as a sign of the age of 'spectacular death'.

Chapter 2 by *Ruth Penfold-Mounce* and *Rosie Smith* provides an examination of how high-profile celebrity death encapsulates the visibility and commercial value of mediated death as a spectacle. The authors show that dead celebrities have significant potential to be financially lucrative for those who commodify and control their posthumous careers. An analysis of Marilyn Monroe's posthumous career is here used as a representative example of spectacular death and the productive celebrity dead through performance after death.

The topic of celebrity is also the main theme in Chapter 3 by *Jacque Lynn Foltyn*. This chapter explores the near-death experiences (NDE) of celebrities through an in-depth analysis of existing literature, biographies and interviews in which living and deceased celebrities talk about their NDE. According to the author, this concern with celebrity NDE is a sign of the new spectacularity of death in contemporary society in which the near-death encounters and recollections of famous people in particular attract increasing attention from the public. In this way, highly profitable NDE accounts have been folded into the consumer–entertainment–celebrity industrial complex and also shape broader cultural and popular understandings of the NDE phenomenon in particular, and death in general.

Chapter 4 by *Michael C. Kearl* is concerned with showing how the skull as a cultural and commercial symbol has changed its meaning throughout time. Kearl observes that we in the early 21st century have witnessed a revival of the skull in contemporary popular and commercial culture, but also that its social meaning has changed significantly. For centuries, depictions of skulls symbolised either warnings of lethal threat or moralistic reminders of the transience of life and the vanity of earthly pleasures. Today, skulls are used solely as commercial ornamentations mostly without any deeper social or cultural meaning. The author thus concludes that the skull in contemporary post-mortal culture no longer serves as a reminder of human mortality.

In Chapter 5, *Daniel William Mackenzie Wright* ventures into the world of 'dark tourism' in order to explore how sites of deaths and disasters increasingly become tourist and consumerist attractions. It is the author's contention that we are in the process already of moving beyond 'spectacular death' and into the age of 'the immersive death' in which technology and digital content will allow individuals to encounter and feel the presence of death in new forms. Virtual and augmented reality technologies have the potential to immerse visitors and dark tourists in new profound levels of storytelling. By way of a multitude of examples from the world of virtual and augmented reality, the author shows how new advances in information technologies also offer opportunities for new experiences and engagements with, and learning about, death in our time.

Chapter 6 by *Dina Khapaeva* digs into the texture of spectacular death by analysing some of the post-humanist and anti-humanist popular cultural expressions from contemporary movies. In the chapter, the author specifically examines the differences in the representations of the end of humankind in secular apocalyptic and post-apocalyptic movies, with a special focus on the ones produced in 2018 and 2019. It is her contention that contemporary movies, as well as computer games and fiction in general, mark an unprecedented way of envisioning death of humanity that may be captured by the notion of *thanatopathia* – a deep-seated longing and passion for violent entertainment that is focused on death. The author suggests that many of these popular cultural products, by making death 'spectacular', prompt millions to consider the ultimate end of humanity a trendy commodity and a popular entertainment.

In chapter 7, *Tal Morse*, by way of empirical cases from New Zealand and Germany, explores the recent rise of terrorism as a spectacular death via new media and the ethical challenges for the players involved. The discussion situates these representations of violent death within a broader historical framework of spectacular death and mediated thanatopolitics (the politics of death), and explicates their adequacy and downsides. It is the author's argument that the removal of news organisations from the chain of circulation of newsworthy events results in the desecration of death.

Chapter 8 by *Arnar Árnason* discusses two contrasting deaths that both happened in Iceland in 2017. These two concrete instances of deaths speak to issues of contested memorialisation in public places and the political lives of the dead. In this chapter, the author shows how the notion of 'spectacular death' can help shed light on these two different cases of reported death from Iceland by drawing on conceptual insights from 'spectacular death', 'scenes of pain' and 'grievability'. It is shown that the way such deaths are publicly mourned and memorialised relate to questions of what counts as grievable lives and to matters of inclusion and exclusion, belonging and non-belonging. In this way, the chapter provides important insights into how what become spectacular or not in the age of 'spectacular death' in many respects has to do the values and normative structure of society.

In Chapter 9, *Michael Hviid Jacobsen, Peter Clement Lund* and *Anders Petersen* look into the way grief in recent years has re-surfaced as a topic of much publicity and debate. If the 1990s was the decade of ethics, and the 2000s was the decade of anxiety (in the post-9/11 world), then the 2010s is the age of grief and memorialisation. As the authors show, grief is no longer a privatised and socially sequestrated phenomenon as it was throughout large parts of the 20th century. Rather, grief has in many ways in the new century become spectacular. In this chapter, the authors document and discuss three dimensions of this contemporary culture of 'spectacular grief': individualisation/singularisation, professionalisation/commercialisation and memorialisation/mediatisation.

The book's final chapter, Chapter 10 by *Carlo Leget*, discusses some of the implications of the age of spectacular death on some of the ethical, philosophical and spiritual dimensions on the way we understand life and death in our time. In this chapter, the author outlines several paradoxes contained within the notion of 'spectacular death', and one of these paradoxes is the basic tension between human freedom and the existential unavailability of death and dying. North Atlantic culture hardly provides any tools for dealing with this tension and these paradoxes at a personal level, unlike previous centuries in which people could fall back upon an art of dying. Therefore, it is subsequently discussed what such a contemporary art of dying might look like, and how it might deal with the basic tension between human freedom and the existential unavailability of death in a fruitful way.

The Postscript by *Michael Hviid Jacobsen* seeks to summarise some of the many important insights and findings from across the book's chapters and to draw some conclusions from these in relation to the notion of 'spectacular death' by focusing on the conception of the notion and some of the complexities and shortcomings involved in it, as well as some of the consequences that can be drawn from it.

All in all, this book thus aspires to provide some food for thought when it comes to understanding the changing cultural significance, visibility and meaning of death, dying and grief in contemporary society. Needless to say, this is not an exhaustive account of death in the beginning of the 21st century, but it does provide a roadmap from which we may get at least a small glimpse of the real landscape of death that it tries to capture.

References

Aaron, Michele (ed.) (2013): *Envisaging Death: Visual Culture and Dying.* Newcastle upon Tyne: Cambridge Scholars Publishing.

Ariès, Philippe (1974a): *Western Attitudes Toward Death from the Middle Ages to the Present.* Baltimore, MD: Johns Hopkins University Press.

Ariès, Philippe (1974b): 'The Reversal of Death – Changes in Attitudes Toward Death in Western Societies'. *American Quarterly*, 26(5):536–560.

Ariès, Philippe (1974c): 'Death Inside Out'. *The Hastings Center Studies*, 2(2):2–18.

Ariès, Philippe (1981): *The Hour of Our Death.* London: Allen Lane.

Árnason, Arnar and Sigurjón B. Hafsteinsson (2003): 'The Revival of Death: Expression, Expertise and Governmentality'. *The British Journal of Sociology*, 54(1):43–62.

Arnold, Michael et al. (2017): *Death and Digital Media.* London: Routledge.

Baudrillard, Jean (1970/1998): *The Consumer Society: Myths and Structures.* London: Sage Publications.

Baudrillard, Jean (1976/2017): *Symbolic Exchange and Death* (Revised Edition). London: Sage Publications.

Bauman, Zygmunt (1992): *Mortality, Immortality and Other Life Strategies*. Cambridge: Polity Press.

Bauman, Zygmunt (2007): *Consuming Life*. Cambridge: Polity Press.

Becker, Ernest (1973/1997): *The Denial of Death*. New York: Free Press.

Berridge, Kate (2002): *Vigor Mortis: The End of the Death Taboo*. London: Profile Books.

Boret, Sébastien P., Susan O. Long and Sergei Kan (eds.) (2017): *Death in the Early Twenty-First Century: Authority, Innovation and Mortuary Rites*. London: Palgrave/Macmillan.

Bryman, Alan (2004): *The Disneyization of Society*. Thousand Oaks, CA: Sage Publications.

Clark, David (2018): *Cicely Saunders: A Life and Legacy*. Oxford: Oxford University Press.

Doka, Kenneth J. (2003): 'The Death Awareness Movement: Description, History and Analysis'. In: Clifton D. Bryant (ed.). *Handbook of Death and Dying, Volume 1: The Presence of Death*. Thousand Oaks, CA: Sage Publications, pp. 50–56.

Doss, Erika (2010): *Memorial Mania: Public Feeling in America*. Chicago, IL: University of Chicago Press.

Dugdale, Lydia (ed.) (2015): *Dying in the Twenty-First Century – Towards a New Ethical Framework for the Art of Dying Well*. Cambridge, MA: The MIT Press.

Dumont, Richard G. and Dennis C. Foss (1972): *The American View of Death: Acceptance or Denial?* Cambridge, MA: Schenkman Publishing Company.

Elliott, Anthony (2018): 'The Death of Celebrity: Global Grief, Manufactured Mourning'. In: Anthony Elliott (ed.). *The Routledge Handbook of Celebrity Studies*. London: Routledge, pp. 109–123.

Feifel, Herman (ed.) (1959): *The Meaning of Death*. New York: McGraw-Hill.

Foltyn, Jacque Lynn (2008): 'The Corpse in Contemporary Culture: Identifying, Transacting and Recoding the Dead Body in the Twenty-First Century'. *Mortality*, 13(2):99–104.

Foltyn, Jacque Lynn (2010): 'To Die for: Skull Style and Corpse Chic in Fashion Design, Imagery and Branding'. *Scan: Journal of Media Arts Culture*, 7(2).

Freud, Sigmund (1918/1963): 'Reflections on War and Death'. In: Philip Rieff (ed.). *Character and Culture*. New York: Collier Books, pp. 107–134.

Gawande, Atul (2015): *Being Mortal: Illness, Medicine and What Matters in the End*. London: Profile Books.

Gibson, Margaret (2007): 'Death and Mourning in Technologically Mediated Culture'. *Health Sociology Review*, 16(5):415–424.

Glaser, Barney G. and Anselm L. Strauss (1965): *Awareness of Dying*. Chicago, IL: Aldine.

Gorer, Geoffrey (1955): 'The Pornography of Death'. *Encounter*, 49–52.

Han, Sam (2019): *(Inter)Facing Death: Life in Global Uncertainty*. London: Routledge.

Hanusch, Folker (2010): *Representing Death in the News: Journalism, Media and Mortality*. London: Palgrave/Macmillan.

Hirschauer, Stefan (2006): 'Animated Corpses: Communicating with Post Mortals in an Anatomical Exhibition'. *Body & Society*, 12(4):25–52.

Höflinger, Laura (2013): 'The Rise of Quirky Gravestones'. *Spiegel Online*, April 9. Available online at: https://www.spiegel.de/international/germany/sociologists-document-rise-of-personalized-gravestones-in-germany-a-892809.html.

Jacobsen, Michael Hviid (ed.) (2013): *Deconstructing Death – Changing Cultures of Death, Dying, Bereavement and Care in the Nordic Countries*. Odense: University Press of Southern Denmark.

Jacobsen, Michael Hviid (2016): '"Spectacular Death' – Proposing a New Fifth Phase to Philippe Ariès's Admirable History of Death'. *Humanities*, 5(19):1–20.

Jacobsen, Michael Hviid (2020): 'Thoughts for the Times on the Death Taboo – Trivialisation, Tivolisation and Re-Domestication in the Age of Spectacular Death'. In: Adriana Teodorescu and Michael Hviid Jacobsen (eds.). *Death in Contemporary Popular Culture*. London: Routledge, pp. 15–37.

Jacobsen, Michael Hviid and Michael C. Kearl (2013): 'Educated to Death – The Disciplinary and National Development of "Death Education": Danish and American Examples, Experiences and Perspectives'. In: Michael Hviid Jacobsen (ed.). *Deconstructing Death – Changing Cultures of Death, Dying, Bereavement and Care in the Nordic Countries*. Odense: University Press of Southern Denmark, pp. 77–110.

Kalanithi, Paul (2016): *When Breath Becomes Air*. New York: Random House.

Kaul, Adam and Jonathan Skinner (eds.) (2018): *Leisure and Death: An Anthropological Tour of Risk, Death and Dying*. Louisville, KY: University Press of Colorado.

Kearl, Michael C. (2015): 'The Proliferation of Skulls in Popular Culture: A Case Study of How the Traditional Symbol of Mortality Was Rendered Meaningless'. *Mortality*, 20(1):1–18.

Leget, Carlo (2017): *The Art of Living, the Art of Dying: Spiritual Care for a Good Death*. London: Jessica Kingsley Publishers.

Leming, Michael R. (2003): 'The History of the Hospice Approach'. In: Clifton D. Bryant (ed.). *Handbook of Death and Dying, Volume 1: The Presence of Death*. Thousand Oaks, CA: Sage Publications, pp. 485–494.

Macdonald, Richard (2005): *Thinking Sociologically: Social Scripts and Everyday Life*. Dubuque, IA: Kendall Hunt Publishing.

Macho, Thomas and Kristin Marek (eds.) (2007): *Die neue Sichtbarkeit Des Todes*. Munich: Wilhelm Fink Verlag.

Maeterlinck, Maurice (1911/2015): *Death*. New York: Jefferson Publication.

McCullough, Matt (2018): 'The New Pornography of Death'. *The Rabbit Room*, September 19. Available online at: https://rabbitroom.com/2018/09/the-pornography-of-death/.

McDaniel, Kathryn N. (ed.) (2018): *Virtual Dark Tourism: Ghost Roads*. London: Palgrave/Macmillan.

Moreman, Christopher M. (2008): 'Introduction'. In: Christopher M. Moreman (ed.). *Teaching Death and Dying*. Oxford: Oxford University Press, pp. 1–13.

Moreman, Christopher M. and A. David Lewis (2014): *Digital Death: Mortality and Beyond in the Online Age*. New York: Praeger.

Morse, Tal (2017): *The Mourning News: Reporting Violent Death in a Global Age*. New York: Peter Lang.

Noonan, Estelle, Miles Little and Ian Kerridge (2013): 'Return of the *Memento Mori*: Imaging Death in Public Health'. *Journal of the Royal Society of Medicine*, 106(12):475–477.

Noys, Benjamin (2005): *The Culture of Death*. Oxford: Berg.

O'Mahony, Seamus (2016): *The Way We Die Now*. London: Head of Zeus Ltd.

Penfold-Mounce, Ruth (2018): *Death, the Dead and Popular Culture*. Bingley: Emerald Publishing Limited.

Prothero, Stephen (2001): *Purified by Fire: A History of Cremation in America*. Berkeley, CA: University of California Press.

Ritzer, George (1993): *The McDonaldization of Society*. Thousand Oaks, CA: Sage Publications.

Simpson, Michael A. (1979): *Death, Dying and Grief: A Critically Annotated Bibliography and Source Book of Thanatology and Terminal Care*. New York: Plenum Press.

Solomon, Sheldon, Jeff Greenberg and Tom Pyszczynski (2015): *The Worm at the Core: On the Role of Death in Life*. New York: Random House.

Stanley, Liz and Sue Wise (2011): 'The Domestication of Death: The Sequestration Thesis and Domestic Figuration'. *Sociology*, 45(6): 947–962.

Stone, Philip R. (2018): 'Dark Tourism in an Age of "Spectacular Death"'. In: Philip R. Stone et al. (ed.). *The Palgrave Handbook of Dark Tourism Studies*. London: Palgrave/Macmillan, pp. 189–210.

Sullivan, Daniel and Jeff Greenberg (2016): *Death in Classic and Contemporary Film: Fade to Black*. London: Palgrave/Macmillan.

Tamm, Ditlev (1992): *Dødens triumf* [The Triumph of Death]. Copenhagen: G.E.C. Gad.

Teodorescu, Adriana and Michael Hviid Jacobsen (eds.) (2020): *Death in Contemporary Popular Culture*. London: Routledge.

Walter, Tony (1994): *The Revival of Death*. London: Routledge.

Walter, Tony (1996): *The Eclipse of Eternity: A Sociology of the Afterlife*. London: Macmillan.

Walter, Tony (2004): 'Plastination for Display: A New Way to Dispose of the Dead'. *Journal of the Royal Anthropological Institute (N.S.)*, 10(3):603–627.

Walter, Tony (2010): 'Jade and the Journalists: Media Coverage of a Young British Celebrity Dying of Cancer'. *Social Science & Medicine*, 71(5):853–860.

Walter, Tony (2012): 'Why Different Countries Manage Death Differently: A Comparative Analysis of Modern Urban Societies'. *The British Journal of Sociology*, 63(1):123–145.

Wouters, Cas (2007): *Informalization: Manners and Emotions Since 1890*. London: Sage Publications.

Zakowicz, Ilona (2011): 'A Postmodern Thanatic Triad: Crisis, Pornography and Renaissance of Death'. *Journal of Education & Culture*, 1:59–72.

Zornado, Joseph (2017): *Disney and the Dialectic of Desire: Fantasy as Social Practice*. London: Palgrave/Macmillan.

1

IF DEATH IS THE SPECTACLE, BIG TECH IS THE LENS

How social media frame an age of 'spectacular death'

Elaine Kasket

Introduction

Nearly everything that was fleeting or intangible in the pre-digital age is now stored, making it harder for us to forget than to remember for the first time in the history of human memory (Mayer-Schoenberger 2011). The global datasphere generated by digital-era humans has swollen to approximately 33 zettabytes (equal to a trillion gigabytes), and by 2025, the world's servers are predicted to heave with five times that much (Reinsel, Gantz and Rydning 2018). The information we store is growing at four times the rate of the world economy, with the processing power of computers growing nine times faster. 'Little wonder that people complain of information overload. Everyone is whiplashed by the changes' (Mayer-Schoenberger and Cukier 2013:9).

As much as we may feel whiplashed by the breakneck pace, we are both active and passive suppliers of this glut of data. The digital footprint that we now make as we traverse the online world makes a far heftier impression than the one of a mere decade ago, which by comparison seems as scant and brief as personalised tombstone inscriptions in the medieval 'one's own death' period (Ariès 1974). Just like the global datasphere, we have expanded exponentially too. To René Descartes' being of body and being of mind, we have added a third, a digital being, a *res digitalis* (Kim 2001). Much of this digital being is comprised of information captured by the surveillance devices that make our environment 'smarter' and that track our movements, health, faces, and voices. Even if certain elements of this passively collected information do not seem personal, in aggregate they can reveal an astonishingly intimate and comprehensive picture of a person's life (Mayer-Schoenberger and Cukier 2013). To assemble this picture, however, one needs big data processes, which more casual observers might not have at their disposal. Instead, what people most often see is the deliberate spectacle of our performative, curated digital personae on sites like Facebook, Twitter, and Instagram.

Public relations crises around the use and misuse of our personal data have done little to curb the social media companies' growth. In 2019, 45% of people around the globe were active users of social media (Chaffey 2019). Even the reputationally beleaguered Facebook remains dominant, having enjoyed a 2% rate of growth in the third quarter of 2019 (Constine 2019). Like other service providers of its type, Facebook's business model rests upon connecting living users, selling them things, and harvesting and profiting from their data. It did not set out to be mixed-use social networking and digital-cemetery platform. But there is no avoiding the inevitable: no matter how hale and hearty they are upon signing up, 100% of users will eventually die. Facebook may now be an empire of social media, but it will eventually become the empire of death: it could find itself hosting the digital remains of 4.9 billion people by the end of the century, dead profiles having far exceeding living users by that stage (Öhman and Watson 2019). Having failed to adequately plan for the end from the beginning, social media companies are now attempting to catch up, often evolving their policies and practices in response to incident-specific bad press and user backlash about how they have handled deceased people's data. For example, in 2014, Facebook made significant changes to their policies after a grieving father – who wanted a 'Lookback' video to be created for his deceased son – spoke directly to the CEO, Mark Zuckerberg, in an emotional YouTube appeal (Griggs 2014).

Until sufficient, clear, and fit-for-purpose systems evolve for the identification, sorting and disposition of data associated with a deceased entity, it will remain an incontrovertible truth that our *res digitalis* outlives our physical self. Posthumously persistent social media profiles, formally memorialised or not, are now a common spectacle online, and people's feelings about this are highly variable. In a 2019 UK YouGov survey, 16% of the 1,616 respondents said that they would like their profiles to remain online and visible to others after death, at least for a time (Ibbetson 2019). A quarter of respondents, however, said that they would like all social media to be deleted entirely at the time of their deaths. This desire is currently inexecutable, in both a practical and legal sense. Even if it were possible, would we seize the opportunity to make provisions for our digital estate when two-thirds of us already fail to make plans for our physical one (Chapman 2018)? The 2017 Digital Death Survey, conducted by the UK's Digital Legacy Association (2017), revealed that 83% of respondents had made no plans for their social media accounts after death. Personal inaction and the data controllers' tendency towards retention combine to mean that physical death does not equal digital death. Our personal data is simply too voluminous, too widely spread throughout the datasphere, and too under the control of innumerable third parties to be able to simply gather it up and 'bury' it, even if that is what the deceased would have wanted.

If we do not know what to do about that, rest assured that the big technology companies that store and control all these data are flummoxed too, and the posthumous persistence of millions of digital identities is starting to constitute a problem for the companies that host them. A former Google advertising strategist turned philosopher and digital ethicist writes that 'Many of the systems we've developed to help guide our lives ... arose in, and still assume, an environment of information scarcity. We're only just beginning to explore ... how [these systems] need to change, in this new milieu of information abundance' (Williams 2018:16). Systems have not changed much yet, and incidentally and by default, rather than by original mission or intention, social media companies have moved into position as the viewfinder, lens, and frame for death, the backdrop against which contemporary 'spectacular death' (Jacobsen 2016) is set.

This chapter will illustrate and argue that posthumously persistent data on social media platforms fuel the contemporary climate of spectacular death, discussing three features of spectacular death as outlined by Danish sociologist Michael Hviid Jacobsen (2016): the mediatisation, commercialisation, and re-ritualisation of death. I will first discuss mediatisation, describing the living's interaction with the dead on social media. I will then describe how social media companies may commercialise death, focusing on Facebook's evolving role as a type of 'funeral director'. Finally, I will critique the practice of memorialising social media profiles, questioning whether this particular re-ritualisation of death is either sustainable or desirable. Some concluding remarks round out the chapter.

Mediatisation – contacting death and the dead through social media

This section further discusses how social media mediate our experience of death and the dead. Throughout cultures and across millennia, we have stayed connected with our dead in various ways, a phenomenon known as *continuing bonds* (Klass and Steffen 2017). Continuing bonds through the medium of communication technologies is, in fact, not a new phenomenon. In the 19th century, the table-rapping of spirits during Spiritualist seances mirrored the tapping of the telegraph. When photography emerged, so did the 'spook picture' industry, producing hoax images in which spirits materialised alongside the sitter(s). Thomas Edison himself hoped to invent a phonograph sensitive enough to capture the voices of the Great War dead, and in modern-day Japan there is a 'wind telephone' connected to nowhere that mourners from around the country visit to talk to their dead (see, e.g., Kasket 2019.) Now, it is easier than ever before to experience a connection to the dead using modern communication technologies, for the deceased live in the technology already, situated cheek by jowl with the living. Rather than removing to a separate space, like a designated online cemetery or data heaven, digital shades on social media currently hold their same place within their network of connections, mingling with the living in closer proximity than at any time since Philippe Ariès' 'tamed death' stage, when the graveyard and the ground for goods, services, and entertainments were one and the same space (Ariès 1974). Our 21st-century online society is composed of both the living and the dead, mingling as 'promiscuously' as in the early Middle Ages.

Social media have rapidly assumed a special significance for bereaved people. Their role in mediating a particular death starts with death notification, for even the closest relatives may hear the news of someone's demise via Facebook or Twitter, which are capable of delivering bad news faster than any police department or family-organised telephone tree, and many people do not subscribe to the still-nascent etiquette around the whens, hows, and whos of revealing a death on social media. In the immediate period after a death, social media have practical uses, organising and informing the network about memorials and other arrangements, but primarily they serve as a significant space for tributes and emotional expression, functions that they may fulfil for many years. People almost always speak in the second person to the deceased person themselves (Kasket 2012). As people express themselves about and to the person they have lost, additional drama flares via correctives from self-appointed 'grief police', who weigh in about who is entitled to feel sad, how this sadness should be expressed, and even whether the deceased can hear them – in essence, telling people to stop making unseemly spectacles of themselves (Gach, Fiesler and Brubaker 2017). Grief policing is an example of the tensions and uncertainty that can arise when highly local conventions around grief collide on a global, visible stage. As people continue to post photos and describe their memories, they negotiate what Tony Walter (1996) calls the *durable biography*, a picture of the deceased person that the community of mourners can comfortably carry forward as they grieve and remember. This process used to happen at the funeral home or wake, presided over by the physical deceased person, and it still does; however, on a once-living person's social media account, the community forms a durable *auto*/biography, significantly contributed to by the digital footprint the deceased person made themselves. People without access to a social media account in the wake of a death, which may include members of older generations like parents and grandparents, may feel acutely isolated from the community of mourners, shut out of the virtual memorials (Bassett 2018).

What explains the ongoing attachment to, and interaction with, posthumously persistent social media profiles, which bereaved people describe as being the last bit of someone that feels *really real* (Kasket 2012)? Without question, the multimedia vividness of these particular digital artefacts may have much to do with it, but it may also be partly down to the fact that these are co-constructed entities, representing and capturing the interaction and hence the *relationship* that existed between the deceased and the bereaved person, not just the deceased in isolation. The most richly developed profiles of erstwhile active social media users may seem, to those who knew the person in life, to contain an essence of their humanity (Bassett 2020). Just as in the romantic period of 'thy death', for many, these profiles constitute the sacrosanct 'tombs of our dear ones' (Ariès

1974:72), sites of ongoing visitation and veneration. Accessibility is also key; the dead are in our very palms, our smartphones serving as portable cemeteries as well as *mobile-emotive devices*, which Kathleen Cumiskey and Larissa Hjorth (2017) describe as having multiple affordances when it comes to managing emotions in the face of grief. Paradoxically, our phones can trigger emotion and help us process it more deeply, or they can provide the distractions and entertainment that blunt our sadness and sense of loss.

Social media platforms like Facebook are also experienced as a kind of medium that gives one access to the inhabitants of the afterlife, a conduit through which the bereaved can communicate directly to the deceased and experience themselves as being heard (see, e.g., Kasket 2012). This belief that messages sent via social media reach the deceased might seem like a kind of death denial, although research participants certainly express no belief that the deceased is not actually gone. It could be argued that for *digital natives* in particular, however, the illusion is understandable. In the terminology of the sociologist Marc Prensky (2001), anyone born before around 1985 is a 'digital immigrant', but anyone who arrived into the world after that year can be considered a 'digital native' who has grown up with digital technologies. People who have always known email and instant messaging have never experienced lack of proximity as a barrier to instantaneous communication. For them, to send a communication into the ether is to assume it will be received, even if there is no direct visual or auditory confirmation. It seems understandable that this felt sense, this article of faith that one's messages will be heard, would not simply dissolve upon the physical death of one's correspondent, especially when their digital presence is still occupying the same online spaces it always did.

On the other hand, perhaps we should not mistake our proximity and exposure to digital remains for a closer acquaintance with death itself, which brings us to the question of whether social media's mediatisation of death more closely resembles 'tamed' or 'forbidden' death. When we see memorialised profiles on social media, we may indeed be exposed to the truth of others' mortality and perhaps more connected to the eventual reality of our own. Yet, we do not experience these entities as we would corpses. When the online dead decompose, as they eventually do, we do not witness fleshly deterioration, like the rotting cadavers and the flayed bones of medieval memorials. Digital remains may gradually break down before our eyes, but they do so silently, cleanly, through a thousand tiny cuts of a data loss here, a broken link there, the cull of a deceased person's account. On social media, the dead confront us everywhere, but in anodyne form, preserved in odourless binary code and viewed at a remove, through the tempered glass of our devices' screens. They appear more as semblances or echoes of life than as something truly dead.

> Death has been dissected, cut to bits by a series of little steps, which finally makes it impossible to know which step was the real death … All these little silent deaths have replaced and erased the great dramatic act of death

wrote Ariès (1974:88–89). He was speaking about the medicalisation of death in the 'forbidden death' stage of the industrial revolution, but it applies just as easily to the current age of 'digital zombies' on social media (Bassett 2018). Their persistence has made death even more of a stepwise process, perhaps not complete until the digital traces – and hence the socially embedded individual – also disappear. Like cremation – which Ariès described as another way of 'getting rid of the body and of forgetting it, of nullifying it, of [death] being "too final"' (Ariès 1974:91), perhaps keeping the vivid, yet non-corporeal, remains of the dead indefinitely available on social media is another means of distancing ourselves from death's finality. Social media may present us with the spectacle of death, but it is the incorruptible dead we encounter, far removed from the 'natural processes of corruption and decay [that] have become disgusting' (Gorer 1955:51). The online dead are not corpses but immortals, like angels. 'The most common place where the angelic dead are encountered is online' (Walter 2016:17), and we are drawn into fantasising that there they can live on 'forever'.

Commercialisation – social media as the new funeral directors

Comforting visions of incorruptibility and fantasies of immortality bring us neatly to the topic of commercialisation, another feature of spectacular death discussed by Jacobsen (2016). Digital-legacy companies exist and are all too eager to promote the idea of living forever online, selling services that claim to preserve digital selves in perpetuity (Kasket 2019). These digital legacy companies, however – which seem to fail as frequently as they emerge – are mere minnows next to the mammoth social media companies that never intended to be legacy companies in the first place. Social media, through their control and management of posthumously persistent data, have considerable power to shape the prevailing death mentality of the 21st century, succeeding the medical establishment as the masters of death of the spectacular death era. I would argue that social media are the new undertakers of our digital remains, and just as with the funeral industry, the potential for profit may drive their efforts.

At one time, undertakers were primarily responsible for the disposition of physical remains and little else. But Ariès (1974) describes the emergence, in the latter days of the 1800s, of *funeral directors*. Funeral directors, as he described, became not simple purveyors of coffins, not merely embalmers (another emergent fashion in the 19th century), not only stewards charged with the efficient and hygienic disposition of physical remains. More than this, they were 'doctors of grief' (Ariès 1974:99), their mission overlapping with that of priests. Funeral directors endeavoured to smooth the rough edges from mourners' experience of death, helping to return 'abnormal minds to normal in the shortest possible time' (Ariès 1974:99). These new professionals of death were particularly prominent in the United States, where open-casket visitations became an integral part of the funeral industry. These visitations involve embalming and making up the dead, placing them in elaborate and expensive caskets, and hosting a kind of party for them in elegant visitation rooms (Mitford 2000). Ariès saw these practices as a kind of play-acting that the dead were not actually dead, a blunting of the harsh reality of death. 'The definitive nature of the rupture has been blurred,' he wrote. 'Sadness and mourning have been banished from this calming reunion' (Ariès 1974:100–102). Americans were willing to pay high prices for funeral directors to relieve them of their overwhelming grief in these ways, he argued.

Ariès never had the chance to become a digital immigrant, as he died well before the watershed year of 1985 (Prensky 2001). Just as the late opera singer Maria Callas was unable to fathom that, years after her death, she would be revivified and embark on a worldwide tour, part of a booming holographic resurrection trend (see, e.g., McLeod 2016), Ariès would have been unable to predict the emergence of social media. If he had been able to observe and analyse the way Facebook handles the data of the dead, he might have remarked that the company – like the funeral directors that emerged to help usher in an era of forbidden death – seems to embody an American attitude towards mortality. The United States, as Jessica Mitford (2000) persuasively and sometimes scathingly argues, has fostered considerable commodification of death concomitant with the growth of the 'funeral industry', satirised in Evelyn Waugh's take on Californian death culture in his 1948 novel *The Loved One* (Waugh 1948/2012). Silicon Valley – the home to the social media giants – is in California too. It is a place where immortalists hope to eventually make ageing and death optional (Pontin 2017), and where nearly every developer is dedicated to developing technologies that increase users' convenience and pleasure, and decrease pain and friction.

No social media platform has embraced responsibility for ongoing stewardship of the visible online dead more than Facebook, representatives of which company demur when asked about the financial incentives behind continuing to manage the data of the dead. Jed R. Brubaker is an academic research partner at Facebook and the co-creator of both the current 'stewardship' memorialisation philosophy (Brubaker and Callison-Burch 2016) and of the 'Legacy Contact' feature on the site, which enables the appointment of a trusted friend to manage one's account in the event of one's death (Gibbs 2015). When I enquired about his vision of Facebook's role in managing the data of the deceased, his reply was interesting. '"The metaphor of the funeral director is not far off, right?", he said. "We don't ask the bereaved to go and embalm their loved ones. A lot of that complexity [can be] taken away. Call it an example of good design, so that people make choices that meet them where they're at"' (Kasket 2019:157).

I challenged him with several examples of family members *not* being able to make choices that meet them where they are at, including the case of the late Hollie Gazzard. Hollie's Facebook profile was memorialised without its having been requested by the family, and the profile featured 72 images of her murderer, who was her ex-boyfriend. When her family contacted Facebook, the company cited its terms and conditions at that time and said that they needed to prioritise the privacy preferences of the deceased by leaving the memorialised profile intact. Brubaker acknowledged this as a 'pain point' (personal communication, 10 October 2017) and assured me that there were changes being planned that would make people's experiences on the site better. At the time, I assumed that he meant 'pain point' in the psychological or emotional sense, and perhaps in one way he did. Since then, however, I have discovered that the phrase has a different meaning, a marketing one that pertains to consumers' experiences of services. It appears in the tongue-in-cheek Silicon Valley Dictionary and is defined elsewhere as 'a specific problem that prospective customers of your business are experiencing' (Shewan 2019).

About a year and a half after our discussion, there was an announcement by the Chief Operating Officer of Facebook, widowed herself after her husband's untimely death. She explained that Facebook would be 'Making it Easier to Honor a Loved One on Facebook After they Pass Away' (Sandberg 2019). After describing a raft of new features to 'minimize experiences that might be painful', the press release made it clear that this was not the final word. Facebook would continue revising their approach based on feedback from users, family members of deceased individuals, academics, and professionals, and their own research. 'We hope Facebook remains a place where the memory and spirit of our loved ones can be celebrated and live on', it concluded, employing a term for the deceased that was invented by the American funeral industry that came to prominence during Ariès' era of 'forbidden death': 'loved one' (Mitford 2000).

Who would have predicted that Facebook, and companies like it, would eventually come to function, and to see themselves, as funeral directors of our online digital remains? But the analogy is incredibly apt. Ariès described the new funeral directors of the last century as people who attempted to manage grief, to make it as painless as possible, to smooth rough edges and return matters to normalcy as soon as possible, and profit in the process. If Brubaker's statements and Sandberg's press release are representative of the general outlook, the social media companies that manage our digital remains are the newest kind of undertaker, committed to the same aims, and potentially just as interested in profit, too.

But how does commercialisation of deceased people's data happen? On Facebook and Instagram, advertising does not appear on memorialised profiles, and the uninitiated often assume that this means there is no financial benefit to the company in their retention. When I put this question to Brubaker, he disavowed the idea that Facebook might have a financial stake in deceased users' data. '"To date, there's pretty good evidence that there are not [commercial incentives]", he said, emphatically. "If there are … they're pretty crappy ones. There's not a lot of money to be made in cemeteries. There's way more money to be made in amusement parks'. (Kasket 2019:159).

Some critics, including scholars from the Oxford Internet Institute, are sceptical of the claim that technology companies do not profit from deceased people's data. As the dead burgeon online and our smartphone-mediated veneration of them burgeons alongside, profile preservation becomes a powerful incentive for living users to remain on a site that they might otherwise gravitate away from. People who have lost loved ones often do not wish to lock themselves out of the online cemetery, with its communities of mourners and sentimentally important digital remains. Deceased users' data can also be mined for market insights and used to train artificial intelligence models, as cogently argued by Carl Öhman and David Watson (2019). It may be true that, both online and off, there is more money to be made in amusement parks than cemeteries – but online at least, cemeteries may prove reasonably profitable too.

I would argue that social media have become new doctors of grief, telling us what the easiest and best ways are for us to honour our loved ones, which generally seems to involve ongoing visibility on the site. More editorial powers in this regard have now been granted to Legacy Contacts (Sandberg 2019). But, just like the funeral professionals who limit what choices the family members can make with respect to preparation, display, and disposition of the body, Facebook still sets the parameters and rules governing how such editing can occur, assuring us that they have made their decisions based on consumer feedback and on well-founded research in collaboration with academic and professional partners. Still, grief is highly idiosyncratic, social media companies are not public health organisations or grief counselling providers, and the profit-making nature of their enterprise might make one argue that they are not best placed to shape and impose new societal rituals and rules around death, mourning, and access to and control over digital remains. Facebook co-founder Chris Hughes has written passionately (Hughes 2019) about how the company in general, and its CEO Mark Zuckerberg specifically, make powerful decisions that affect billions of people based on personal values. Whether their intentions are humanitarian, mercenary, or both, when social media companies commercialise the data of the deceased and mediate death's visibility, the values, assumptions, and motivations of a handful of people affect the whole planet. The ratio of data controllers to data subjects is sobering. In 2019, a well-known specialist in post-mortem privacy law visited the people responsible for memorialisation at Facebook at their headquarters in California. She informed me that the team making the decisions about how we encounter the deceased on Facebook consisted of less than a dozen Facebook employees – residents of the very particular American subculture of Silicon Valley (personal communication, Edina Harbinja, 13 July 2019). In the third quarter of 2019, there were 2.45 billion users of Facebook worldwide. How many of them will be contributing in some way to Facebook's fortunes after their demise? How many will eventually be subject to social media's re-ritualisation of death?

Re-ritualisation – the dilemma of memorialisation on social media

The third characteristic of 'spectacular death' that I will discuss is *re-ritualisation* (Jacobsen 2016). Jacobsen describes how the mania for online memorialisation resembles the Victorian 'death of the other' stage described by Ariès (1974). The re-ritualisation I will focus on here is of a particular type: memorialisation through the preservation of in-life profiles on social media, rather than through the construction of new-built online memorials.

The practice of memorialising profiles in a way that ensures their continuing visibility was initiated by Facebook. It was not their policy from the start, however, and upon its inception Facebook featured a delete-upon-death policy for in-life profiles, advising that any memorialisation on the site should take the form of 'RIP' or 'In Memory' groups (Brubaker 2015). These groups were visited and used by mourners in much the same way as the virtual memorials found in places like the World Wide Cemetery, the world's first online 'graveyard', created in 1995 as a place where people could post photos, memories, and various tributes like virtual flowers (Kasket 2019). In fact, it was an 'In Memory' group on Facebook that first sparked my own interest in this topic when I stumbled upon it in late 2006. Jed R. Brubaker describes Facebook's original deletion-upon-death policy as 'horrible' (Kasket 2019:153), but it did not last long. The policy was abruptly changed after the Virginia Tech massacre of April 2007, when mourners contacted Facebook pleading for the profiles of the dead to be memorialised. Indeed, they have been ever since, although designs and policies for memorialised profiles have evolved. Over time, the number of virtual interments in dedicated online cemeteries has dwindled, while memorialisation of social media profiles created in life has proliferated on Facebook and Instagram. People have come to expect every digitally stored piece of information to arise at their command – 'consumers are ... resetting their expectations for data delivery' (Reinsel, Gantz and Rydning 2018) – and the data of the dead are no exception. Bereaved people have come to expect that they will continue to see the data of the dead in the place where they expect them to be, as illustrated by a public relations incident with Twitter in November 2019.

Twitter's character and mission are expressed in its perpetual motion newsfeed, the character limit on tweets, and its emphasis on textual data. This social media site is all about speed, immediacy, and transience. Perhaps it makes sense, then, that at time of writing it has never offered a mechanism to memorialise deceased users' Twitterfeeds for ongoing accessibility and visibility. It could be argued that a platform with a remit to capture in-the-moment, of-the-moment commentary is under no moral responsibility to memorialise anything, when preservation of information over the long term was not in its business plan. While it already had an inactive account policy (Digital Legacy Association 2019), this did not trouble the news media much. That changed in November 2019, when multiple news outlets reported that Twitter was due to commence a cull of inactive accounts the following month (see, e.g., Welch 2019). Anyone who had not signed in for six months would soon have their account wiped from the network. Although Twitter has no explicit delete-upon-death policy, this was tantamount to it, for a user's inactivity could be due to the fact that they are no longer alive.

In the latter case, the person behind the profile is no more, but their family, friends, and followers may still experience close ties to their ongoing digital presence through continuing bonds (Klass and Steffen 2017). When Stephanie Wittels Wachs heard the news about Twitter's impending cull, she knew that it would likely affect the profile of her late brother, Harris Wittels, a well-known public figure with a Renaissance-man panoply of talents: comedian, actor, producer, writer, and musician. Over four years after his death, his account was still there, complete with 89,000 followers and a blue tick to verify his account as belonging to the actual Harris. There was nothing in the design of the account to indicate that Harris was gone other than the tweet at the top, posted by his sister on 27 November 2019. Intuiting that the tweet would materialise like a haunting in the feeds of her brother's followers, she was careful to identify herself and her purpose straightaway.

'Hi! This is a weird, shitty thing. This is Harris's sister, Stephanie', she wrote. 'Twitter is going to start deleting inactive accounts in December, and it would be a goddamn tragedy if this account got sucked into oblivion. So I'm tweeting to ensure that doesn't happen. Signing off now' (Wachs 2019). Hundreds replied and thousands retweeted and liked the post. Many people thanked Stephanie for keeping the account 'alive' and described how much they enjoyed going back and reading it. Some people used language that implied it was Harris himself that was being kept alive, like the individual who said, 'Thanks for keeping *him* around for us' [emphasis added]. But not all bereaved family members have the power that Stephanie did – through whatever means, she apparently had her brother's Twitter password and/or one of his devices that was still logged on to the site. In one of Harris' last tweets, he encouraged people to come and see his band in a week's time. The band's name uncannily echoes what could have happened if Twitter had gone ahead with its inactive-account cull: Don't Stop or We'll Die. Stephanie's actions prevented that eventuality. For the 89,000 people still watching Harris Wittels' Twitter feed, his persistent digital reflection will now live another day. Drew Olanoff was not in Stephanie's position and was panicked at what such a cull would mean for the way he liked to remember his father. 'I don't have my dad's login,' he wrote on TechCrunch. 'I can't "wake up" his account to keep it safe' (Olanoff 2019).

On 27 November 2019, the day of Stephanie's tweet and just one day after their initial announcement, Twitter hastily back-pedalled in the face of widespread upset, saying that they would hold off on the cull and prioritise developing policies and mechanisms for memorialisation (Lee 2019). A representative confessed that Twitter 'had not considered the potential upset that would be caused by the removal of accounts belonging to users who had died' (Lee 2019). This professed surprise at the user backlash is rather interesting, for the potential importance of digital remains to the bereaved should not be news to anyone in Silicon Valley. A decade ago, the spectacle of an online ghost would have come as a surprise, but now people have come to expect these persistent hauntings, often reacting with outrage when the spectacle is removed, when a loved one's digital remains unexpectedly disappear from the social space.

Given the mounting evidence that digital legacies feel important to many mourners, does this mean social media platforms should memorialise accounts as a matter of course? Perhaps not, for there are issues with the practice that should prompt us to heavily manage our expectations that social media platforms will or should take ongoing responsibility for preserving the profiles of the deceased as sites of mourning and memorialisation. The data that we generate over the course of our lives are costly, energy-sucking, and heat-producing to store. It is difficult to imagine how we can be responsible towards the global environment and its living inhabitants while simultaneously storing massive archives of the lives of every digital citizen who has ever walked the earth. The Oxford Internet Institute's estimates about the potential size of Facebook's cemetery in 2100 (Öhman and Watson 2019) is only one illustrative example, a microcosm of a much larger issue. For our global datasphere to be sustainable, culls will be needed and are already occurring. The photo-based social media site Flickr started culling its old free accounts in February 2019, having explained on its website several months prior that 'storing tens of billions of Flickr members' photos is staggeringly expensive' (Stadlen 2018).

Data protection is a major factor here too. Part of Twitter's initial decision was driven by compliance with the EU's General Data Protection Regulation (GDPR) (Lee 2019). GDPR gives no guidance on what to do with the data of the deceased, but it does stipulate that companies should not retain our data for longer than is necessary. This is only safe, pragmatic, and wise in a time when we are drowning in a suffocating surfeit of personally identifiable and sensitive information. Whatever your views on whether the persistent digital selves of physically dead people deserve an ongoing right to privacy, when the digital dead remain on social media sites or when their email and message accounts remain open, the privacy and data of the living users with whom they are connected can sometimes be compromised. On one hand, memorialisation can mitigate against this risk, keeping the existing content visible whilst preventing anyone (whether friends or hackers) from logging into the account and accessing living users' data. On the other, living users might not always be happy with data pertaining to them – comments, photos, shared posts – being inalterably preserved on a deceased friend's memorialised social media profile. It is not easy for companies to juggle all of these competing interests: keeping their servers from overheating while simultaneously upholding data protection law for living users *and* deciding how to best respect and handle the digital remains of the dead ones. As I write this, I do not envy Twitter for the deliberations that lie ahead. But something must be decided, for as the data mount up and more digital-age citizens with social media accounts die, the dilemma of what to keep and what to cull is only going to get worse, and the idiosyncrasy of grief makes it impossible for a social media company to design a one-size-fits-all policy that works for everyone. The spectacle of the dead on social media is exquisitely beautiful or exquisitely painful, depending on the eye of the beholder.

Conclusion

In this chapter, I have critically examined the role of big technology companies in framing death and grief, and I have also contemplated the question or paradox posed by Michael Hviid Jacobsen (2016) about the 'spectacular death' of this book's title. At first blush, the ongoing visibility of the online dead would appear to force a partial re-reversal of Philippe Ariès' (1974) 'forbidden death', the last stage he conceptualised before his own demise in 1984. There is scant separation between the living and the dead on those social media sites that engage in memorialisation, which already include Facebook and Instagram, and which may soon include Twitter. As long as social media policies are biased towards the retention rather than the deletion of the dead, the digital shades will proliferate quickly, like memorial crosses liberally scattered throughout the streets of a busy city. When we see them, we may choose to stop and remember, perhaps even interact, and at other times we will circuit around them and get on with the business of the living. This choice exists partly because our posthumously persistent digital identities retain a certain spark of vitality, lifelike within themselves and/or through the ongoing life breathed into them by the communities in which they continue to be embedded.

Online, death is not sequestered, and when the dead remain on our list of connections on a social media platform, and when we continue to interact with their digital remains, it seems straightforward to call death 'tame' and plausible to compare our modern relationships with the online dead to the citizens of the Middle Ages and the ready familiarity with finitude that Ariès argues they experienced. On the other hand, it could be just as accurate to say that the 'fifth phase of "spectacular death" just as its historical predecessor is also haunted by a denial and sequestration of death' (Jacobsen 2016:2). The lifelike nature of digital remains recalls Jessica Mitford's (2000) and Ariès' descriptions of encounters with embalmed bodies in America, presented by the funeral directors in their open caskets as 'almost-living [people] ... still present, as if [they] were awaiting you to greet or take you off on a walk' (Ariès 1974:102). When even secular people assume that the digitally embalmed dead are still reading messages that the bereaved write to them on WhatsApp or Facebook (Kasket 2012), it is difficult not to draw parallels with this description.

It may be inaccurate to say that 'sadness and mourning have been banished from this reunion' (Ariès 1974:102), partly because it is difficult to achieve a 'reunion' with a continuous digital entity that has been uninterruptedly available, like a psychologically comforting 'transitional object' (Winnicott 1953) that carries one through a loss, as a teddy comforts a child who is separated from a parent. The hypothesis that the existence of vivid and comprehensive digital remains has blurred the definitive separation or rupture between death and life is persuasive, however, and in these early days, it remains to be seen how far and how long the power of these new 'masters of death' will extend. For now, though, they are free to manage, as they see fit, the modern stage on which the drama that is modern spectacular death is performed.

References

Ariès, Philippe (1974): *Western Attitudes Toward Death from the Middle Ages to the Present.* Baltimore, MD: Johns Hopkins University Press.

Bassett, Debra (2018): 'Ctrl+Alt+Delete: The Changing Landscape of the Uncanny Valley and the Fear of Second Loss'. *Current Psychology.* DOI:10.1007/s12144-018-0006-5.

Bassett, Debra (2020): 'You Only Live Twice: A Constructivist Grounded Theory Study of the Creation and Inheritance of Digital Afterlives'. PhD Dissertation. University of Warwick.

Brubaker, Jed R. (2015): 'Death, Identity and the Social Network'. Doctoral Thesis. UC Irvine. Available online at: https://escholarship.org/uc/item/6cn0s1xd.

Brubaker, Jed R. and Vanessa Callison-Burch (2016): 'Designing and Implementing Post-Mortem Stewardship at Facebook'. *CHI'16: Proceedings of the 2016 CHI Conference on Human Factors in Computing Systems*, pp. 2908–2919.

Chaffey, Dave (2019): 'Our Compilation of the Latest Social Media Statistics of Consumer Adoption and Usage'. *Smart Insights.* Available online at: https://www.smartinsights .com/social-media-marketing/social-media-strategy/new-global-social-media-r esearch/.

Chapman, Ben (2018): 'Nearly Two-Thirds of Adults Don't Have a Will, Research Finds'. *Independent*, January 9. Available online at: https://www.independent.co.uk/ news/business/news/nearly-two-thirds-of-uk-adults-dont-have-a-will-research -finds-a8148316.html.

Constine, Josh (2019): 'Facebook Shares Rise on Strong Q3, Users Up 2% to 2.45B'. *TechCrunch*, October 20. Available online at: https://techcrunch.com/2019/10/30/f acebook-earnings-q3-2019/.

Cumiskey, Kathleen and Larissa Hjorth (2017): *Haunting Hands: Mobile Media Practices and Loss.* Oxford: Oxford University Press.

Digital Legacy Association (2017): 'Digital Death Survey 2017 Overview Report'. Digital Legacy Association. Available online at: https://digitallegacyassociation.org/ wp-content/uploads/2018/07/Digital-Death-Survey-2017-HQ.pdf.

Digital Legacy Association (2019): 'Twitter Guide'. Digital Legacy Association. Available online at: https://digitallegacyassociation.org/twitter-guide/.

Gach, Katie Z., Casey Fiesler and Jed R. Brubaker (2017): '"Control Your Emotions, Potter": An Analysis of Grief Policing on Facebook in Response to Celebrity Death'. *PACM on Human Computer Interaction*, Article 47. DOI:10.1145/3134682.

Gibbs, Samuel (2015): 'Facebook "Legacy Contact" Can Take Over Your Account When You Die'. *The Guardian*, February 12. Available online at: https://www.the guardian.com/technology/2015/feb/12/facebook-legacy-contact-can-take-over-y our-account-when-you-die.

Gorer, Geoffrey (1955): 'The Pornography of Death'. *Encounter*, 5:49–52.

Griggs, Brandon (2014): 'Facebook Answers Grieving Dad's Emotional Plea'. CNN Business, February 10. Available online at: https://edition.cnn.com/2014/02/06/ tech/social-media/facebook-dad-video-appeal/index.html.

Hughes, Chris (2019): 'Opinion: It's Time to Break Up Facebook'. *The New York Times*, May 9. Available online at: https://www.nytimes.com/2019/05/09/opinion/sunday/ chris-hughes-facebook-zuckerberg.html.

Ibbetson, Connor (2019): 'What Do Brits Want to Happen to Their Data and Social Media Accounts When They Die?'. *YouGov*, November 1. Available online at: https:/ /d25d2506sfb94s.cloudfront.net/cumulus_uploads/document/brc97100i4/YouGov %20-%20Data%20after%20Death%20Results.pdf.

Jacobsen, Michael Hviid (2016): '"Spectacular Death" – Proposing a New Fifth Phase to Philippe Ariès's Admirable History of Death'. *Humanities*, 5(19):1–20.

Kasket, Elaine (2012): 'Continuing Bonds in the Age of Social Networking: Facebook as a Modern-Day Medium'. *Bereavement Care*, 31(2):62–69.

Kasket, Elaine (2019): *All the Ghosts in the Machine: Illusions of Immortality in the Digital Age*. London: Robinson/Little Brown.

Kim, Joohan (2001): 'Phenomenology of Digital-Being'. *Human Studies*, 24(1/2):87–111.

Klass, Dennis C. and Edith Steffen (eds.) (2017): *Continuing Bonds in Bereavement: New Directions in Research and Practice*. New York: Routledge.

Lee, Dave (2019): 'Twitter Deletions on 'Pause' After Outcry'. *BBC News*, November 27. Available online at: https://www.bbc.co.uk/news/technology-50581287.

Mayer-Schoenberger, Viktor (2011): *Delete: The Virtue of Forgetting in the Digital Age*. Princeton, NJ: Princeton University Press.

Mayer-Schoenberger, Victor and Kenneth Cukier (2013): *Big Data: A Revolution That Will Transform How We Live, Work and Think*. London: Hachette/John Murray Publishers.

McLeod, Ken (2016): 'Living in the Immaterial World: Holograms and Spirituality in Recent Popular Music'. *Popular Music and Society*, 39(5):501–515.

Mitford, Jessica (2000): *The American Way of Death Revisited*. London: Virago.

Öhman, Carl and David Watson (2019): 'Are the Dead Taking Over Facebook?: A Big Data Approach to the Future of Death Online'. *Big Data and Society*, April 23. DOI:1 0.1177%2F2053951719842540.

Olanoff, Drew (2019): 'You Can Take My Dad's Tweets Over My Dead Body': *TechCrunch*, November 27. Available online at: https://techcrunch.com/2019/11/26/you-can-take-my-dads-tweets-over-my-dead-body/.

Pontin, Jason (2017): 'Silicon Valley's Immortalists Will Help Us All Stay Healthy'. *Wired*, December 15. Available online at: https://www.wired.com/story/silicon-vall eys-immortalists-will-help-us-all-stay-healthy/.

Prensky, Marc (2001): 'Digital Natives, Digital Immigrants'. *On the Horizon*, 9(5):1–6.

Reinsel, David, John Gantz and John Rydning (2018): 'The Digitization of the World: From Edge to Core'. *IDC Information and Data*, November. Available online at: https:/ /www.seagate.com/files/www-content/our-story/trends/files/idc-seagate-dataage-whitepaper.pdf.

Sandberg, Sheryl (2019): 'Making It Easier to Honor a Loved One on Facebook After They Pass Away'. Available online at: https://about.fb.com/news/2019/04/updates -to-memorialization/.

Shewan, Dan (2019): 'Pain Points: A Guide to Finding and Solving Your Customer's Problems'. *Wordstream*, November 25. Available online at: https://www.wordstream .com/blog/ws/2018/02/28/pain-points.

Stadlen, Anthony (2018): 'Why We're Changing Flickr Free Accounts'. *Flickr Blog*, November 1. Available online at: https://blog.flickr.net/en/2018/11/01/changing-fli ckr-free-accounts-1000-photos/.

Wachs, Stephanie Wittels (2019): [Post on Twitter.] *Harris Wittels' Twitter Account*, November 27. Available online at: https://twitter.com/twittels?lang=en.

Walter, Tony (1996): 'A New Model of Grief: Bereavement and Biography'. *Mortality*, 1(1):7–25.

Walter, Tony (2016): 'The Dead Who Become Angels: Bereavement and Vernacular Religion'. *Omega: Journal of Death and Dying*, 73(1):3–28.

Waugh, Evelyn (1948/2012): *The Loved One*. London: Hachette Books.

Welch, Chris (2019): 'Twitter Will Remove Inactive Accounts and Free Up Usernames in December'. *The Verge*, November 26. Available online at: https://www.theverge .com/2019/11/26/20984328/twitter-removing-inactive-accounts-usernames-avail able-date.

Williams, James (2018): *Stand out of Our Light: Freedom and Resistance in the Attention Economy*. Cambridge: Cambridge University Press.

Winnicott, Donald W. (1953): 'Transitional Objects and Transitional Phenomena – A Study of the First Not-Me Possession'. *The International Journal of Psycho-Analysis*, 34(2):89–97.

2

RESISTING THE GRAVE

Value and the productive celebrity dead

Ruth Penfold-Mounce and Rosie Smith

Introduction

On 23 December 2016, on a flight back from her book tour, actress Carrie Fisher experienced a medical emergency and died four days later in hospital as a result of cardiac arrest. Tragically, the following day whilst planning her daughter's burial arrangement, her mother, Debbie Reynolds (of *Singin' in the Rain* fame) died following a severe stroke. Reynolds' son Todd Fisher reported that only 15 minutes before her death she had said she longed to be with Carrie again. Fisher and Reynolds had a joint private funeral service and were subsequently buried together in Los Angeles. Following their deaths, there was widespread public hysteria as members of the public followed events using both social and mass media platforms. Outpourings of grief were rife across twitter with hashtags such as #Debbie&Carrie being used as anchors for a globalised sense of loss and tragedy. In an age defined by mediated spectacle, the deaths of Reynolds and Fisher epitomised how celebrities can become spectacularised right through the end of their lives. Even the public memorial for mother and daughter was streamed live on Reynolds' website. For such high-profile individuals, dying is not the end of their highly mediated spectacle-based careers, but can instead be a new stage of productivity and value.

The mediated spectacle of high-profile celebrity deaths and outpourings of grief and memorialisation have become prominent in the 21st century, to the extent that Glennys Howarth (2010:103) declared that 'death has replaced sex as a source of pornographic entertainment'. Nowhere is death more entertaining, titillating and a stimulant of raw emotion than the death of a high-profile celebrity figure. However, for many high-profile celebrity individuals, death is not the end, but the beginning of a new stage of existence – a posthumous career (see Penfold-Mounce 2018). Although the celebrity body is dead and gone, celebrity 'traces' (Skeggs 2011; Penfold-Mounce 2019b) linger, leaving a legacy amongst the living that continue to have symbolic and commercial value as consumable goods. These traces refer here to the celebrity image, including name, likeness, voice, signature, photographs and film footage etc. which act as a proxy for the celebrity after their death. Celebrity as a form of popular culture reveals that despite 'concealment of the realities of death and dying … popular culture increasingly focuses on the body in death' (Howson 2013:203), positioning it as a site of both spectacle and productivity. The dead body is both object and subject. To best understand the productivity of celebrity death, and celebrities' ability to have posthumous careers (see Penfold-Mounce 2018, 2019a, 2019b; Jones and Jensen 2005; Petty and D'Rozario 2009; D'Rozario 2016) that are, in some cases, even more profitable and consumable than in life, we must consider the social and cultural dynamics that facilitate this ability to resist the grave.

We argue that contemporary culture is defined by mediated spectacles of all shapes and forms making it unsurprising, and even predictable, that even death has become spectacularised. Drawing upon Michael Hviid Jacobsen's (2016) notion of spectacular death, we provide an examination of how dead celebrities encapsulate the visibility and commercialisation of mediated death. Notably, we develop Jacobsen's work and take it further, arguing that it is not the actual dying and death of a celebrity that is spectacular but rather their transition into a valuable and consumable posthumous career. For high-profile dead celebrities, the commercialised and mediated productivity they achieve after death as 'the productive dead' is an exemplar of spectacular death. Dead celebrities as a mediated spectacle have significant potential to be financially lucrative for those who commodify and control their traces after death. We build upon Beverley Skeggs's (2011) concepts of 'bodies of value' and 'traces' by applying them to dead celebrities allowing a focus upon their posthumous careers. A case study of Marilyn Monroe is used as a clear example of the productive celebrity dead, as she reveals and encapsulates so many of the facets of what it is to be a dead celebrity who continues to be productive after death. Monroe is used to exploring the productivity of the celebrity dead through performance after death. Further, we address the conflict and challenges surrounding Monroe as a member of the productive dead who resist the grave and work amongst the living, contributing to contemporary culture as an age underpinned by the spectacle of death and the dead.

The age of mediated spectacle and spectacular death

The saturation of contemporary culture with mediated spectacle is a defining feature of the 21st century global north (Kellner 2003). For Douglas Kellner, the global north is definable as an age of mediated spectacle where the mass media reports on, reacts to, and makes visible a myriad of social issues and events as part of its relentless pursuit of news and entertainment. Writing in the early 21st century, Kellner identifies key, yet notably diverse, cases of media spectacle, including the commodity spectacle as embodied within McDonald's; sports icon Michael Jordan; the murder trial of O.J. Simpson; the spectacle of popular culture such as *The X-Files* and aliens; and the political and cultural spectacle of US President John F. Kennedy. Each of these cases represents the global reach of media spectacle and their function within systems of globalisation and celebrity culture. They speak of how living under conditions of a mediated, globalised society creates an insatiable desire for entertainment, commercialisation and consumption. We are witnessing the coming together of 'media and computer culture and of entertainment and information in a new networked and multimedia infotainment society' (Kellner 2003:13).

A sense of mercilessness characterises this mediated spectacle age as multiple arenas of social existence from politics, sport, crime, commodities and even death become spectacularised and made consumable through visually striking performance. Media spectacle pursues almost all corners of the social world, taking even the most mundane instances of social life and transforming them into an object to watch, survey and consume. An age of mediated spectacle is underpinned by Guy Debord's 1967 seminal text on the subject of spectacle – *Society of the Spectacle* – where spectacle is most prominently a product of capitalism. Much like Kellner (2003), Debord's (1967/2012) spectacle is ubiquitous, operating at the intersection between capitalism and media technologies. Taking a critical Marxist perspective, *Society of the Spectacle* presents readers with a reflexive and critical assessment of the capitalist motivations behind media spectacle. It calls on us to recognise the reach of media technologies and their spectacle almost as capillaries running through the institutions and relationships of society. Thus, not only are media spectacles a product of capitalist forces and changes in production and consumption practices, but they also serve as mouthpieces through which ideologies are communicated by the capitalist elite and hegemonic ideals are solidified. Although Debord never explicitly defines what he means by 'spectacle', we can understand it as a phenomenon that has the power to cement and justify social structures by demanding obedience; the spectacle has turned appearance into a commodity to which social actors are enslaved. Echoing Orwellian narratives (Orwell 1948/2013), *Society of the Spectacle* not only describes how modernity is defined by a media, technological and capitalist spectacle, but also how contemporary media spectacles are bound up with the manufacturing of dominant ideologies and the commercialisation of social life.

Media spectacle is therefore less about the glamorisation of social life, the visually powerful, entertaining or connecting distant individuals, but more an example of how capitalist structures dominate and demand obedience from consumers and observers. Consequently, society is being defined by mediated spectacle that is driven by capitalist-driven consumerism and the visual commodification of everyday existence. As such, living in a spectacle-based society is somewhat bleak, as capitalist motivations result in the isolation and loneliness of individuals 'linked solely by their one-way relationship to the very centre that keeps them isolated from each other. The spectacle thus reunites the separated, but it reunites them only in their separateness' (Debord 1967/2012:40). From this perspective, the age of mediated spectacle is more than an example of frippery or an indulgent interest of the media scholar. The spectacle is triumphing in all arenas of contemporary life, so much so that it has become 'one of the organizing principles of the economy, polity, society, and everyday life' (Debord 1967/2012:1). We are witnessing the 'spectacularization of ... consciousness' (Debord 1967/2012:14), where our social world is steeped in readily consumable profit-driven mediated content.

Building on the work of Kellner (2003) and Debord (1967/2012), it is not only important to examine media spectacles because of the snapshot they offer into the intimate workings of a capitalist system, but also because of the power they hold to make everyday life visible and visual. Indeed, it is hard to avoid mediated spectacles due to the visual impact of these striking events and performances, ranging from international sporting events such as the Olympics to political debates such as the Brexit process in the United Kingdom, or criminal cases such as the #MeToo campaign and the trial of Harvey Weinstein. As John Urry (2002) writes, the visualising powers of the camera and its ability to accelerate time–space compression has meant that 'almost all environments across the globe have been transformed, or are being transformed, into diverse and collectable spectacles' (Urry 2002:149). The technological interconnectivity of a globalised mass media, combined with the rise of social media and citizen journalists (Thurman 2008), allows mediated spectacle to thrive, turning the mundane into the glossy (see Beer and Penfold-Mounce 2010). The media technology's ability to spectacularise the everyday sculpts and directs consumers' understanding of the world around them. The media (both social and mass) do not lie dormant, passively functioning in the background of social structures (see Adorno and Horkheimer 1944/2002) but rather, cultivate and generate spectacle. Nothing and no-one are unworthy of becoming spectacularised and death is no exception. Considering the pervasive reach mediated spectacle has, it is not surprising that human mortality has become spectacularised; it is in fact a rather predictable development. Death itself is becoming 'spectacular death' as it becomes embraced and domesticated, making it safe and familiar whilst colonising chunks of our earthly and mortal lives (Jacobsen 2016:16).

The notion that mediated spectacle involves an active audience and fluid dialogue between the public and objects of spectacle is conspicuous in a society defined by what Jacobsen (2016) coined as 'spectacular death'. Here, two of the characteristics that define spectacular death – the new mediated/mediatised visibility of death and the commercialisation of death – are explored before being examined in relation to celebrity death later in the chapter. In his review of Philippe Ariès's (1974) historical analysis of death, Jacobsen argues that Ariès's 'forbidden/invisible death' is no longer accurate, but rather, redundant in contemporary culture. Our contemporary world is different to that of the 1980s described by Ariès, there have been vast social and cultural developments that mean that rather than suppressing death and banishing it from the social imagination, 'we increasingly witness death ... through the media' (Jacobsen 2016:10).

In an age of mediated spectacle, there is according to Jacobsen (2016:10) a 'new mediated/mediatized visibility of death'. Death is not forbidden or invisible; instead it is seen and encountered in multiple media-facilitated forms. The age of spectacular death does not mean that death has re-established its place at the dinner table of families around the world, but rather, because of new media technologies, we experience death vicariously. Death is simultaneously everywhere, on our mobile phones, our TVs, our computers, but also kept at a safe distance; it is 'present whilst being bizarrely absent' (Jacobsen 2016:11). Death is an object of mediated spectacle, but spectacular death is arguably a sanitised era of death in which individuals are separated from the reality of death by a screen. The forbidden death that Ariès discusses is 'challenged by a death that is gradually coming out of the closet' (Jacobsen 2016:10), and reflects Zygmunt Bauman's contention that death is spectacularly present although we manage to live 'as if death was not or did not matter' (Bauman 1992:231).

The new mediated visibility of death is not alone in contributing to spectacular death, according to Jacobsen, but is also supported by the rise in 'commercialisation of death'. Jacobsen (2016) focuses on how the death industry has become commercialised; however, it is not only funeral directors and other death industry workers that commercialise death. Instead, death has become commercialised through mediated spectacle as a source of media curiosity and a means to increase sales (Jacobsen 2016:12) in a capitalist, technologically saturated social world. Death has moved away from being something that the public get up close and personal with in everyday life, and is also no longer a constant, paralysing source of fear and anxiety. Instead it has become a commonplace consumable, often for entertainment purposes, as death and the corpse are being 'recoded, desacralized, and transacted by those who view it as a worldly commodity to exploit for profit' (Foltyn 2008:100). Themes of the macabre, death and dying are being 'constructed and circulated as ... object[s] of consumption, knowledge, and desire' (Elliott 1999:148). The public does not simply passively consume the death and the dead, watching them on the television or on their computer. Rather, new technologies such as the growth of social media and global mass media enable the public to have a front row position at all moments of death. We gaze, we surveil, we are voyeurs that consume as the boundary between us and them, subject and object, becomes blurred (Kristeva 1982).

A key route for the commercialisation of death is through the catapulting of celebrity death into the public eye. The lives of celebrities are lived out in the spotlight and subsequently so too are their deaths. Sitting at the heart of 21st century glossy, mediated culture, celebrities are highly consumable and bound up with meaning-making, representation and symbolisation (Rojek 2001, 2012). Both living and dead celebrities feed a world where the ordinary are transformed into the extraordinary, and every aspect of existence has the potential to be 'uploaded and downloaded, copied and cross-posted, Flickr-ed, Facebook-ed and Photoshop-ped' (Hayward 2010:1). Mediated spectacle-based culture (Jewkes 2015) is constantly, and simultaneously, balancing its ability to 'record the truth authentically and to represent a radically new way of seeing the world' (Carrabine 2014:135) as well as its power to construct an 'image [as] ... contingent and metaphorical, standing in for an infinite number of alternative imaginings' (Young 2010:94). As such, mediated spectacle has become so all-consuming that it can perhaps be argued that no longer do we interact with the social world as a 'simple pre-existing reality simply waiting "out there"' (Urry and Larsen 2011:1); rather, the social world has been constructed into an all-too-often sparkling mediated environment in which people navigate being simultaneously individuals, audiences and influencers, and wherein the distant are made familiar, and the unimaginable become the everyday. Online platforms, in particular social media, serve as 'active *mediators* between users, technologies and content' (van Dijck 2013:142) and the spectacle of death is not exempt from this dialogue.

This section has made clear how, firstly, we are living in a mediatised society characterised by spectacle and a complete saturation of technology and popular representation. Beyond this, it has demonstrated that death is a core feature of this society of the spectacle, and that the media industry and popular culture not only represent death and dying as part of its thick catalogue of content to attract audiences, but rather the visibility of death and its commercialisation is perhaps one of the most powerful weapons in its arsenal aimed at generating profit and attracting audiences. In essence, the media draw upon the celebrity traces (see Skeggs 2011; Penfold-Mounce 2019a) that linger after death, cultivating certain high-profile deaths to hold a unique place in our cultural imagination.

Value, 'traces' and the productive dead

In a media spectacle-driven society, where the high-profile celebrity is central to the consumer gaze, the celebrity is a 'body of value'. For Beverley Skeggs (2011), bodies of value are interwoven with imagining personhood differently. She highlights how people can be excluded from possibilities of accruing and attaching value to themselves if they are outside the dominant cultural understanding of value. In the case of dead celebrities, being excluded from the accruement of value is not the issue, but rather how this value is actively cultivated and maximised for financial gain after death. As bodies of value, dead celebrities are able to generate commercial value through control of their personhood (or celebrity image) as a form of bodily capital. Celebrities as bodies of value produce 'traces' of their personhood that embody value, and this value is not dispelled by death (see Penfold-Mounce 2019a). The value of celebrity goes beyond the physical body and is bound to the 'traces' of the celebrity dead. It is these traces that can be owned and managed by the living, reviving celebrity careers, for although the body is gone, the celebrity image and the value they acquired in life continues. Notably, the traces of the celebrity dead become a significant resource within the entertainment industry (Baker and Faulkner 1991), as they offer capitalism a new realm for profit and productivity. Celebrities in life become brands and this extends beyond the grave, confirming their value as a consumable good for the living and their embodiment of spectacular death. Acting as a proxy after death, celebrity traces create and reinforce continuing bonds with the living, meaning the celebrity dead do not undergo a social death where they disappear from living memory (Mulkay 1992; Jonsson 2015). Instead these traces, as a consumable for the living, suggest a degree of activity and productivity that does not end with death. Being dead is merely an inconvenience for the careers of many celebrities who exist after death through their posthumous careers rooted in the traces they leave behind. The celebrity dead remain and display remarkable productivity as they continue to work with the aid of the living. They become the productive dead (Penfold-Mounce 2019b).

The posthumous careers of the productive dead are driven by the living, namely family who are left in charge of the estate of the dead or professional management groups, such as CMG Worldwide and Authentic Brands Group (ABG), who own and control the traces of dead celebrities. These cultural intermediaries (Smith-Maguire and Matthews 2012) manage the dead celebrity as a brand enabling them to facilitate dead celebrities to become highly visible pawns in a spectacular capitalist society and as a result, effectively 'the productive dead' (see Penfold-Mounce 2018, 2019b). Much like the raw materials and machinery of a Marxian capitalist society, dead celebrities become a means of production for those that control and possess their traces after death, meaning that their financial and symbolic value is interwoven with the management of their bodily capital (see Mears and Finlay 2005). This capital is not just tied to the body, but the performance of skills and talents that define their celebrity image and career in both life and death. For example, Fred Astaire controversially continued to perform in 1997 when his dancing props from *Easter Parade* (1948) and *Royal Wedding* (1951) were replaced with Dirt Devil vacuums for television advertisements. Astaire's widow Robyn agreed to the commercial deal, but it led his daughter, Ava to claim she was 'saddened that after his (Fred's) wonderful career he was sold to the devil' (Archerd 1997). The productivity of the dead is heavily directed by the cultural intermediaries who manage the celebrity dead's posthumous careers and who direct the consumers' gaze.

The posthumous careers of celebrities as the productive dead through their lingering 'traces' enable them to resist the grave. Life for the celebrity body might be over but existence and productivity continue, reflecting Loïc Wacquant's (1995:67) argument, in reference to boxers, that bodily capital, if properly managed, is able to produce more value than was put into it. The celebrity dead were a consumable in life and, more importantly here, death, and as a consumable spectacle they are highly productive. The actual presence of the celebrity is unnecessary, for the traces of the dead celebrity can replace them: for example, through body doubles and computer-generated (CG) face replacement which are infused with the value of the dead celebrity's body capital acquired in life (Penfold-Mounce 2019b). This value is evident through the performances of the dead in film and television, highlighting how the thanatological imagination of the entertainment industry is stimulated by the celebrity dead resisting the grave (Penfold-Mounce 2019b). The celebrity dead are productive in producing new and original performances after death that go beyond inserting past performances into television adverts. Performing live on stage is achieved by the productive celebrity dead. For example, Michael Jackson's performance on stage at the Billboard Music Awards in 2014 entailed not just his hologram performing on stage but in the context of an elaborate set with backing dancers who performed with him. Jackson's traces produced a new and unique performance under live conditions which had not been achieved before. This feat of the 'productive dead' on stage has been replicated and expanded by the dead going on tour, such as in 2019 when Roy Orbison toured as a hologram accompanied by fellow hologram Buddy Holly, as well as living musicians.

These on-stage performances to living audiences by the celebrity dead offer a challenge to post-mortem social death (see Jonsson 2015), as the dead are both absent and present. They are the dead who interact with the living but with no direct personal agency or sense of the self – similar to the monstrous Undead such as the zombie, but with no cannibalism (Penfold-Mounce 2018). The participation of the celebrity dead in the acting and music world expands the dimensions and understanding of performance and productivity in the arts, along with a ripple effect into related industries. The celebrity dead now continue to labour within the film industry, as legal professionals along with marketing and advertising experts work to keep celebrities' posthumous careers going, turning and maintaining them as 'the productive dead' (Penfold-Mounce 2019b). The implication of the productive dead is that they blur the boundaries of life and death and potentially increase the competition for film and television roles for the living as the dead compete for them. In November 2019, actor James Dean, who died in 1955 in a car accident aged 24, was cast in a co-starring role in Vietnam film called *Finding Jack*. Mark Roesler, CEO of CMG Worldwide (a company specialising in managing celebrity posthumous careers) said: 'This opens up a whole new opportunity for many of our clients who are no longer with us' (Ritman 2019).

The possibility of dead celebrity traces being productive and valuable is leading to a growth in posthumous career planning. Digital Domain, the firm that was responsible for special effects in films including but not limited to *X-Men* (2000), *Thor* (2011), *Maleficent* (2014), *Beauty and the Beast* (2017) and even *Avengers: Endgame* (2019) also works with actors preparing for a day when their life is over but their traces continue to work. Darren Hendler, digital effects supervisor for *Digital Domain*, has revealed that the firm has a

> digital archive menu … [in which] you can archive how your face works and every single expression you make, full body scans. You can archive your voice and the way your voice sounds. You can archive different wardrobes and scans of wardrobes that you may wear.
>
> *(Sydell 2018)*

High-profile actors, it would seem, are already being faced with their own demise, and the productive posthumous career they can enjoy after death. In the future, living actors may be competing for roles against not just icons of the 20th century, such as James Dean and Marilyn Monroe, but potentially a digital Meryl Streep or Al Pacino. The celebrity dead do not 'rest in peace', as they do not truly cross the boundary into death; instead, they resist the grave and linger amongst the living (see Králová 2015).

The ability of dead celebrity traces to work reveals that there are substantial rewards for being productive after death, as evidenced by the Forbes Top Earning Dead Celebrity List otherwise known as the Dead Rich List (DRL). Published in October on an annual basis since 2001, the DRL provides a significant and rare insight into celebrity earnings as an elite global group. It is the DRL that highlights that the most successful route to a posthumous career is by being a singer-songwriter, such as Elvis Presley, Richard Rodgers and Oscar Hammerstein, John Lennon or Michael Jackson. Writing and recording songs in life enables the person to keep performing and earning after death. Death is far from the end of a career; it is just a diversion towards a different manner of working. For example, Elvis Presley still sells more than one million albums every year and he is hugely productive in terms of tourism surrounding his traces and brand by enabling fans to access Graceland and an entertainment complex called Elvis Presley's Memphis. Presley has also had significant success in releasing new material after death through the reuse of his vocals, helping him achieve four posthumous number ones. This productivity has resulted in him consistently holding 2nd to 4th place on the DRL since losing first position (which he has never regained) in 2009, to Yves Saint Laurent and subsequently Michael Jackson. Meanwhile, golfer Arnold Palmer is so productive from beyond the grave via his beverage line, that he achieved 3rd place in 2019 on the DRL with US$30 million, whilst Bob Marley earned an impressive US$20 million aided not only by music sales but also House of Marley headphones and Marley Natural cannabis and smoking accessories.

The DRL reveals more than that celebrities can have immense incomes through posthumous careers. It unveils evidence that gender inequality continues even after death (Penfold-Mounce 2019a). Since its inception, the DRL has published the earnings of 52 dead celebrities all of whom have been men, barring five women: actor/model Marilyn Monroe; actor Elizabeth Taylor; model Bettie Page; singer-songwriter Jenni Rivera; and singer-songwriter Whitney Houston. The representation of dead celebrity women on the DRL is particularly significant in terms of gender inequality amongst posthumous careers in terms of actual income and the types of labour they conduct after death. Women are scarce on the DRL; for example, it was not until 2011 that more than one woman was present – Monroe was joined by Taylor and Page – and 2013 was a landmark year when four women featured for the first and only time – Monroe, Taylor, Page and Rivera. Since this peak of four women, numbers have declined again with three women appearing between 2014–2015 (Monroe, Taylor and

Page) and reducing to just two in 2016–2017 (Taylor and Page), in 2018 (Monroe and Page) and in 2019 (Monroe and Houston). The DRL reveals not only how few dead women celebrities achieve financially successful posthumous careers, but how precarious their position is amongst the huge earnings of many male posthumous careers. Women on the DRL struggle to maintain a position on the list (for example, Rivera appeared for a single year in 2013 and Houston made her first appearance in 2019) or to hold the top positions on the top ten earners list, with only Elizabeth Taylor having achieved the number one slot for a single year in 2012. From the five women who appear on the DRL, it is Monroe who stands out as a successful productive dead female celebrity due to her longevity on the list. She has appeared on the DRL since its first publication in 2001 and every year since apart from 2009–2010 and 2016–2017, leading to the question: what is the secret of her posthumous success? The final section of this chapter uses Monroe as a case study of how a dead female celebrity can have a successful posthumous career as the productive celebrity dead. She is used to explore the ways the celebrity dead continue to be productive from beyond the grave and to highlight the conflict that can ensue over the ownership and control of post-humous careers. Monroe has an impressive capacity to encapsulate spectacular death through her productivity.

Dead famous, dead successful, dead productive: Marilyn Monroe

In 1962, at the age of just 36, actor/model Marilyn Monroe died of a barbiturate overdose. She had been a huge sex symbol and popular Hollywood star during the 1950s and early 1960s, despite grappling with mental illness and eventually, substance abuse. Monroe was in life, and has continued to be in death, an icon (see Rollyson 2005); she cultivated her celebrity personhood forming a revered and idolised status. She uniquely captured vulnerability, difficulty and provocation; whilst being a high-profile star, she still managed to remain elusive. Monroe's death was the death of an icon. Her death led to a variety of conspiracy theories suggesting murder and links to President John F. Kennedy and his brother Robert, as well as union leader Jimmy Hoffa and even mob boss Sam Giancana. In both life and death Monroe courted controversy and speculation. Therefore, it is unsurprising that her posthumous career, although financially and symbolically successful, has been defined by both productivity and conflict. Monroe is an exemplar of spectacular death, not through the spectacle of her demise, but rather through the spectacular nature of her posthumous career.

In death Monroe has become a lucrative brand that is proving to have longevity in terms of earnings. For example, Monroe is the first and only woman to feature in the first eight years of the publication of the DRL (2001–2008) hovering between 6th and 12th place whilst earning up to US$10 million a year before ultimately achieving 8th place in 2018 with US$14 million her highest income on the DRL. Monroe's posthumous career as a brand has certainly demonstrated an ability for longevity; however, she has failed to climb to the top of the DRL, highlighting that the top dead celebrity earners are men. This lack of success in rising to the economic top amongst dead celebrities is interrelated with conflict over the possession and management of the value of her traces and her bodily capital. Several earning blips are evident on the DRL, including between 2009–2010 and also 2016–2017 when she disappeared from the list. Both of these absences on the list reveal how conflict over the control of Monroe's celebrity traces, and subsequently her posthumous career, have impacted on her productivity and financial success. 2009–2010 marked the first substantial disappearance of Monroe from the DRL and coincides with the culmination of a litigation battle over who owned Monroe's image, particularly relating to photographs. This resulted in Anna Strasberg, the widow of Monroe's acting coach Lee Strasberg to whom was left 75% of Monroe's estate and CMG Worldwide (the company hired by Strasberg to license Monroe's name and image) losing a court battle in 2008. This litigation battle resulted in Authentic Brands Group (ABG) purchasing the licencing rights to Monroe in 2011 for a rumoured US$20–30 million. ABG now control and manage Monroe's traces which led to the second disappearance of Monroe from the DRL in 2016–2017 as new licensing deals, including with Montblanc pens, were negotiated (Kirsta 2012).

Following ABG purchasing the rights to manage her posthumous career, Monroe's value has become substantially more financially lucrative than it was between 2001–2008. Their management of products rooted in her bodily capital has been hugely economically successful since 2011. Monroe has become very active with a previously unheard recording of her stating that she only wore Chanel No.5 to bed being used in 2012 to advertise the perfume, whilst in 2015 she appeared in Coca-Cola adverts (alongside Elvis Presley), Max Factor and Dior perfume (with Grace Kelly and Marlene Dietrich) and even launched a clothing line with US retailer Macy's. A significant development for Monroe's posthumous career has been her conversion into an animated character in order to 'make the world a better place by inspiring others through her creative mindset and individuality'. This cartoon character called Mini Marilyn is described by ABG: 'She's dazzling, she's vivacious, and she's bursting to meet the world! With her trademark blonde hair and red lips, Mini Marilyn is the epitome of all things glamorous'. Mini Marilyn is an extension of the value of Monroe's bodily capital, having been designed to target those aged between 17–34 (Young 2015); and to serve as an 'engine for licensing, retail and other brand opportunities' particularly in film, television, video games and live venue attractions (Frater 2015) whilst having a major appeal to the Chinese market. Monroe's traces continue to work extensively through the symbolic, and subsequently financial, value generated by her physical attractiveness (see Gottschall 2008; Stephens, Hill and Hanson 1994). Monroe's bodily capital endows her posthumous traces with value that can be marketed to the consumer's gaze. In life, Monroe was an iconic spectacle to be consumed through the news media, photographs and films. In death, she epitomises spectacular death – a spectacle facilitated by the media to be gazed upon and consumed.

In life Monroe's celebrity status was rooted in being beautiful, young, sexy and unattainable. She was the ultimate 'blonde bombshell', who was emotionally complex and unpredictable which made her difficult to control. In death, the control and ownership of her traces have continued to affirm the difficulty in controlling Monroe through an extensive barrage of litigation that has extended beyond her death. In 2007 a series of lawsuits were filed by the children of three of Monroe's photographers (Sam Shaw, Milton Greene and Tom Kelley who were deceased) challenging the right of Anna Strasberg (who owned 75% of the Monroe estate following the death of her husband Lee, to whom Monroe left much of her estate) and CMG Worldwide to control all rights to Monroe's image. The complaint was that the photographers owned the copyright to thousands of Monroe images and had the right to license the images for publishing and merchandising deals without sharing profits with CMG Worldwide and Strasberg. The photographer's descendants no longer wished to pay the hugely inflated 75–90% of gross receipts of royalties to the licence-holder, namely, CMG Worldwide and Strasberg, when most US merchandising agreements involved paying only up to 15%. Shaw, Greene and Kelley's descendants also claimed their dismay at the tawdriness of much of the Monroe licencing granted by CMG Worldwide (Kirsta 2012).

Monroe's financially lucrative posthumous career raised the question of who owns her? And did Monroe have the legal power to bequeath her publicity rights to Strasberg? Notably, when she died America did not recognise posthumous rights of publicity, meaning that the right to control or profit from commercial use of a celebrity's name and likeness died with them. The state of California had introduced the Celebrities Rights Act in 1985 creating publicity rights for dead celebrities whose names, signatures, photographs or likenesses had commercial value but was only valid for those who died after January 1985 and lasted up to 70 years (Decker 2009). Within the six weeks after the Monroe ruling in May 2007 in favour of Monroe's photographers' descendants, a new bill was introduced in California allowing any star who had died since 1 January 1938 to transfer their publicity rights to their heirs (Decker 2009). Unfortunately, Monroe's legal executor filed her will for probate in New York, making her a New York citizen at the time of her death, meaning her estate (Strasberg) and CMG Worldwide could not claim her publicity rights (Krista 2012). Ultimately, Authentic Brands Group (ABG) purchased Monroe's publicity rights from CMG Worldwide, but legal battles continue to threaten Monroe's posthumous career and the value of her traces (see *AVELA, Inc v Estate of Marilyn Monroe, LLC*, SDNY, No 12-cv-4828).

At the time of her death, Monroe was not in a position to predict the conflict that would engulf her posthumous career. However, more contemporary actors are thinking about their future working life after death, such as actor Al Pacino who expressed that 'I feel like one's likeness and image should be protected in some way and not abused or denigrated for the sake of profit' (Kirsta 2012). Meanwhile, actor Liza Minnelli stated 'I believe only family or those entrusted with this right [legal rights over the ownership of dead celebrities' images] can truly know how to maintain the integrity, respect and dignity of a loved one's name, image and likeness' (Kirsta 2012). Facing the prospect of becoming the productive dead is leading celebrities to plan for their posthumous careers. They are seeking to exert control and ownership over their traces from beyond the grave. They are effectively resisting death and not fully trusting the living to work in their best interests. No longer do celebrities after death have to pass over full control of their traces to family or a brand management company and trust they will act in a way that they would approve. Instead, dead celebrities can remain in control of themselves by leaving strict instructions for how they wish their posthumous career to be conducted and thus direct how their value is to be used and accrued after death. Actor and comedian Robin Williams set a precedent for controlling traces after his death in 2014 by leaving his rights of publicity to a foundation set up in his name and denying them the right to benefit from this legacy until 2039. What was distinctive about this move was twofold: firstly, Williams asserted control over his posthumous career and how his traces could be exploited, and secondly, he recognised the value of the productive dead and took steps to mitigate the tax contribution his traces would have to pay to the US Internal Revenue Service (IRS) (Anon 2015).

Conclusion

When Norbert Elias wrote: 'Death is the problem of the living. Dead people have no problems' (2001:3), he did not consider that although the dead might have no problems, they are very able to cause problems. In an age of globalised spectacular death, the high-profile celebrity dead become highly consumable as a brand and product, making them extremely financially and symbolically valuable. Drawing on Beverley Skeggs's (2011) concept of 'bodies of value', the 'traces' which are left behind by dead celebrities as consumables enable posthumous careers to thrive. It is the leaving behind of traces imbued with bodily capital after the death of their physical body, that reveals dead celebrities to encapsulate spectacular death that expands Michael Hviid Jacobsen's (2016) vision of new visibility and commercialisation of human mortality. We have argued that spectacular death is not about the actual dying and death of a celebrity, but their transition into a posthumous life and career and the productivity they display after death as the productive dead. Subsequently, whether dead celebrities' process of dying may or may not be a visual spectacle (see Walter 2009; Woodthorpe 2010), the traces that linger after death enable them to achieve spectacular death through lucrative and highly productive posthumous careers.

As the productive dead in an age of mediated spectacle, dead celebrities are a catalyst for spectacular death, as their posthumous careers are spectacles producing products and images available to be consumed globally. As such, the value of dead celebrities reveals a particular form of 'spectacular death' in an age of the spectacle. In using Marilyn Monroe as an exemplar of the productive dead, it is apparent that conflict over control and ownership does not end with death. Instead, the spectacular death of dead celebrities such as Monroe opens new channels for debate over ownership, control and the dignity of the dead in terms of preventing tawdry commodification. It is through the labour of celebrity traces and their commercial value that the deceased celebrity becomes the productive dead who resist the grave and co-exist amongst the living, embodying spectacular death. The key to the spectacular death experienced by many high-profile celebrities through posthumous careers rooted in the traces they leave behind is that you need to be more than dead famous to be dead successful after death. To have a successful posthumous career in the age of mediated spectacle and spectacular death, a celebrity needs to be dead productive, dead in control and ultimately have imbued their traces with drop dead gorgeous bodily capital too.

References

Adorno, Theodor W. and Max Horkheimer (1944/2002): *Dialectic of Enlightenment*. London: Verso.

Anon. (26 May 2015): '4 Lessons from the Robin Williams Estate Litigation'. *Law 360*, Available online at: https://www.law360.com/articles/659532/4-lessons-from-the -robin-williams-estate-litigation.

Archerd, Army (1997): 'Astaire Won't Deal with the Devil'. *Variety*, February, 25. Available online at: https://variety.com/1997/voices/columns/astaire-won-t-deal-w ith-the-devil-1117863031/.

Ariès, Philippe (1974): *Western Attitudes Toward Death from the Middle Ages to the Present*. Baltimore, MD: Johns Hopkins University Press.

AVELA, Inc vs. Estate of Marilyn Monroe, LLC, SDNY, No 12-cv-4828.

Baker, Wayne E. and Robert R. Faulkner (1991): 'Role as Resource in the Hollywood Film Industry'. *American Journal of Sociology*, 97(2):279–309.

Bauman, Zygmunt (1992): *Mortality, Immortality and Other Life Strategies*. Cambridge: Polity Press.

Beer, David and Ruth Penfold-Mounce (2010): 'Researching Glossy Topics: The Case of the Academic Study of Celebrity'. *Celebrity Studies*, 1(3):360–365.

Carrabine, Eamonn (2014): 'Seeing Things: Violence, Voyeurism and the Camera'. *Theoretical Criminology*, 18(2):134–158.

Debord, Guy (1967/2012). *Society of the Spectacle*. East Sussex: Soul Bay Press Ltd.

Decker, Michael (2009): 'Goodbye, Norma Jean: Marilyn Monroe and the Right of Publicity's Transformation at Death'. *Cardozo Arts & Entertainment Law Journal*, 27(1):243–272.

D'Rozario, Denver (2016): 'Dead Celebrity (Deleb) Use in Marketing: An Initial Theoretical Exposition'. *Psychology & Marketing*, 33(7):486–504.

Elias, Norbert (2001): *The Loneliness of the Dying*. London: Continuum.

Elliott, Anthony (1999): *The Mourning of John Lennon*. Berkeley, CA: University of California Press.

Foltyn, Jacque Lynn (2008): 'The Corpse in Contemporary Culture: Identifying, Transacting and Recoding the Dead Body in the Twenty-First Century'. *Mortality*, 13(2):99–104.

Frater, Patrick (2015): 'China's DMG Teams with Authentic Brands to Launch Mini Marilyn Character'. *Variety*, April 9. Available online at: http://variety.com/2015/biz/asia/chinas-dmg-teams-with-authentic-brands-to-launch-mini-marilyn-character-1201469245/.

Gottschall, Jonathan (2008): *Literature, Science and a New Humanities*. New York: Palgrave/Macmillan.

Hayward, Keith (2010): 'Opening the Lens: Cultural Criminology and the Image'. In: Keith Hayward and Mike Presdee (eds.). *Framing Crime: Cultural Criminology and the Image*. London: Routledge, pp. 1–16.

Howarth, Glennys (2010): *Death and Dying: A Sociological Introduction*. Cambridge: Polity Press.

Howson, Alexandra (2013): *The Body in Society*. Cambridge: Polity Press.

Jacobsen, Michael Hviid (2016): '"Spectacular Death" – Proposing a New Fifth Phase to Philippe Ariès's Admirable History of Death'. *Humanities*, 5(19):1–20.

Jewkes, Yvonne (2015): *Media and Crime*. London: Sage Publications.

Jones, Steve and Joli Jensen (eds.) (2005): *Afterlife as Afterimage: Understanding Posthumous Fame* (Volume 2). New York: Peter Lang.

Jonsson, Annika (2015): 'Post-Mortem Social Death – Exploring the Absence of the Deceased'. *Contemporary Social Science*, 10(3):284–295.

Kellner, Douglas (2003): *Media Spectacle*. London: Routledge.

Kirsta, Alix (2012): 'Selling the Dead'. *Telegraph*, February 3. Available online at: https://www.telegraph.co.uk/finance/9056455/Selling-the-dead.html.

Králová, Jana (2015): 'What is Social Death?' *Contemporary Social Science*, 10(3):235–248.

Kristeva, Julia (1982): *Power of Horror: An Essay on Abjection*. New York: Columbia University Press.

Mears, Ashley and William Finlay (2005): 'Not Just a Paper Doll: How Models Manage Bodily Capital and Why They Perform Emotional Labour'. *Journal of Contemporary Ethnography*, 34(3):317–343.

Mulkay, Michael (1992): 'Social Death in Britain'. *The Sociological Review*, 40(1_suppl):31–49.

Orwell, George (1948/2013) *1984*. London: Oberon Books.

Penfold-Mounce, Ruth (2018): *Death, the Dead and Popular Culture*. Bingley: Emerald Publishing.

Penfold-Mounce, Ruth (2019a): 'Value and Gender Inequality after Death'. *Sociological Research Online*. DOI: 10.1177/1360780419883297.

Penfold-Mounce, Ruth (2019b): 'The Thanatological Imagination and Celebrity Death'. In: Adriana Teodorescu and Michael Hviid Jacobsen (eds.). *Death in Contemporary Popular Culture*. London: Routledge, pp. 51–64.

Petty, Ross D. and Denver D'Rozario (2009): 'The Use of Dead Celebrities in Advertising and Marketing: Balancing Interests in the Right of Publicity'. *Journal of Advertising*, 38(4):37–49.

Ritman, Alex (2019): 'James Dean Reborn in CGI for Vietnam War Action-Drama'. *The Hollywood Reporter*, November 6. Available online at: https://www.hollywoodreporter.com/news/afm-james-dean-reborn-cgi-vietnam-war-action-drama-1252703.

Rojek, Chris (2001): *Celebrity*. London: Reaktion Books.

Rojek, Chris (2012): *Fame Attack: The Inflation of Celebrity and Its Consequences*. London: Bloomsbury.

Rollyson, Carl (2005): *Female Icons: Marilyn Monroe to Susan Sontag*. New York: iUniverse.

Skeggs, Beverley (2011): 'Imagining Personhood Differently: Person Value and Autonomist Working-Class Value Practices'. *The Sociological Review*, 59(3):496–513.

Smith-Maguire, Jennifer and Julian Matthews (2012): 'Are We All Cultural Intermediaries Now? An Introduction to Cultural Intermediaries in Context'. *European Journal of Cultural Studies*, 15(5):551–562.

Stephens, Debra Lynn, Ronald Paul Hill and Cynthia Hanson (1994): 'The Beauty Myth and Female Consumers: The Controversial Role of Advertising'. *Journal of Consumer Affairs*, 28(1):137–153.

Sydell, Laura (2018): 'In the Future Movie Stars May Be Performing Even After They Are Dead'. *NPR: All Tech Considered*. Available online at: https://www.npr.org/secti ons/alltechconsidered/2018/03/05/590238807/in-the-future-movie-stars-may-be -performing-even-after-their-dead.

Thurman, Neil (2008): 'Forums for Citizen Journalists? Adoption of User Generated Content Initiatives by Online News Media'. *New Media & Society*, 10(1):139–157.

Urry, John (2002): *The Tourist Gaze* (2nd edition). London: Sage Publications.

Urry, John and Jonas Larsen (2011). *The Tourist Gaze 3.0* (3rd edition). London: Sage Publications.

Van Dijck, José (2013): 'Facebook and the Engineering of Connectivity: A Multi-Layered Approach to Social Media Platforms'. *Convergence*, 19(2):141–155.

Wacquant, Loïc J. D. (1995): 'Pugs at Work: Bodily Capital and Bodily Labour Among Professional Boxers'. *Body & Society*, 1(1):65–93.

Walter, Tony (2009): 'Jade's Dying Body: The Ultimate Reality Show'. *Sociological Research Online*, 14(5):1–11.

Woodthorpe, Kate (2010): 'Public Dying: Death in the Media and Jade Goody'. *Sociology Compass*, 4(5):283–294.

Young, Alison (2010): 'The Scene of the Crime: Is There Such a Thing as 'Just Looking'?' In: Keith Hayward and Mike Presdee (eds.). *Framing Crime: Cultural Criminology and the Image*. London: Routledge, pp. 83–97.

Young, Vicki M. (2015): 'Authentic Brands Group Introduces Mini Marilyn'. *Women's Wear Daily*, April 9. Available online at: http://wwd.com/business-news/marketing -promotion/authentic-brands-group-introduces-mini-marilyn-10109393/.

3

TOURING HEAVEN AND HELL

Spectacular encounters by celebrities in near-death experiences

Jacque Lynn Foltyn

Introduction

In the 21st century, Near-Death Experiences (NDE) are a recognised social category and publishing phenomenon. In January 2020, over 4,000 NDE titles were listed on Amazon. Bestselling memoirs by clergy, atheist, child, and physician 'experiencers' (NDErs) provide spectacular tales of their dying, deaths, and resurrections; encounters with divinities, the dead, and corpses; and their return to life, transformed. Since the publication of *Life After Life* (1975) by Raymond A. Moody, a philosopher, psychologist, and physician teaching ethics at a medical school, accounts of NDE have been growing steadily. Consider the following titles: *90 Minutes in Heaven: A True Story of Death and Life* (Piper 2004) and *Imagine Heaven: Near-Death Experiences, God's Promise, and the Exhilarating Future that Awaits You* (Burke 2015). Over ten million copies of three-year-old Colton Burpo's *Heaven Is for Real: A Little Boy's Astounding Story of His Trip to Heaven and Back* (2010) have been sold, and his tale of seeing Jesus riding on a rainbow-coloured horse was made into a 2014 film. Since Moody's studies, NDE accounts by other physicians have further legitimised NDE accounts; among them are *Proof of Heaven: A Neurosurgeon's Journey into the Afterlife* (Alexander 2012) and *To Heaven and Back: A Doctor's Extraordinary Account of Her Death, Heaven, Angels, and Life Again* (Neal 2012). NDE are not only a central subject of contemporary popular culture, they are the focus of study by experts. There are NDE workshops and conferences, the peer-reviewed *Journal of Near-Death Studies*, and academic studies published in medical and scientific journals, all of which reflect a more nuanced consideration of what happens to consciousness after death.

Growing interest in NDE is a subcategory of the increasing beguilement with dying, death, the dead, and corpses. In the 21st century there is a Western cult of death. Halloween rivals Christmas in popularity, 'dark tourism' is a growing industry, fictional human-eating monsters are fêted as pop culture heroes, and elements of gothic, horror, and torture porn stream into conventional genres (Khapaeva 2017, 2019). In the world of fashion, skull style and 'corpse chic' have gone mainstream (Foltyn 2008b, 2010, 2013). Not only is death 'worn', it is the focus of international 'mournathons' after pop stars die unexpectedly (Foltyn 2008b, 2016). Death has been 'revived' (Walter 1994), is no longer denied or hidden away, as it was after the Victorian Era, or proclaimed the 'failure of a cure' (Ariès 1974). In the mid-20th century, after this interdiction began to fade, fictive death appeared as a form of entertainment in popular culture (Gorer 1955). Death went 'pop' (McIlwaine 2005), and in the 21st century it has become a place where the dead exert agency while entertaining the consumer, engaging them with issues of mortality (Penfold-Mounce 2018). Complementing these developments in popular culture, the growth of death studies and conferences reflects a more open attitude about death, a reaction, perhaps, to the 'rationalisation' that Max Weber (1958) claimed had wrung the mystery out of modern life, disillusionment with technology, and a desire to re-enchant the world, exploring confines beyond the physical world (Lee 2003).

Death, the dead, corpses, dead celebrities, and NDE have seized the popular imagination, which is where this chapter, a study of 37 celebrity NDE, comes in. In the chapter, I argue that these accounts have been folded into a consumer–entertainment–celebrity industrial complex focused on death (Foltyn 2008a) and are a feature of death in a spectacular age, late-modern or postmodern society, specifically in terms of the following dimensions identified by Danish sociologist Michael Hviid Jacobsen (2016): the mediation/mediatisation, commercialisation/commodification, re-ritualisation, and specialisation of death. This period overlaps with the growth of spectacularity in other dimensions of social life, including the growth of social media and celebrities of the A-D list imagination. The chapter unfolds as follows: a review of the literature and of historical accounts of famous individuals who have had what have come to be known as NDE. Next, the study methodology, results, and data analysis followed by a discussion. Finally, a conclusion about how the chapter may inform our understanding about death in contemporary culture.

Near-death experiences

Accounts of individuals dying and coming back to life have figured in worldwide transcendental beliefs for thousands of years (Shushan 2009; Sleutjes, Moreira-Almeida and Greyson 2014), have been reported by 95% of world cultures (Holden, Greyson and James 2009), and transcend history, religious beliefs, culture, age, class, gender, and sexuality.

While the term 'Near-Death Experience' was first used by the physician John C. Lilly in 1972 (Schlieter 2018), Moody, with his imposing credentials, popularised the term. Before Lilly or Moody, military physician Pierre-Jean Du Monchaux (1766) described NDE in *Anecdotes de Médecine* (Charlier 2014).

In 1892, Swiss geologist Albert Heim wrote of falling down a mountain and seeing a 'heavenly light'; the event was so compelling that he gathered accounts from others (as cited in Noyes and Kletti 1972:50). In 1896, epistemologist-psychologist Victor Egger shared NDE accounts he gathered with a group of philosophers (Bogousslavsky et al. 2010). With modern medical technology's ability to bring people back from death, NDE reports are increasing. Heart-lung machines, medically induced comas, reviving the bodies of those who died while submerged in freezing water, and chilling patients to stop heart, breathing, and brain activity to perform dangerous operations have provided more evidence of NDE.

Historical records about famous individuals who had NDE go back to the 'The Story of Er'. In *The Republic* 10 (375 BC), Plato writes of a soldier who died, visited the afterlife, revived on his funeral pyre with macabre and marvellous tales of the hereafter, and became a celebrity. In *The Republic* 9, Plato reports that Timarchus, a student of Socrates, died, had an out-of-body experience (OBE) and descended into a place of roaring animals, wailing babies, and lamenting people, before a light led him to a beauteous landscape and return to life. In 'The Divine Vengeance' 563D–568D, Plutarch provides the account of Aridaeus, who died, had an OBE, witnessed the dead suffering horrific punishments, resurrected on the day of his funeral, and earned fame and a new name, Thespesius (van der Sluijs 2009). In the 6th century CE, Pope Gregory the Great offered 'proofs' of the soul's immortality in 42 accounts of deathbed visions, including NDE in Book 4.37, *Dialogues* (Zaleski 1988). Fast-forward to the 16th century to Michel de Montaigne who had an NDE after being thrown from a horse (Danticat 2017) and to the 18th century, when British Navy Admiral Francis Beaufort saw his life pass before his eyes while nearly drowning (Friendly 1977).

In the 20th century, novelist Ernest Hemingway and psychoanalyst Carl Jung enter the NDE fame roster. In 1918, while serving with the Red Cross in Italy during the First World War, Hemingway was wounded by a mortar shell, had an OBE, and a sudden return to his body (Villard and Nagel 1989). Hemingway's experience was so profound, it shaped plotlines in *A Farewell to Arms* (1929), 'In Another Country' (1927), 'Now I Lay Me' (1927), and 'The Snows of Kilimanjaro' (1936) (Vardamis and Owens 1999). After a heart attack in 1944, Jung had an OBE during which he claimed he floated into outer space, was surrounded by a bright light, witnessed efforts to revive him, had a life review, encountered spiritual and historical figures, experienced bliss, was told to return to life, and had no desire to return to life. After the sudden return to his body, Jung no longer feared death, felt reborn, and had a new willingness to take intellectual risks (Jung 1961/1989).

A growing body of research by physicians studying NDE finds that consciousness survives death and is independent but closely connected to the brain. Among these are critical care physician Laurin Bellig (2015), radiation oncologist Jeffery Long (2010), paediatrician Melvin L. Morse (1986), and cardiologists Michael Sabom (1982) and Pim van Lommel et al. (2001). Since 2008, pulmonologist

Sam Parnia has headed the Aware Study (I, 2008–2012 and II, 2016–concluding in 2020) of a team of medical professionals in the United Kingdom, United States, and Austria. Critics of these physician-led studies claim the investigators use their professional status to lend legitimacy to their claims and their true purpose is to eliminate death (Zaleksi 1988).

Explanations for the origins of NDE fall into three categories: (1) spiritual-transcendental, (2) psychological: dissociative defence mechanism (Blackmore 1993), and (3) organic/biological meltdown (French 2001). For some researchers, NDE are merely a lens for understanding consciousness (Crick 1995). Those looking for non-metaphysical explanations have found a strong relationship between psychedelic-induced NDE-like experiences and NDE, pointing to biochemical disturbances in the brain (Timmermann et al. 2018).

While there are studies to support any of the above viewpoints, there are recurring NDE patterns. Psychiatrist Bruce Greyson (1983) developed a 16-point scale, and philosophers John Martin Fischer and Benjamin Mitchell-Yellin (2016) found that NDE follow an expected script: OBE, travelling in a tunnel, encountering a celestial light, meeting divine beings, reunions with deceased loved ones, experiencing a glorious afterlife, a reluctant return to life, and profound transformation. In their study of 154 NDE narratives, Charlotte Martial et al. (2017) found the eight most common features are: a feeling of peace (80%), seeing a bright light (69%), OBE (53%), encounters with spirits/[dead] people (64%), experiencing a tunnel (47%), coming to a point of no return (40%), unearthly environment (37%), and returning to the body (37%). While NDE have usual patterns, there is no sequence to the events and not all NDE share the same features (Martial et al. 2017).

Post-NDE personal transformation is another area of study. Among changes reported are a greater appreciation for life; increased spirituality and concern for others; decreased materialism, competitiveness, and fear of death (Sabom 1982); strengthened belief in post-mortem existence (Noyes 1980); and renewed purpose, greater confidence, increased value of love, and greater compassion (Ring 1980, 1984). In NDE scholarship, this pattern of transformation is linked to the Hero's Journey, outlined by Joseph Campbell (1949), in which the hero is wrenched out of normal life, takes a journey to an unfamiliar realm, struggles and faces death, and returns, transformed, to former life.

Less discussed are unpleasant NDE. These comprise about 50% of NDE, according to some studies (Rawlings 1978), and 23% in a more recent study (Litchfield 2015). Plato, Plutarch, and Pope Gregory the Great recount terrifying as well as blissful NDE; Montaigne found his NDE unbearable (Danticat 2017); and Hemingway's NDE made him fear his spirit would slip out of his body as he slept. Before entering a beautiful after-world in his NDE, neurosurgeon Eben Alexander claimed he was trapped in a filthy claustrophobic place where he encountered grotesque animal faces. A temporary sojourn in hell is a common report (Rawlings 1978). About 15% of adults and 3% of children NDErs enter 'a threatening void or stark limbo or hellish purgatory' (Atwater 2009). For them, the afterlife is a dark place of encounters with demonic beings where one experiences grief, depression, and fear (Kellehear 2002). Researchers describe post-NDE negative changes in attitudes and behaviour that can lead to psychosocial and psychospiritual problems and other unbeneficial after-effects (Orne 1995).

Methodology

For this study, accounts of celebrity NDE come from several sources, specifically, content analysis of published interviews, autobiographies, memoirs, and social media, and from secondary sources such as NDE publications and websites. My subjects are individuals whose renown, prestige, and ineffable 'x-factor' moved them into the realm of celebrity. Each had an NDE – or spoke of a past NDE – in the era of 'spectacular death'. My rationale for limiting the sample in this way is the celebrities whom I have chosen not only have familiarity with the NDE concept, but have applied the label to interpret their encounter with death.

In defining NDE, I use the criteria developed by scholars. My subjects survived imminent death or clinical death. Limiting my sample allowed me to weed out celebrities who have had a 'brush' with death, rather than an NDE, but whose accounts nevertheless regularly appear in NDE journalism and websites.

The study goal was to test whether the NDE of these individuals fill the most prevalently occurring NDE features found by Martial et al. (2017), described in the previous section, and to identify other patterns. Other goals were to compare post-NDE value and belief changes to the findings of Noyes (1980), Ring (1980, 1984), and Sabom (1982), also discussed above, and to analyse whether celebrity NDE accounts have elements of the Hero's Journey.

Limitations for this study include its small sample and relying on published interviews and excerpts of published interviews that may or may not provide the entire narrative of the NDE. One of the problems with NDE research is that most accounts are retrospectives, raising the question of reliability of memories (French 2001) and embellishment (Greyson 2007).

Subjects

My 37 subjects are/were public figures in the world of entertainment, sports, politics, or religion, whose renown made them celebrities during their lifetimes:

Roseanne Barr (1952–), actor, comedian. NDE: age 16/17, hit by car, traumatic brain injury.
Tony Bennett (1926–), singer. NDE: 1979, drug overdose.
Gary Busey (1944–), actor. NDE: 1988, motorcycle accident, while undergoing brain surgery.
Johnny Cash (1932–2003), singer-songwriter, musician. NDE: 1988, after bypass surgery, double pneumonia.

Jim Caviezel (1968–), actor. NDE, lightning strike, while filming crucifixion scene in *The Passion of the Christ* (2004).

Chevy Chase (1943–), actor, comedian. NDE: electrocution while filming *Modern Problems* (1981).

William Jefferson (Bill) Clinton (1946–), 42nd President of the USA. NDE: 2004, during bypass surgery, while on heart-lung machine.

James Cromwell (1940–), actor. NDE: age 5, near drowning.

Roger Daltrey (1944–), singer, founder of *The Who*. NDE: 2015, meningitis, a fall.

Rebecca De Mornay (1959–), actor. NDE: age 7, peptic ulcer, blood loss.

Erik Estrada (1949–), actor. NDE: 1979, motorcycle accident, while working on the set of *CHiPs*, massive internal bleeding.

Louis Farrakhan (1933–), minister-leader of Nation of Islam. NDE: 1999, while battling cancer.

George Foreman (1949–), boxer. NDE: 1977, heat exhaustion collapse suffered after a boxing match.

Louis Gossett Jr (1936–), actor. NDE: age 12, fall.

Larry Hagman (1931–2012), actor. NDE: 1995, post-liver transplant surgery complications.

Niels Hausgaard (1944–), singer-songwriter, comedian. NDE: 2016, heart attack.

Roy Horn (1939–2020), animal trainer and performer at Siegfried & Roy. NDE: 2003, neck bite by white tiger while performing, blood loss, stroke.

Sally Kirkland (1941–), actor. NDE: 1966, suicide attempt, drug overdose.

Tracy Morgan (1968–), actor, comedian. NDE: 2014, multi-vehicle accident.

Lamar Odom (1979–), basketball player and reality TV star. NDE: 2015, cardiac arrest, seizures, coma caused by drug overdose.

Ozzy Osbourne (1948–), singer-songwriter and reality TV star. NDE: 2003, ATV accident.

Robert Pastorelli (1954–2004), actor. NDE: 1973, car accident, while in ER.

William Petersen (1953–), actor. NDE: early 1980s, blood loss, severed finger.

Amy Purdy (1979–), actress, model, para-athlete. NDE: 1999, bacterial meningitis.

Ronald Reagan (1911–2004), 40th President of the United States, actor. NDE: two events: after being shot by John Hinckley in 1981; and while suffering from pneumonia, while shooting *That Hagen Girl* (1947), with Shirley Temple.

Della Reese (1931–2017), singer, actor, minister. NDE: two events: n.d., exsanguination after walking into a glass door; 1979, brain aneurysm, while filming *The Tonight Show*.

Christopher Reeve (1952–2004), actor. NDE: 1995, anaphylactic shock after being given the drug Sygen, after fall from horse that made him quadriplegic.

Burt Reynolds (1936–2018), actor, former football player. NDE: two events: once as teen, after a car accident; and again after an accident while working on *City Heat* (1984).

Eric Roberts (1956–), actor. NDE: 1981, car accident, coma.

Peter Sellers (1925–1980), actor. NDE: 1964, during a series of eight heart attacks.

Jane Seymour (1951–), actor. NDE: 1987, allergic reaction to penicillin

Nikki Sixx (1956–), musician, songwriter in Mötley Crüe. NDE: 1987, heroin overdose.

Sharon Stone (1958–), actor. NDE: 2001, brain haemorrhage during an MRI.

Donald Sutherland (1935–), actor. NDE: meningitis, coma/pneumonia while filming *Kelly's Heroes* (1970).

Elizabeth Taylor (1932–2011), actor, AIDS activist. NDE: 1957 during back surgery.

Clint Walker (1927–2018), actor. NDE: ski pole impaled his heart.

Debra Winger (1955–), actor: NDE: New Year's Eve, 1973, cerebral haemorrhage.

Results

Below is a summary of results, in numbers and percentages, organised by frequency, with noteworthy examples from celebrity NDErs of what they claimed occurred during their NDE.

The near-death experience

Encounters with spirits and the dead (19/51%): Busey, Cash, Daltrey, De Mornay, Estrada, Farrakhan, Foreman, Hagman, Horn, Morgan, Pastorelli, Petersen, Purdy, Reagan, Reese, Sellers, Seymour, Stone, and Taylor claim they encountered spiritual entities and the deceased. Peter Sellers met God (MacLaine 1983), Tracy Morgan conversed with God (Winfrey 2016), Jane Seymour (2010a, 2010b) met angels, and Roger Daltrey saw a 'green exit sign' doorway to heaven (Law 2018). Gary Busey says that he 'was surrounded by angels. And they don't look like what they look like on Christmas cards. They're big balls of light that float and carry nothing but love and warmth' (Rosen 2012). During their NDE, Sharon Stone visited with friends (Winfrey 2014), Roy Horn was reunited with his beloved deceased animals (Shriver 2004), Erik Estrada visited with dead family members and friends, and Elizabeth Taylor spent time with her deceased husband, the producer Michael Todd (Near-Death Experiences of the Hollywood 2016).

Bright light (18/49%): seeing a bright light is a classic NDE event, and Barr, Bennett, Busey, Cash, Caviezel, Clinton, Estrada, Gossett, Horn, Osbourne, Petersen, Purdy, Reynolds, Sellers, Sixx, Stone, Sutherland, and Taylor described their encounters with a light source. According to Sharon Stone, 'this kind of giant vortex of white light was upon me and I kind of – poof! Sort of took off into this glorious, bright, bright, bright white light' (Winfrey 2014). Tony Bennett

(2007) recounted 'a golden light enveloped me in a warm glow', and Bill Clinton saw 'circles of light containing the faces of Hillary, Chelsea and others ... They smiled and flew away toward a brightness' (Powers 2005). Jim Caviezel claims he saw a light and was lit up by a light (Burden 2019).

Out-of-body experience (15/41%): Barr, Caviezel, Daltrey, Estrada, Horn, Pastorelli, Reeve, Reynolds, Roberts, Sellers, Seymour, Sixx, Stone, Sutherland, and Taylor reported OBEs. Elizabeth Taylor felt weightlessness, like 'being in liquid mercury' (Elizabeth Taylor's Near-Death Experience 1992). Nikki Sixx revealed he 'felt as if something very gentle was grabbing my head and pulling me upward ... I shot upright, as if I weighed nothing' (Lee et al. 2002).

Felt peace (14/38%): Barr, Bennett, Busey, Cash, Estrada, Hagman, Haussgaard, Pastorelli, Petersen, Reagan, Sellers, Stone, Sutherland, and Walker experienced a blissful afterlife. As reported by William Petersen:

> I could tell it was a great, great place. Full of love and peace and crap like that. You know, postcard stuff. I remember the whole rest of the night I was sort of blissed out by having seen that.
>
> *(Near-Death Experiences of the Hollywood 2016)*

Unearthly environment (12/35%): Barr, Busey, Cash, Estrada, Foreman, Hagman, Morgan, Petersen, Sellers, Stone, Taylor, and Walker felt they had entered an unearthly environment. Larry Hagman (2011) heard celestial music:

> Everyone has their own unique song, an inner melody that fuses each of us to the deep, modulating, harmonious hum of the celestial orchestra that's the collective energy of everything that's ever lived and ever going to live. It's our life force.

Coming to a point of no return, a border (12/32%): Busey, Daltrey, Foreman, Hagman, Morgan, Pastorelli, Reeve, Sellers, Seymour, Stone, Taylor, and Walker found themselves at a point of no return during their NDE.

Witnessed resuscitation efforts (11/30%): Estrada, Osbourne, Pastorelli, Purdy, Reeve, Reynolds (2), Sellers, Seymour, Sixx, Taylor, and Walker witnessed efforts by others to revive them. As Jane Seymour (2010a, 2010b) revealed:

> I literally left my body. I had this feeling that I could see myself on the bed, with people grouped around me. I remember them all trying to resuscitate me. I was above them, in the corner of the room looking down. I saw people putting needles in me, trying to hold me down, doing things.

And according to Christopher Reeve (1999):

> I looked down and saw my body stretched out on the bed, not moving, while everybody – there were fifteen or twenty people, the doctors, the

EMTs, the nurses – was working on me. The noise and commotion grew quieter as though someone were gradually turning down the volume. I watched myself lying still and saw everyone swirling around with blood pressure cuffs, stethoscopes, and needles.

Sudden return to body (10/27%): Bennett, Estrada, Pastorelli, Estrada, Foreman, Reeve, Roberts, Seymour, Stone, and Sutherland felt themselves suddenly return to their bodies. Sharon Stone's experience is representative: 'It was very fast – whoosh! Suddenly, I was back. I was in my body and I was in the room' (Winfrey 2014).

Not ready to die or given choice (10/27%): Barr, Busey, Estrada, Foreman, Hagman, Pastorelli, Purdy, Reynolds, Seymour, and Walker realised they were dying and decided not to die. Gary Busey heard a voice: 'You may come with us now or return to your body and continue your destiny. It's your choice' (Near-Death Experiences of the Hollywood 2016). When Burt Reynolds (2015) realised he was dying, he said: '"Fuck this! I'm going back!"'. Jane Seymour (2010a, 2010b) pleaded with God to spare her life:

> The only thing I cared about was that I wanted to live because I did not want anyone else looking after my children. I was floating up there thinking, "No, I don't want to die. I'm not ready to leave my kids". And that was when I said to God, "If you're there, God, if you really exist and I survive, I will never take your name in vain again".

Not your time (9/24%): Bennett, Busey, Estrada, Hagman, Morgan, Petersen, Sellers, Taylor, and Walker were told by a deceased family member or a spiritual entity, or simply understood, it was not their time to die. While encountering the spirit of Michael Todd, Elizabeth Taylor wanted to stay with him, but he said: '"No, Baby. You have to turn around and go back because there is something very important for you to do. You cannot give up now". It was Mike's strength and love that brought me back with America's AIDS magazine' (Near-Death Experiences of the Hollywood 2016).

Saw grieving living family and friends (6/16%): During their NDE, Estrada, Pastorelli, Sellers, Seymour, Sixx, and Taylor were aware of the living people witnessing their deaths. Consider the experience of Erik Estrada:

> At the foot of my bed were four people that I knew: a friend of mine from New York, my Dad … my mother, and a friend of the family … And they were looking at me; but they had really sad faces on them. My mother was crying. So I got out of the bed and walked towards them. And I was maybe three, four inches away, five inches away from them. And they didn't see me. They just kept looking, like looking through me. They were looking past me. And I turned around and I saw what they were looking at [his dead body].
>
> *(Near-Death Experiences of the Hollywood 2016)*

Tunnel (5/14%): During their NDE, Estrada, Petersen, Stone, Sutherland, and Taylor entered the proverbial NDE tunnel. Donald Sutherland says: 'I began to glide down a long tunnel, away from the bed' (Ritchie 1996).

Last rites (3/8%): Estrada, Kirkland, and Pastorelli saw the 'last rites' (the Catholic sacrament, Anointing of the Sick) administered. Consider the recollection of actor Robert Pastorelli as he watched ER staff working on him: 'I could see tubes down my nose and throat. I knew I was dying, and I thought: "Well, this must be death". I even saw a priest giving me the last rites' (Near-Death Experiences of the Hollywood 2016).

Life review (3/8%): Foreman, Osbourne, and Seymour experienced a life history. 'I remember my whole life flashing before my eyes, but I wasn't thinking about winning Emmys or anything like that', said Jane Seymour (2010b).

Past lives (3/8%): Cromwell, Gossett, and Sellers came to believe they had encountered their past lives. His near-drowning caused James Cromwell to have past life memories of the Middle Ages in days of King Arthur (Dovel 2003). Louis Gossett, Jr. saw his past incarnation as a pirate with a harem off the coast of Morocco (Williams 2019), and Peter Sellers became convinced he was a reincarnated soul whose acting powers 'of mimicry' sprang from memories of past lives (Walker 1982).

Experience of horror/hell (2/5%): Foreman and Horn experienced the afterlife as a dreadful place. Roy Horn was hoping it was 'just a bad nightmare' (Shriver 2004). Aspects of George Foreman's post-fight NDE are petrifying, a descent into a hell:

> I knew I was dead, and this wasn't heaven … Sorrow beyond description engulfed my soul, more than anyone could ever imagine … If you multiplied every disturbing and frightening thought that you've ever had during your entire life, that wouldn't come close to the panic I felt … Although I couldn't see anyone, I was aware of other people in this terrible place – the place reeked with the putrid smell of death … This place was a vacuum without light, love, or happiness … In that place, I had no hope for tomorrow – or of ever getting out.
>
> *(Foreman 2007,* Duel with Death *n.d.)*

The aftermath

The after-effects of my subjects' NDE took a variety of forms:

Rebirth, better person (19/51%): Barr, Bennett, Busey, Cash, Chase, Estrada, Farrakhan, Kirkland, Morgan, Odom, Osbourne, Petersen, Sellers, Sixx, Stone, Sutherland, Taylor, Walker, and Winger claim their NDE radically changed their lives. Louis Farrakhan, minister-leader of the Nation of Islam, who in the past was often accused of intolerance towards other religions, stopped demonising Jews and Orthodox Muslims (Johnson 2000). Sharon Stone says her NDE changed everything: 'Every death is a rebirth' (Winfrey

2014). Nikki Sixx celebrated the 25th anniversary of his NDE in December 2012 in a Facebook posting: '25 years ago today I had two almost-fatal drug overdoses that changed my life forever. I can't even see myself these days as that kid who was running head strong into the abyss' (Near-Death Experiences of the Hollywood 2016). While Ozzy Osbourne's NDE was unremarkable except for seeing a white light, it changed his life: 'There were 'no f##king angels, no one blowing trumpets and no man in a white beard', but the ATV crash made him 'grow up'. 'You are bopping along through life and have your ups and downs, but it is amazing how two or three seconds can totally change your life' (Dovel 2003). For Peter Sellers, repeatedly dying during his eight heart attacks became the most important experiences of his life (Walker 1982). After her NDE, Sally Kirkland rose like a phoenix: 'A miracle happened; I was given a second chance' (Dovel 2003).

No more fear of death (8/22%): Cash, Foreman, Haussgaard, Pastorelli, Petersen, Sellers, Stone, and Taylor no longer feared death. Danish songwriter-musician Niels Haussgaard understood that death is 'nothing to fear':

> I know people who struggle at trying to repress the thought of death, but you just cannot do that. It just peeks out in other ways. As angst or stress … When one is freed from one's fear of death, it makes room for so much more life.
>
> *(Aggersbjerg 2019)*

After his NDE, Johnny Cash (2003) was angry that he was made to return to life and was convinced of the reality of heaven:

> I just don't have any fear of death … I'm very much at peace with myself and with God … and when he sees fit to take me from this world, I'll be reunited with some good people I haven't see for a while.

Understands that life is love (8/22%): Busey, Foreman, Hagman, Morgan, Petersen, Sellers, Seymour, and Foreman learned the meaning of life is love. As Tracy Morgan says:

> I feel like I tapped into humanity and love. I told my wife that the other day: "Something's different. The way I am with people". I find myself saying: "I love you" 200 times a day to strangers. I don't care. I don't have to know you to love you! That's how we're supposed to be as human beings. We're supposed to take care of each other.
>
> *(Winfrey 2016)*

Became spiritual, more spiritual and introspective (8/22%): Busey, Cash, Caviezel, Cromwell, Foreman, Kirkland, Reese, and Sellers reoriented their lives toward spiritual transcendence. Practising Christian Jim Caviezel became an evangelist (Burden 2019). Peter Sellers became a 'seeker', and while born a Jew, developed a serious interest in Christianity and consulted spiritualists and past-life mediums (Walker 1982). Gary Busey, George Foreman, Sally Kirkland, and Della Reese became ordained ministers, and Johnny Cash (2003) began recording more gospel music. James Cromwell claims that his entire life since his NDE has been a mystical event (Dovel 2003).

Took life-enhancing risks (8/22%): Bennett, Cash, Kirkland, Pastorelli, Sixx, Stone, Sutherland, and Winger claim their NDE made them take risks. Tony Bennett (2007) ended his addictions and reshaped his music to appeal to younger audiences. Debra Winger stopped studying criminology and took a chance on an acting career (Italie 1990). After his NDE, Robert Pastorelli said:

> Things like a secure job and pension suddenly became meaningless … A goal like acting − which I thought was unattainable − became the only thing I focused on. If I hadn't had the accident, I'd probably be dead or just sleepwalking through life … It was my destiny to have that accident.
>
> *(Near-Death Experiences of the Hollywood 2016)*

Nikki Sixx's NDE made him sober up, and the two adrenalin shots that revived him inspired him to write the 1989 *Mötley Crüe* song 'Kickstart My Heart' (Lee et al. 2002). Tracy Morgan says his NDE made him funnier. 'These jokes I'm giving y'all − they're gifts!' (Winfrey 2016).

Negative (2/5%): Only two of 37 subjects, Chase and Sellers, report their NDE as ultimately troubling. Chevy Chase reportedly suffered from deep depression, not wanting to return from his NDE (Sunfellow 2019), and Peter Sellers no longer knew who he was, his purpose, or why he was returned to the living; he felt restless, adrift (Walker 1982; MacLaine 1983).

Reluctant to talk about it (2/5%): Petersen and Taylor. At first William Petersen talked about his NDE, but 'the more I talked about it, the more freaked out people got. Some of them were like, "Okay, whatever: You took too many drugs"' (Near-Death Experience of the Hollywood 2016). Elizabeth Taylor became circumspect about her NDE, after seeing the reaction of others. 'Wow, this sounds really screwy. I think I'd better keep quiet about this. For a long time I didn't talk about it; and it's still hard for me to talk about' (Near-Death Experience of the Hollywood 2016). After Taylor became a supporter of AIDS causes, she began to share her story to comfort the dying.

Summary

The results from this study of celebrity NDE show some correspondence with the work of Martial et al. (2017) in 7 of 8 NDE features, commonly found in the NDE 'script', three in the same ranking (bright light, border, return to body).

Feature	Peace	Bright light	Encountered spirits and people	Out-of-body	Tunnel	Border	Return to body	Unearthly place
Rank & % (Martial et al. 2017)	1: 80	2: 69	3: 64	4: 53	5: 47	6: 40	7:37	8: 37
Rank & % (Foltyn 2020)	4: 38	2: 49	1: 51	3: 41	11: 14	6: 32	7: 32	5: 35

Only 14% of my subjects experienced a tunnel, but a significant percentage described other prominent features, such as witnessing their resuscitation (30%), not being ready to die or given a choice whether to die or not (27%), or being told it was not the time to die (24%).

Findings about the aftermath of the NDE fulfil commonly reported aspects of the NDE script (Noyes 1980; Ring 1980, 1984; Sabom 1982), and are structurally like Campbell's Hero's Journey (1949). Among my celebrity subjects, 51% felt reborn, 22% no longer feared death, 22% understood that life is about love, 22% became more spiritual, and 22% took more risks. Only 5% found their NDE ultimately troubling, and 5% found themselves at some point reluctant to talk about their NDE, fearing ridicule.

Discussion

The results of this study suggest that celebrity NDE follow the overall script outlined by Charlotte Martial et al. (2017), with iconic features such as a bright light, encounters with divinities and the deceased, OBE, sudden return to the body, and a sense of rebirth. That said, however, celebrity NDE accounts often included other dramatic features, such as witnessing one's resuscitation or the last rites, and watching family and friends grieve at one's deathbed. The narrative structure of the celebrity NDE dovetails with the Hero's Journey, a mythic story of starting in one place, being cast into another world where one faces trials and death, and then returning to one's former life transformed. The Hero's Journey appeals to modern audiences, just as it did ancient ones, and lends itself to the theatrics of Hollywood entertainment. Strikingly, this meshing of entertainment, Hollywood, and the NDE was eerily apparent in the fact that 27% (10 of 37) of my celebrity subjects had their NDE while filming or otherwise performing (Caviezel, Chase, Estrada, Foreman, Horn, Petersen, Reagan, Reynolds, Reese, and Sutherland).

Celebrities who have had an NDE are not only sharing the details of an intense experience, they are offering another performance (Foltyn 2018). While bestselling accounts of NDE of ordinary individuals have also made some famous, celebrities have an advantage in having theirs told/sold. NDE make for good storytelling, with their high drama, 'special effects', and Hollywood 'happy endings'. In a spectacle-oriented era (Jacobsen 2016), celebrities are not only having gripping NDE, theirs unfold with theatrical details, for they are articulate, accustomed to following a script, holding the attention of the public, and being offered starring roles.

It also is clear that celebrity NDE accounts have testimonial expectations that are shaped by culture, history, and personal beliefs, as well as widely reported characteristics of NDE. As with other NDE accounts, those of celebrities, ever mindful of their image, reveal much about their religious or philosophical orientation. It is not surprising that Ozzy Osbourne, formerly of the heavy metal group Black Sabbath, a rocker known to have bitten off the heads of doves, but also a discreet member of the Church of England, says his NDE did not include angels or God, but the NDE of Jane Seymour, who talks openly about her spiritual life, did. That said, it was unexpected to learn that George Foreman, who once thought those who are religious pitiful, changed his mind after his NDE and became a minister. Typically, NDE that feature deities, heaven, and/ or hell are shaped by the degree of involvement in religion that the person has. Christians tend to see angels, Jesus, and the Virgin Mary, while Hindu see Yama, god of death, or Krishna, his messenger (Osis and Haraldson 1977).

Arguably, the celebrity association with an alluring life and having a certain authority has made it possible for the famous to cash in on the popularity of NDE accounts as well as the current death celebratory climate. Celebrity NDE present death as what Jacques Lacan (1992/2006:62) would call a 'dazzling sight'. The overall picture is to glamorise death, to present the hereafter as a peaceful and pleasant place, where the self continues, joining deceased loved ones and companion animals. While traditional religion continues to supply this message, it is lost for many members of Western secular society for whom death is a terrifying unknown. Celebrities often seem larger than life, authoritative, and magical to ordinary people, and their NDE surely provide legitimacy and comfort to some of those who have existential angst about death. Since 'The Story of Er', celebrity NDE accounts have influenced spirituality and conceptions of the soul, heaven, and hell, including in Western philosophy and Christianity.

While the isolated features of celebrity NDE differ little from those of the un-famous, what is different is the attention given them. In the 21st century, the public profiles and performative power of celebrities have expanded through various digital media, from YouTube interviews and social media, as well as traditional publishing venues. Modern communications technology has not only changed the way people attain information and entertainment, it has transformed how people become and remain famous, and created platoons of celebrities, some enduring, others fleeting (Foltyn 2016). Celebrities shape conversation, politics, style, and behaviour, and influence individual and community identity (Blake 2002), and, perhaps the increasing social acceptability of talking about NDE. Celebrities have parasocial relationships with their fans (Horton and Wohl 1956), who follow their every move, identify with them, and may find their NDE not only believable, relatable, and heroic, but entertaining.

Consuming celebrity is an important aspect of popular culture, which not only constructs the celebrity and the celebrity's audience, but documents the celebrity's ascent, decline, and demise (Holmes and Redmond 2006; Ward 2011). Celebrity depends upon this continual reinvention (James 1993), the selling of 'new chapters' of famous lives, including, it would seem, NDE. The question arises: should we view celebrity NDE accounts as another chapter in the life of a performer, a way to tap into the market for NDE, and perhaps achieve another kind of notoriety before their eventual deaths and possible posthumous fame (Foltyn 2018)?

A fascination with the changing bodies of celebrities is a key element of the modern cult of celebrity (Foltyn 2008b), and celebrity NDE accounts, with their stories of damaged, sometimes savaged corpses, can be viewed as not only another way to consume death, but another chapter in the trope of the celebrity body, e.g. weight gains and losses, pregnancies, plastic surgery, and illnesses (Foltyn 2016). The NDE body is the chapter before the final one, when one officially becomes a corpse (Foltyn 2018). If the human body is the 'story' of the postmodern era (Foucault 1990), the celebrity is the central body of our entertainment society (Foltyn 2016), and the dead body is 'Other', then the celebrity corpse is the ultimate 'Other' (Foltyn 2013). Cultural values are inscribed on the dead as well as the living body (Foucault 1979), and our fascination with celebrity NDE reveals much about current cultural obsessions and anxieties about the body, celebrity, death, and the afterlife.

Talented, creative, imaginative, wealthy, and often beautiful and charismatic, accustomed to public adulation and being taken seriously, celebrities are idols of consumption (Lowenthal 1961), stars of the contemporary consumer–industrial–entertainment complex that Jean Baudrillard (1970/1998) argued positions us as 'consumers' to be seduced into buying things and experiences, both real and simulated. From *Game of Thrones* to the endless production of zombie, war, horror, and suspense films, this complex is preoccupied with death, a highly profitable, and particularly American export (Foltyn 2008a). Not only do many celebrity actors portray the dead or dealers of death, they can now re-enact their NDE, telling them in perpetuity on YouTube. Because NDE are *en trend*, celebrities no longer need to be circumspect about revealing them, in the way in which Elizabeth Taylor and William Petersen once were. In fact, an NDE may enhance the status of a celebrity, keep him or her relevant, and become part of the carefully crafted celebrity image, handled not only by managers, but by celebrities themselves via social media.

Similar to those I call 'dead famous' who are the subjects of mournathons and who have lucrative post-mortem 'lives' (Foltyn 2008b), celebrities whose NDE have captured the public imagination share common elements: (1) they encourage identification and strong emotion in people, (2) their NDE were sudden, unexpected, and dramatic, (3) their NDE contribute to their fame, and (4) their deaths and return to life were transformed into news and entertainment commodities.

This coming together of celebrity and death is a feature of another NDE research project of mine, the appearance of celebrities like Elvis Presley, Kurt Cobain, Michael Jackson, Marilyn Monroe, and Princess Diana in the NDE of fans (Foltyn 2018). Many observers have noted that in a secular era, celebrities have acquired a kind of divinity and people connect with the dead famous in the ways some do martyred saints. Dead or alive, celebrity is a sacred status for some. Hyped as god-like beings, celebrities evoke Jungian archetypes and a longing for the divine. So it is that in a secular age, the dead famous are replacing saints and divine entities in NDE. Clearly, there are famous people that culture cannot let go. While the overall roster of the dead famous changes, and will likely change in the NDE of fans, others seem to live on indefinitely (Foltyn 2018).

Conclusion

Celebrity NDE shine a heavenly and hellish spotlight on not only a growing cultural phenomenon, but death in a spectacular age (Jacobsen 2016). Folded into the consumer–entertainment–celebrity industrial complex, celebrity NDE – with this study – have become a sub-speciality of a speciality, NDE research. My study found that the individual features of celebrity accounts overlap with the findings of NDE scholars, but also provide other audience-ready details. Framed as transformative experiences, celebrity NDE are myth-like in their narrative structure, the stuff of the Hollywood blockbuster. The celebrification of NDE through bestselling memoirs, high-profile interviews, and social media has provided publicity and authority for NDE and created entrepreneurial opportunities. As celebrity NDE are mediated through media screens, they not only commercialise and commodify NDE as a subcategory of death, they re-re-ritualise death, de-tabooing it, making it meaningful, less frightening, perhaps preferable to life.

Celebrity NDE call attention to dying, death, the dead, the undead, and celebrity afterlives, all of which are features of death in a spectacular age. For moments or minutes, celebrities who have had an NDE join the ranks of the 'undead'. Perhaps their NDE accounts offer a preview of the otherworldly after-life they expect, another kind of celebrity 'afterlife' where their consciousness continues, rather than being 'revived', after their physical deaths by heritage groups, heirs, and entertainment executives devoted to keeping the dead famous 'live' and lucrative in the material world. After a celebrity's permanent death, the NDE may be folded into their dead famous storyline, e.g. Elizabeth Taylor.

Celebrity NDE challenge binaries established by modernity, presenting another explanation for what happens to identity after death: the possibility of unity, of continuity, rather than a bifurcation of life and death, body and mind/soul, consciousness and annihilation of self. This is important for members of individualistic secular societies, where the annihilation of self is a major concern. While participation in mainstream Christian churches is declining, and members of Western culture are likely to call themselves 'spiritual' rather than religious, belief in an afterlife, particularly heaven, remains high (Religious Landscape Study 2019). For atheists, agnostics, and the spiritual, as well as the religious, uncertainty about death, the great existential unknown, from which no-one returns – except those who purport to have had an NDE – is a source of anxiety. No wonder NDE research tends to focus on Western iterations of the phenomenon and interest in NDE of celebrities and others is high.

We humans have always developed many strategies to fend off awareness of our mortality and convince ourselves we are immortal (Becker 1973). NDE may thus serve as a prototype for an evolutionary theory of religion, according to philosopher Michael Grosso, and be 'a vehicle for the mythic renewal of our idea of death as a journey rather than as a termination' (Grosso 1991:49). According to sociologist Raymond L.M. Lee (2003), metanarratives about consciousness, space, and time that circumscribe the reality of our existence are being challenged as faith in modernity has eroded. The mass media has decentred NDE as an experience available only to those with paranormal powers; this democratisation as well as increasing reporting of NDE and acceptance of their authenticity suggests that denial and fear of death are diminishing. NDE challenge former strict boundaries between life and death and serve to re-enchant the effects of modernity's disenchantment.

References

Ariès, Philippe (1974): *Western Attitudes Toward Death: From the Middle Ages to the Present.* Baltimore, MD: Johns Hopkins University Press.

Atwater, P. M. H. (2009): *Beyond the Light: What Isn't Being Said About Near-Death Experience: From Visions of Heaven to Glimpses of Hell.* Kill Devil Hills, NC: Transpersonal Publishing.

Baudrillard, Jean (1970/1998): *The Consumer Society: Myths and Structures.* Thousand Oaks, CA: Sage Publications.

Becker, Ernest (1973): *The Denial of Death.* New York: Free Press.

Bellig, Laurin (2015): *Near Death in the ICU: Stories from Patients Near Death and Why We Should Listen to Them.* Cornwall on Hudson, NY: Sloan Press.

Blackmore, Susan (1993): *Dying to Live: Science and Near-Death Experience.* London: Grafton.

Blake, David Haven (2002): 'Campbell McGrath and the Spectacle Society'. *Michigan Quarterly Review,* 41(2):249–273.

Bogousslavsky, Julien, Michael G. Hennerici, Hansjörg Bäzner and Claudio L. Bassetti (eds.) (2010): *Neurological Disorders in Famous Artists, Part 3.* Basel: Karger Publishers.

Burpo, Todd and Lynn Vincent (2010): *Heaven Is for Real: A Little Boy's Astounding Story of His Trip to Heaven and Back.* Nashville, TN: Thomas Nelson.

Campbell, Joseph (1949): *The Hero with a Thousand Faces.* New York: Pantheon.

Charlier, Philippe (2014): 'Letter to the Editor: Oldest Medical Description of Near-Death Experience (NDE), France, 18th Century'. *Resuscitation.* Available online at: https://www.academia.edu/19113041/Oldest_medical_description_of_a_near_death_experience_NDE_France_18th_century.

Crick, Francis (1995): *Astonishing Hypothesis: The Scientific Search for the Soul.* New York: Scribner.

Danticat, Edwidge (2017): *The Art of Death: Writing the Final Story*. Minneapolis, MN: Graywolf Press.

Du Monchaux, Pierre-Jean (1766): *Anecdotes de médecine, ou choix de faits singuliers qui ont rapport à l'anatomie, la pharmacie, l'histoire naturelle, et aux quelles on a joint des anecdotes concernant les Médecins les plus célèbres*. Lille: J. B. Henry.

Fischer, John Martin and Benjamin Mitchell-Yellin (2016): *Near-Death Experiences: Understanding Visions of the Afterlife*. Oxford: Oxford University Press.

Foltyn, Jacque Lynn (2008a): 'The Corpse in Contemporary Culture: Identifying, Transacting, and Recoding the Dead Body in the Twenty-First Century'. *Mortality*, 13(2):99–104.

Foltyn, Jacque Lynn (2008b): 'Dead Famous and Dead Sexy: Popular Culture, Forensics, and the Rise of the Corpse'. *Mortality*, 13(2):153–173.

Foltyn, Jacque Lynn (2010): 'To Die For: Skull Style and Corpse Chic'. *Scan: Journal of Media Arts Culture* 7(2). Available online at: http://scan.net.au/scan/journal/display.php?journal_id=151.

Foltyn, Jacque Lynn (2013): 'Corpse Chic: "Dead" Models and "Living" Corpses in Mainstream Fashion Magazines'. In: Jacque Lynn Foltyn (ed.). *Fashions: Exploring Fashion through Cultures*. Oxford: ID Press, pp. 269–294.

Foltyn, Jacque Lynn (2016): 'Bodies of Evidence: Criminalizing the Celebrity Corpse'. *Mortality*, 21(3):246–262.

Foltyn, Jacque Lynn (2018): 'Touring Heaven: Near-Death Experiences of Celebrities and Their Fans'. In: *Death & Culture II* (Book of Abstracts). UK: University of York, September 6–7, 2018, pp. 29–30.

Foucault, Michel (1979): *Discipline and Punish: The Birth of the Prison*. New York: Vintage Books.

Foucault, Michel (1990): *The History of Sexuality: An Introduction* (Volume 1). New York: Vintage Books.

French, Christopher C. (2001): 'Dying to Know the Truth: Visions of a Dying Brain, or False Memories?' *The Lancet*, 358(9298):2010–2011.

Friendly, Alfred (1977): *Beaufort of the Admiralty: The Life of Sir Francis Beaufort, 1774–1857*. London: Hutchinson.

Gorer, Geoffrey (1955): 'The Pornography of Death'. *Encounter*, 5:49–52.

Greyson, Bruce (1983): 'The Near-Death Experience Scale: Construction, Reliability and Validity'. *Journal of Nervous and Mental Diseases*, 171(6):369–375.

Greyson, Bruce (2007): 'Near-Death Experiences: Clinical Implications'. *Archives of Clinical Psychiatry*, 34(Supplement 1):49–57.

Grosso, Michael (1991):'The Myth of the Near-Death Journey'. *Journal of Near-Death Studies*, 10(1):49–60.

Holden, Janice Miner, Bruce Greyson and Debbie James (2009): 'The Field of Near-Death Studies: Past, Present and Future'. In: Janice Miner Holden, Bruce Greyson and Debbie James (eds.). *The Handbook of Near-Death Experiences: Thirty Years of Investigation*. Westport, CT: Greenwood Publishing Group, pp. 1–16.

Holmes, Su and Sean Redmond (eds.) (2006): *Framing Celebrity: New Directions in Celebrity Culture*. London: Routledge.

Horton, Donald and R. Richard Wohl (1956): 'Mass Communication and Para-Social Interaction: Observations on Intimacy at a Distance'. *Psychiatry*, 19(3):215–229.

Jacobsen, Michael Hviid (2016):'"Spectacular Death" – Proposing a New Fifth Phase to Philippe Ariès's Admirable History of Death'. *Humanities*, 5(19):1–20.

James, Clive (1993): *Fame in the 20th Century*. London: BBC Books.

Jung, Carl. G. (1961/1989): *Memories, Dreams, Reflections*. New York: Vintage Books.

Kellehear, Allan (2002): 'Near-Death Experiences'. In: Robert Kastenbaum (ed.). *Macmillan Encyclopedia of Death and Dying*. Farmington Hills, MI: The Gale Group, pp. 611–616.

Khapaeva, Dina (2017): *The Celebration of Death in Contemporary Culture*. Ann Arbor, MI: University of Michigan Press.

Khapaeva, Dina (2019): *Man-Eating Monsters: Anthropocentrism and Popular Culture*. Bingley: Emerald Publishing.

Lacan, Jacques (1992/2006): 'The Mirror Stage as Formative of the Function of the I as Revealed in Psychoanalytic Experience'. In: Jacques Lacan (ed.). *Escrits: A Selection*. New York: W.W. Norton, pp. 75–81.

Lee, Raymond L. M. (2003): 'The New Face of Death: Postmodernity and Changing Perspectives of the Afterlife'. *Illness, Crisis and Loss*, 11(2):134–147.

Lilly, John C. (1972): *The Center of the Cyclone: An Autobiography of Inner Space*. Munich: Julian Press.

Litchfield, Gideon (2015): 'The Science of Near-Death Experiences: Empirically Investigating Brushes with the Afterlife'. *The Atlantic*, April 15. Available online at: https://www.theatlantic.com/magazine/archive/2015/04/the-science-of-near-death-experiences/386231/.

Long, Jeffrey and Paul Perry (2010): *Evidence of the Afterlife*. New York: HarperOne.

Lowenthal, Leo (1961): *Literature, Popular Culture and Society*. Palo Alto, CA: Pacific Books.

Martial, Charlotte, Helena Cassol, Georgios Antonopoulos, Thomas Charlier, Julien Heros, Anne-Francoise Donneau, Vanessa Charland-Verville and Steven Laureys (2017): 'Temporality of Feature in Near-Death Experience Narratives'. *Frontiers of Human Neuroscience*, June 13. Available online at: https://www.frontiersin.org/articles/10.3389/fnhum.2017.00311/full.

McIlwaine, Charlton D. (2005): *When Death Goes Pop: Death, Media & the Remaking of Community*. New York: Peter Lang.

Moody, Raymond A. (1975): *Life After Life: The Investigation of a Phenomenon – Survival of Bodily Death*. Tracy, CA: Mockingbird Books.

Morse, Melvin, Paul Castillo, David Venecia, Jerrold Milstein and Donald C. Tyler (1986): 'Near Death Experiences in a Pediatric Population'. *American Journal of Diseases in Children*, 140(11):1110–1115.

Noyes, Russell and Roy Kletti (1972): 'The Experience of Dying from Falls'. *Omega - Journal of Death and Dying*, 3(1):45–52.

Noyes, Russell (1980): 'Attitude Change Following Near-Death Experiences: A Neurophysiological Explanatory Model'. *Psychiatry*, 43(3):234–242.

Orne, Roberta M. (1995): 'The Meaning of Survival: The Early Aftermath of a Near-Death Experience'. *Research in Nursing and Health*, 18(3):239–247.

Osis, Karlis and Erlendur Haraldson (1977): *At the Hour of Death*. New York: Avon.

Penfold-Mounce, Ruth (2018): *Death, the Dead and Popular Culture*. Bingley: Emerald Publishing.

Rawlings, Maurice (1978): *Beyond Death's Door*. Nashville, TN: Thomas Nelson.

'Religious Landscape Study' (2019). *Pew Research Center*. Available online at: https://www.pewforum.org/religious-landscape-study/.

Ring, Kenneth (1980): *Life at Death: A Scientific Investigation of the Near-Death Experience*. New York: Coward, McCann & Geoghegan.

Ring, Kenneth (1984): *Heading Toward Omega: in Search of the Near-Death Experience*. New York: William Morrow.

Sabom, Michael (1982): *Recollections of Death: A Medical Investigation*. New York: Harper & Row.

Schlieter, Jens (2018): *What Is It Like to Be Dead? Near-Death Experiences, Christianity and the Occult*. New York: Oxford University Press.

Shushan, Gregory (2009): *Conceptions of the Afterlife in Early Civilizations: Universalism, Constructivism and Near-Death Experience*. London: Continuum.

Sleutjes, Adrianna, Alexander Moreira-Almeida and Bruce Greyson (2014): 'Almost 40 Years Investigating Near-Death Experiences: An Overview of Mainstream Scientific Journals'. *Journal of Nervous and Mental Diseases*, 202(11):833–836.

Timmermann, Christopher, Leor Roseman, Luke Williams, David Erritzoe, Charlotte Martial, Héléna Cassol, Steven Laureys, David Nutt and Robin Carhart-Harris (2018): 'DMT Models the Near-Death Experience'. *Frontiers in Psychology*, 15(9):1–12.

Van der Sluijis, Marinus (2009): 'Three Ancient Reports of Near-Death Experiences: Bremmer Revisited'. *Journal of Near-Death Studies*, 27(4):223–253.

Van Lommel, Pim, Ruud van Wees, Vincent Meyers and Ingrid Elfferich (2001): 'Near-Death Experience in Survivors of Cardiac Arrest: A Prospective Study in the Netherlands'. *The Lancet*, 358(9298):2039–2045.

Vardamis, Alex A. and Justine E. Owens (1999): 'Ernest Hemingway and the Near-Death Experience'. *Journal of Medical Humanities*, 20(3):203–217.

Villard, Henry and James Nagel (1989): *Hemingway in Love and War: The Lost Diary of Agnes Von Kurowsky, Her Letters, and Correspondence of Ernest Hemingway*. Boston, MA: Northeastern University Press.

Walter, Tony (1994): *The Revival of Death*. London: Routledge.

Ward, Peter (2011): *Gods Behaving Badly: Media, Religion and Celebrity Culture*. Waco, TX: Baylor University Press.

Weber, Max (1958): *From Max Weber: Essays in Sociology*. edited by C. Wright Mills and Hans H. Gerth. New York: Oxford University Press.

Zaleski, Carol (1988): *Otherworld Journeys: Accounts of Near-Death Experiences in Medieval and Modern Times*. Oxford: Oxford University Press.

Bibliography of study subjects

Aggersbjerg, Marcus (2019): 'Lune Ritter: Signe Svendsen og Niels Hausgaard'. *UD & SE*, November, pp. 22–32 [Translation from the Danish by Michael A. Langkjær].

Bennett, Tony (2007): *The Good Life: The Autobiography of Tony Bennett*. New York: Atria Books.

Burden, Ralph (2019): 'Jim Caviezel – Passionate about Playing Christ'. *REAL Life Stories*. Available online at: http://www.reallifestories.org/stories/jim-caviezel/Real Life Stories.

Cash, Johnny (2003): *Cash: The Autobiography*. New York: HarperOne.

Chen, Joyce (2017): 'Lamar Odom Recalls Near-Death Experience: "I Couldn't Control" Cocaine Use'. *Rolling Stone*, July 27. Available online at: https://www.rollingstone.com/culture/culture-news/lamar-odom-recalls-near-death-experience-i-couldnt-control-cocaine-use-125443/.

'Clint Walker on His Near-Death Experience'. *Youtube Emmytvlegends.Org*. Available online at: https://www.youtube.com/watch?v=03mt7C8-fJg.

'Della Reese: Near Death Experience'. *YouTube Visionary Project*. Available online at: https://www.youtube.com/watch?time_continue=46&v=b3tsEUFbkCY&feature=emb_title.

Dovel, Matthew D. (2003): *My Last Breath*. Frederick, MD: PublishAmerica.

'Duel with Death: George Foreman's [NDE] Testimony'. *YouTube 700: Club*. Available online at: https://www.youtube.com/watch?v=MLvkndz9OPs.

'Elizabeth Taylor's Near-Death Experience' (1992): *The Oprah Winfrey Show*, March 4. Available online at: http://www.oprah.com/own-oprahshow/elizabeth-taylor-on-her-near-death-experience.

Foreman, George (2007): *God in My Corner: A Spiritual Memoir*. Nashville, TN: Thomas Nelson.

Goddard, Audrey (2018): 'Roseanne: My Nine Months in Psych Ward and Why I Gave Up My Baby'. *New Idea*, April 12. Available online at: https://www.newidea.com.au/roseanne-barr-my-nine-months-in-psych-ward-and-why-i-gave-up-my-baby.

Hagman, Larry (2011): *Hello Darlin': Tall (and Absolutely True) Tales About My Life*. New York: Simon & Schuster.

Italie, Hillel (1990): 'Debra Winger Sums Up Her Life: "No Regrets"'. *Los Angeles Times*, December 28. Available online at: https://www.latimes.com/archives/la-xpm-1990-12-28-ca-7664-story.html.

Johnson, Dirk (2000): 'Farrakhan Ends Longtime Rivalry With Orthodox Muslims'. *New York Times*, February 28. Available online at: https://www.nytimes.com/2000/02/28/us/farrakhan-ends-longtime-rivalry-with-orthodox-muslims.html.

Law, Sophie (2018): 'The Who Singer Roger Daltrey Reveals He Feared He Was Dying After Meningitis Scare Cancelled Tour'. *The Daily Mail*, October 15. Available online at: https://www.dailymail.co.uk/news/article-6274939/The-singer-Roger-Daltrey-feared-dying-meningitis-scare.html.

Lee, Tommy, Vince Neil, Mick Mars, Nikki Sixx and Neil Strauss (2002): *The Dirt: Confessions of the World's Most Notorious Rock Band*. New York: Dey Street Books.

MacLaine, Shirley (1983): *Out on a Limb*. New York: Bantam Books.

'Near-Death Experiences of the Hollywood Rich and Famous' (2016): *Near-Death Experiences and the Afterlife*. Available online at: https://www.neardeath.com/experiences/hollywood.html.

Powers, Lindsay (2005): 'Bill: I Saw the Light Before My Heart Op'. *New York Post*, September 25. Available online at: https://nypost.com/2005/09/25/bill-i-saw-the-light-before-my-heart-op/.

Reagan, Ronald (1990): *Ronald Reagan: An American Life*. New York: Simon & Schuster.

Reeve, Christopher (1999): *Still Me*. New York: Ballentine Books.

Reynolds, Burt (2015): *But Enough about Me: A Memoir*. New York: G. P. Putnam's Sons.

Ritchie, Jean (1996): *Death's Door: True Stories of Near-Death Experiences*. New York: Dell.

Rosen, Christopher (2012): 'Gary Busey on Heaven: Actor Reportedly Recalls Near-Death Experience, Says There Are No Mirrors in Afterlife'. *HuffPost*. Available online at: https://www.huffpost.com/entry/gary-busey-heaven-no-mirrors_n_1387487.

Seymour, Jane (2010a): *Among Angels*. Danbury, CT: Guideposts.

Seymour, Jane (2010b): 'On Her New Book, Among Angels'. *Guideposts/YouTube*. Available online at: https://www.youtube.com/watch?v=IQTnoctk09M.

Shriver, Maria (2004): 'Siegfried & Roy: The Miracle', *NBC*. Directed by Jason Raff.

Sunfellow, David (2019): 'Celebrity Near Death Experiences'. Available online at: https://the-formula.org/celebrity-near-death-experiences/.

Walker, Alexander (1982): *Peter Sellers: The Authorized Biography*. New York: Macmillan.

Williams, Kevin R. (2019): 'Near Death Experiences and the Afterlife'. *Near Death*. Available online at: https://www.near-death.com/.

Winfrey, Oprah (2014): 'Soul to Soul 3 Primetime Special: Pharrell Williams, John Legend, Tina Turner, Sharon Stone and David Oyelowo'. *Super Soul Sunday*, December 21. Oprah Winfrey Network.

Winfrey, Oprah (2015): 'Oprah & Paralympian Amy Purdy: How to Create a New Vision for Your Life'. *Super Soul Sunday*, February 22. Oprah Winfrey Network.

Winfrey, Oprah (2016): 'Oprah and Comedian and TV Star Tracy Morgan'. *Super Soul Sunday*, April 3. Oprah Winfrey Network.

4

THE PROLIFERATION OF SKULLS IN POPULAR CULTURE

A case study of how the traditional symbol of mortality was rendered meaningless[1]

Michael C. Kearl

Introduction

For centuries, depictions of skulls symbolised either warnings of lethal threat or moralistic reminders of the transience of life and the vanity of earthly pleasures. However, by the first decade of the 21st century, skulls adorned women's clothing, expensive men's watches, baby bags and even the belt-buckle of a California governor. As words with continuous repetition are reduced to mere sounds, so too are visual symbols – even traditional and emotionally potent ones – rendered meaningless when differently framed by various agencies. Developed in this chapter is a social history of how this symbol was largely emptied of its traditional connotations owing to a 'perfect storm' of cultural trends, ranging from the skull's increasing use in popular culture, a doomsday millennial zeitgeist, the death-accepting ethos of Latino immigrants filling a vacuum within a death-denying (and -defying) culture, to the growing public expectations of a forthcoming post-mortal world.

Appearing in the Neiman Marcus's Spring 2007 online catalogue was the 'Skull Cutout Flat' shoe, from the Loeffler Randall collection. Price: $395. Why would women pay such money to have on their feet the symbol that appears on old New England tombstones, rat poison and drain cleaners? Who are its wearers? Certainly, the point of being fashionable is to attract attention to oneself, but what kind of attention is being garnered here? What messages, both intended and unintended, does the footwear convey (especially given that the season of the shoe's debut was not Halloween, but rather coincided with the mass murder at Virginia Tech)? Might these messages include commentary on the Iraq and Afghanistan wars, satire on the proliferation of warning labels or that the wearer is a victim of AIDS, recently bereaved or simply an adult Goth? The focus here is not the shoe, but rather, its adorning symbol, one that has become a ubiquitous image in the new millennium.[2] It is a case study of how and why this traditional symbol of death – the 'king of bones' (Kastenbaum 2004:146), the longest-surviving remnant of an identifiable self – has historically morphed, eventually to be rendered meaningless owing to a 'perfect storm' of cultural trends. Also explored are the sociocultural implications of the skull being stripped of its associations with mortality.

A brief history of skull meanings in art and popular culture

Humanity's interest in skulls undoubtedly dates back to the human primate's unique awareness of its inevitable fate. It became a symbol of many ideas, of life's transience, of the corporeal body being but carrion for vultures and worms and of death being the great equaliser. The skull is an intermediary between the worlds of the living and dead, and hence, the respect, dread and even veneration it receives around the world. It is the object of meditation for Tibetan Buddhists and to which Hamlet delivered his famous soliloquy. Now it adorns the jackets and helmets of Hells Angels, covers of Grateful Dead albums, Andy Warhol prints, posters of social protest, logos of gymnasiums, high-end men's and women's accessories, baby bags and children's linen. Skulls' meanings are shaped by the cultural ethos of their depictions. Social historians' timelines and demarcations of these death systems are variable; best known is that of Philippe Ariès (1981), whose death epochs of Western history integrate a broad variety of mortuary practices. His epochs change, given major cultural shifts in conceptions of selfhood, social bonds and institutional hegemony over everyday life, as well as in changing demographics of groups most likely to die and how. To give brief historical context to the present, we begin our skull story during the late Middle Ages and the beginning of the Renaissance, a period when traditional communal ties were dissolving as feudal orders faded. Epidemics and plagues were periodically decimating European populations, their virulence magnified by growing urbanisation and expanding trade routes. Religion monopolised the meanings and rituals associated with the dying and the dead. Countering the emergent individualism of the time were its ideas of post-mortem judgement, featuring resurrection hopes for the just and damnation fears for the wicked. The religious hegemony of the Church and its *contemptus mundi* outlook on existence, however, were undergoing challenge by the Reformation. The wealth and luxuries of an emergent mercantile class raised questions of the Old World's understanding of an inherently superior hereafter as opposed to the vile and loathsome here-and-now.

The morphing of vanitas art from the sacred to the profane

Legacies of the era include relic skulls and reliquaries of saints – as well as their artistic depictions – presently found throughout Europe. On the exteriors of Catholic cathedrals, sculptures show priests holding the skulls of saints, such as the statuaries of St Francis of Assisi and St Francis Borgia.[3] A skull is often found at the base of the cross of old crucifixion paintings. These spawned the *vanitas* still-life genre of art, which rose to prominence in 16th- and 17th-century Danish and Flemish painting.[4] Arising with the emergence of Calvinism and the Counter-Reformation, they feature collections of objects symbolic of the inevitability of death, and the transience and vanity of earthly achievements and pleasures.[5] Viewers are exhorted to consider mortality and to repent.

Though its popularity had largely waned by 1650, the genre survived and mutated with the times. During the 17th and 18th centuries, an era marked by the Enlightenment with growing interest in physical death and the corpse as a means to further scientific knowledge, a new variant of *memento mori* arose. Its skull motif featured 'half and half' anatomical images, with half the head being a living image and the other a skull. Toward the end of the nineteenth century,[6] the death ethos of the West was influenced by the late Victorian romanticisms,[7] epitomised by Henry Alexander Bowler's 'The Doubt: Can These Dry Bones Live?', with a black-shawled young woman leaning over a tombstone and viewing the surfaced bones of the grave's occupant. But something new was percolating. Skulls were becoming less morbid, as in Vincent van Gogh's 'Skull of Skeleton with Burning Cigarette' (1886) – which played off smoking associations with death and the fleeting sensuous pleasures admonished within *vanitas* paintings (Mitchell 1987). In addition, James Ensor's 'Skeletons Fighting Over a Pickled Herring' (1891) and 'The Skeleton Painter' (1885–1886) and Edvard Munch's 'The Kiss of Death' (1899) appeared. New meanings, more sensuous meanings were evolving. From these cultural currents arose a new *memento mori* genre, one combining the half-and-half images of the 18th century with less morbid skull depictions. Here, by employing the new ideas of gestalt, a scene of life can simultaneously be perceived as a visage of death. Best known is Charles Allan Gilbert's 'All is Vanity' (1892), where one sees either a large skull or a beautiful young woman at her dressing table. Published in *Life Magazine* in 1902, the optical illusion spawned numerous ambiguous skull-based imitations.[8] Such pairings of skulls with youth and early loves continued until the First World War, the motif of the popular German metaphoric postcards. While the intended and inferred meanings of such images for their senders and recipients can only be surmised, it seems clear that the message was becoming secularised. Given the playful and romantic images juxtaposed against the skeletal craniums, one does not live with death, but rather faces it at the end of well-lived existences. The gestalt-based interplay of meanings – specifically, whether death is to be understood as the background or foreground of life – hints at the existential thought of the time, decrying the excessive psychic energies expended repressing death, and thereby diminishing abilities to live life fully. By the post-war mid-century, images of the life–death duality became highly eroticised. The genre had been initiated in erotic *vanitas* variants, such as the photographs by H. von Jan (1900) and John Everard (e.g. '*Étude de nue: Jeune femme aux vanités*').[9] A transition in skull meaning is evident in a 1942 military venereal disease-warning poster. Painted by Dali, it utilised the gestalt illusion of Gilbert and other turn-of-century illustrators, but here forming the skull are two ladies of the night, skirts raised in front of a large lamp. The shift is complete in Philippe Halsman's 1951 *'Voluptas Mors'* photograph. Created in collaboration with Dali, the fusion of death and sensuality is created with seven nude females positioned to form a skull image. Becoming known as 'Dali's Skull', the concept was broadly replicated for decades. Whether or not it entered into Dali's inspiration for *'Voluptas Mors'*, one broadly disseminated image that possibly set up its meaning seven years earlier is the photograph of a young woman admiring a Japanese trophy skull sent from her Navy boyfriend in New Guinea (Crane 1944). Appearing in *Life* in 1944, one observes the adoring glance of a loved one toward the trophy skull sent by the naval officer of her affections. The look is not that of one pondering the existential predicaments posed by death nor is it one of horror or disgust.[10] As such 'souvenirs' were stripped of flesh and marrow, here the skull is stripped once and for all of any *vanitas* residue.

20th-century skull symbolisations of war, pogroms and protest

Over the past century, traditional religious and existential meanings associated with skulls were frequently overwhelmed by political connotations. Instead of being reminders of life's finiteness and the need to live morally worthy existences, the symbol became one of the needless brutalities and injustices served by political regimes. Following the Great War, skulls and skeletons were to signify deep disillusionments with the technological slaughter produced – and the Lost Generation created. An Italian anti-German *'La Morte'* propaganda poster features a German officer, standing erect with certain pride atop a pile of skulls. Photographs of the horrific consequences of trench warfare include piles of harvested bones and skulls from battlefields like Gallipoli. Decay accentuates Otto Dix's 'Skull' (1924), with worms and maggots infesting a largely decomposed human head. The Second World War outdid the First in the symbol's appearance. Sometimes its use and connotations of death and terror were intentional, as when employed on German Nazi SS banners, officer visors, stickpins and rings. In addition to the costs of war, the skull further connoted political injustice and oppression. They appeared on anti-capitalist propaganda posters of the early Bolsheviks and the International Workers of the World, and decades later during the anti-war protests against Tony Blair and George W. Bush, and before the meeting places of the World Economic Forum. In Mexico City, sex workers gathered, faces covered by skull masks, to commemorate their colleagues who were violently murdered, two days prior to the Day of the Dead festival. While the evils of Nazism were to be symbolised by the crematoriums of its death factories, the later, cruder genocides of the developing world became associated with huge mounds of actual human skulls. They were constructed with the victims of Pol Pot in Cambodia, where over 21% of the population lost their lives between 1975 and 1979. On the other side of the world, similar mounds have sprouted in Rwanda, where in 1994, extremists of the Hutu majority attempted to 'cleanse' the nation of its Tutsi minority.

The rise of the commercialised and commodified skull

Despite its long-term associations with humanity's existential fate, danger and political injustice and savagery, this potent symbol was not immune to alternative meanings of mass media and the marketplace. As words become drained of their symbolic content when endlessly repeated, so ubiquitous alternative framings of the skull were to render its visage, if not meaningless, then at least largely void of its connotations of mortality and horror. As the century moved to conclusion, advertisers discovered death's power to attract attention and stimulate buying[11] – particularly when linked with sex. Such companies as Versace, Duncan Quinn, Louis Vuitton, Jeorge Napolean Hair Salon and Madeline began featuring dead women, victims of murder, suicide, auto accidents and, in the case of American Express, shark attack.[12] Christian Dior came out with its 'Poison' perfume line in 1985. Among the product line's ads print ads was the updated 'All is Vanity' image (Peters 1985). Instead of extinguishing the skull fad, the deadly terrorist attacks of 11 September 2001 were shortly followed by an increasing ubiquity of skulls in both high and low culture. No longer limited to women's footwear and perfumes, the king of bones now adorned their swimsuits, shirts, scarves, corsets and jewellery. The first decade of the new millennium found skull prints being seized upon by fashion designers Alexander McQueen, Thomas Wylde, Clements Ribeiro, Fred Flare, Paula Thomas and Ed Hardy. For men, the symbol was no longer confined to the leather jackets and tattoos of Hell Angels bikers or to the garb of anti-regime protestors. Instead, it came to carry the message of masculinity and physical fitness. In the author's city of San Antonio, a skull adorns the logo of a strength-and-conditioning facility for athletes. Among an array of ski masks worn by US Marines to protect eyes from desert sand during a 2003 Kuwait exercise were Grim Reaper skull masks. Reinforcing the fashion genre was, of course, Disney, with the skull symbolising the pirate craze triggered by its *Pirates of the Caribbean* trilogy: *The Curse of the Black Pearl* (2003), *Dead Man's Chest* (2006) and *At World's End* (2007). Even society's youngest members were to be adorned with the symbol and not just with Halloween pirate outfits. Hot Topic advertised its Pink Skull Infant Bodysuit as 'Perfect for your little punkette! This white infant bodysuit features a front screen of pink skull n' crossbones'. Similarly designed were Tutti Bella's line of infant wear and $65 diaper bags from Diaper Dude. Older siblings could be tucked into beds covered with skull-and-crossbones linen and comforters from such companies as Street Revival, Kids Bedding, Veratex, David and Goliath, Skater and Sin and Linen. There is considerable irony marketing the symbol to society's youngest members. For not-too-distant ancestors, it would be equivalent to using such garments and linens for nursing home residents. Up until the past century, children were the culture's 'death lepers', the age group most associated with death. During the latter half of the 1800s, daguerreotypes of their lifeless bodies ranked among the leading genres of the new photographic arts. Nowadays, with infant mortality rates being less than 7% of what they were a century earlier in the developed world, the skull symbol (along with the 'Now I lay me down to sleep, I pray the Lord my soul to keep, And if I die before I wake, ...' prayer)[13] is shorn of its mortal connotations. In the marketplace, other transformations in skull meanings were to occur. As the symbol secured a successful statement of fashion, inevitable market dynamics led to expensive variations for the elite, producing new opportunities for conspicuous consumption (in an era of increasing class inequalities). Timepieces, which for centuries have been personal objects allowing for status displays and invidious comparisons, quickly adopted the image. The Corum Bubble XL Privateer Black Diamond Men's Automatic Watch appeared on the market. Originally priced for slightly less than $9000, it is ornamented by a pirate's skull atop crossed sabres within the dial. For those desiring to demonstrate even greater status, one can purchase the Nixon skull-print Rotologs, whose band is encrusted with 764 white and 1,087 black diamonds together forming a skull pattern. Not to be left out of the fad, Ralph Lauren quickly sold out its $10,000 white gold skull cufflinks with diamond eyes in 2011. The symbolism of skull watch dials on the wrists of the wealthy deserves reflection. The association of hourglasses and skulls is common on old New England tombstones. The meaning of the pairing nowadays is no longer that of life's brevity. The statement made is not only the conspicuous ability to spend large sums on something worn infrequently or on what may be a short-term fad. In addition, these timepieces are informed by the publicised studies of the elites' greater and growing life-expectancy advantage over those on the lower rungs of the social hierarchy. Time indeed is on their side. But why limit one's skull statement to small watch faces? The mega-rich must distinguish themselves from the merely rich. Instead of flaunting timepieces with skulls shaped out of diamonds, why not just encrust the real thing with valuable gems? For the uber-wealthy, Damien Hirst created 'For the Love of God' (2007), a platinum skull encrusted with 8,601 fine diamonds. The piece sold to an investment conglomerate in August of 2007 for a reported $100 million. Taking further advantage of the trend, Hirst produced the controversial 'For Heaven's Sake', an authentic infant skull covered in platinum and diamonds that listed for $50 million.[14] No longer is death the great equaliser. The trend was acknowledged in a 2006 *New York Times* article, 'The Heyday of the Dead', observing how the skull has lost virtually all of its fearsome meaning (Colman 2006). A disconnect has occurred between the symbol for, and the actual meaning of, mortality. The American death ethos has been described as being death-denying. But in the new millennium, it appears to be in the midst of being superseded by something different. Change is occurring owing to changing demographics of death (e.g. primarily the deaths of society's oldest members, perishing of chronic disease), minimalist funerals (often themed as 'celebrations of life'), dramatic increases in rates of cremation and new levels of death defiance owing to advances in the medical arts.

Deep cultural trends underlying the skull proliferation in the early 21st century

There has arisen a perfect storm of cultural confluences producing the skull genre in popular culture – and the draining of its traditional meanings in the United States and many late-modern societies. Owing to deep cultural trends detailed below, conditions were ideal for the skull to be stripped of its *memento mori* (remember your mortality) signification and replaced by variations of *mors mortua est* (death is dead) messages. Symbols are icebergs of meaning. On the surface, their connotations and denotations are contextualised, framed by varying definitions of the situation. However, at deeper levels, their meanings tap into a realm of collective memory and conscience. These memories and associations vary by the generations that carry them – and by the cultural importance given to the past. As global warming calves an increasing number of ice flows, reducing their size and depth, so globalisation of diverse cultural meaning systems, coupled with communication technologies eviscerating the past and markets monetising everything, have increased the number of skull meanings, while reducing their symbolic depth. Consider, for instance, when the then-California Governor Arnold Schwarzenegger, born in post-war Austria, appeared on the 25 June 2007 cover of *Time* magazine wearing a skull belt-buckle. The symbol was not that of Jack Sparrow, but rather a stylised version of the Nazi SS *Totenkopf* buckle with the motto 'God's with us'. Had he lived another quarter century to witness this, Michel Foucault might have written: '*Ceci n'est pas une crâne*', 'This is not a skull'. Instead of developing the distinction between a pipe and the reality of its signification, he could have similarly developed Schwarzenegger's skull before excavating the layers of ironies and contradictions of the governor's claims that the *Totenkopf* he wore was not real (and thus only carrying the meaning of fashion). On first thought, the easiest explanation is to attribute to Disney the proliferation of skulls and their being rendered meaningless. However, there are too many layers of underlying precedent. While the glut of commercialised skull images appeared mid-decade in the new century in the midst of the *Pirates* trilogy – such as designer Alexander McQueen's skull scarves, which first appeared in 2003 – the cultural receptivity toward the trend was already well underway. Other usual suspects include the maturation of the Goth generation, whose tastes have gone mainstream, or an additional 'holiday creep', the prolongation of the increasingly popular Halloween season.[15]

Transplantation of the Latin death system with immigration

In addition to dramatic changes in the age structure of American society owing to declining fertility and increasing life expectancies, perhaps the greatest demographic change is owed to the massive Hispanic immigration of the past few decades. From 2000 to 2010, the US Hispanic population grew 43%, four times faster than the total population, amounting to more than one-half of the total population over the period. The cultural impacts of over 50 million inhabitants being of Hispanic origin have yet to be totally fathomed by social scientists. One transplanted tradition leaving its mark on mainstream American society, specifically on its death ethos, is *Día de los Muertos* (Day of the Dead). The increasing frequency of Day of the Dead or All Soul's Day observances is owed to cultural physics, where a death-accepting orientation is filling the spiritual voids existent within a death-denying ethos. These voids include the privatisation of grief and the disappearance of the dead – two trends that run counter to long-established rituals to mitigate personal grief and to reaffirm social solidarities (Bottum 2007).[16] These festive death ceremonies are neither positive nor negative, but rather 'an existential affirmation of the lives and contributions made by all who have existed … (and) the affirmation of life as the means for realising its promise while preparing to someday die' (Sanchez 1985).[17] Interwoven with this Latin ethos are images of skulls. They, too, carry a number of deep levels of meaning, reflecting not only Mexico's Mayan and Aztec cultural heritage,[18] but also a fusion with economic and political exigencies. The famous skulls and skeletal caricatures of José Guadalupe Posada served to raise political consciousness in Mexico before the revolution, and those of José Clemente Orozco did so afterwards. In a country historically marked by unstable, corrupt, authoritarian regimes, honouring the dead has given individuals licence to comment on the living. A satirical magazine, *La Calavera* (The Skull), is published in even the smallest hamlet that owns a print shop. The publication is filled with satirical poetic eulogies of living members of the community, ranging from the town drunk to the mayor's wife. Perhaps, most ubiquitous are the small whimsical skulls made of sugar, pottery and papier-mâché or punched out in decorative banners (*papel picado*). Typically stripped of meanings when transplanted and commodified in the US, they become but quaint folk art.

Apocalyptic chic

It is hypothesised that skulls' proliferation in popular culture is also interwoven with the apocalyptic zeitgeist of our times. This is a collective foreboding of the collapse of the entire socio-economic order owing to its inability to survive capitalism's materialism and disposability ethos, extreme pathological individualism, secularism's moral bankruptcy (hence the resurgence of religious fundamentalism throughout the world), growing inequalities and injustices, environmental degradation, dramatic climate change, accelerating extinction rates and so forth. Similar obsessions with death have historically coincided with the demise of old cultural orders and the emergence of new ones.[19] A 1994 survey, conducted for US News and World Report, found nearly six in ten Americans believe the world will come to an end or be destroyed – with one-third of those thinking the cataclysm will occur within a few years or decades (Associated Press 1994). This end-of-time mindset arose from a variety of sources, making death and its symbolic associations in vogue, particularly skulls. Two decades and the endings of the old millennium and a Mayan calendar cycle did not temper apocalyptic enthusiasm. A Barna Group OmniPoll of 2013 revealed over 40% of American adults believing that they are living during the end times, with three-quarters of Evangelicals and more than half of all Protestants agreeing 'the world is currently living in the "end times" as described by prophecies in the Bible' (cited in Chumley 2013). Religion contributed a significant role in reinforcing doomsday anticipations beyond the calendrical year with three zeroes. The premillennialists' end-of-world Requiem Mass continued to capture the collective cultural ear; before Paradise, a massive Armageddon housecleaning of evil must occur. With the Iraq Wars, fears of a nuclear Iran and heightened tensions involving Israel and Palestine, books on Armageddon and Jesus Christ's Second Coming returned to bestseller status in 2003 (Eckerman 2003). In 2009, respected pastor and bestselling author David Wilkerson posted 'An Urgent Message' on his blog, noting how 'an earth-shattering calamity is about to happen' (2009). The natural and social sciences were not about to be left out of this eschatological frenzy. The former found a most receptive audience for its stories on human overpopulation and ecological devastation, global warming, accelerating extinction rates, global pandemics and catastrophism. In November of 2007, the UN's Intergovernmental Panel on Climate Change prophesised how nearly one-third of the world's species face extinction if greenhouse gas emissions continue to rise. In its 2008 Living Planet Index, the World Wildlife Fund reported that between 1970 and 2005 land-based species fell by 25%, marine species by 28% and freshwater species by 29%.[20] Stories of extinction-inducing asteroids lurking in our cosmic neighbourhood and of those historically scoring direct hits on the planet have proliferated over the past two decades. Publicity given to the remnants of Comet Shoemaker-Levy 9 smashing into Jupiter in 1994 and the December 2005 Southeast Asia tsunami that killed more than 200,000 set the stage for the 2006 story of evidence that an asteroid smashed into the Indian Ocean 4,500–5,000 years ago, producing a 600-foot-high tsunami. One of the grimmest forecasts comes from James Lovelock of Gaia fame, who predicts the demise of six billion people by the century's end owing to mega-droughts, famine and mass migrations northward leading to political instabilities and war (Goodell 2007). The cultural monitors of social scientists were similarly detecting their own doomsday trends, such as at Boston University's Centre for Millennium Studies, instituted in 1998, where 'groups who focus on any date, since fascination with dates is characteristic of the millennial mindset' are tracked. Declines in Americans' civic involvements and charitable contributions, and general losses of personal integrity, along with profound cynicism and disaffection with those at the throttles of power were observed. One of the most-read social science pieces of the 1990s was Robert Putnam's (1995) *Bowling Alone* thesis of the unravelling of the social fabric. The percentage of Americans agreeing that 'most people can be trusted' declined by nearly one-third between 1972 and 2010 – most notably among political Independents, those under 40, religious conservatives and the lesser educated (Smith Marsden and Hout 2011). One manifestation of this endism genre is the corpsification of popular culture (Foltyn 2008). The dead became regular fare in such movies as *Death Becomes Her* (1992) and former Disney animator Tim Burton's *The Nightmare Before Christmas* (1993) and *Corpse Bride* (2005). The trend largely followed and was interwoven with cinema's ghost genre (e.g. *Poltergeist* (1982), *Ghostbusters* (1984), *Ghost* (1990), *The Sixth Sense* (1999)) during the final two decades of the 20th century. The gruesome yet highly rated *CSI* television series, featuring backstage autopsies by coroners and corpse encounters with investigators, began in 2000. Gunther von Hagen's 'Body Worlds' tour, first presented in Tokyo in 1995, generated considerable publicity with its displays of plastinated cadavers. Public attention had also been directed to the body farms scattered around the nation, beginning in 1981 with the one near Knoxville, Tennessee, which was described in Patricia's Cornwell's (1994) novel *The Body Farm*. Numerous other books on these gruesome gardens followed (Amazon.com's search engine reports 2199 'results'), including Bass and Jefferson's (2004) *Death's Acre: Inside the Legendary Forensic Lab the Body Farm Where the Dead Do Tell Tales* and photographer Sally Mann's (2003) images of decomposing remains at a Federal Forensic Anthropology facility in *What Remains*.[21] When contrasted with such grotesque images of decomposition and decay, sensualised for heightened emotional effect, the skull no longer conveys its traditional macabre message. Because of its commodification and secularisation, the symbol's ability to instil death fears and to inspire moralistic endeavours has largely dissipated. Also associated with the zeitgeist has been the growing popularity of zombies. Zombies, observes Max Brooks (2003), reflect a collective foreboding of broad social collapse. As children personify their conceptions of death, so for many young adults, zombies personify this sense of social entropy. The zombie phenomenon became so mainstream that even the federal government could not resist their allure: to engage the American public with its hazards preparedness messages, during the summer of 2012, the Centers for Disease Control (CDC) included on its website a page humorously devoted to 'Zombie Preparedness'.[22] Having a genre of its own are zombie skulls, featured in product lines of video games, clothing and accessories. They are the heads of the living dead, zombies of advanced decomposition, skulls having agency limited to the killing of the living.

The culmination of American death denials and defiance: skull mockery as symptom of an emerging post-mortal society

Historian Arnold Toynbee famously observed how 'death is un-American … [an] affront to the American dream' (Toynbee 1969). Forty-two years later, British biomedical gerontologist Aubrey de Grey announced that the first person who will live to see her 150th birthday was already alive and that 20 years later, in 2031, will appear one who will live for 1,000 years. Also in 2011, the caption on the February 11 cover of *Time* magazine proclaimed '2045: The Year Man Became Immortal'. For avid sympathisers of Americans' war against death, the end is finally in sight. The contest has been long, with politically declared wars against smallpox, polio, cancer, auto accidents, terrorism and suicide. With this death-of-death framing, the human skull is becoming something akin to that of the short-lived Neanderthal: an extinct predecessor of *homo immortalis*.[23] Further, with dramatically increasing cremation rates and the rise of opportunities for symbolic immortality (Kearl 2010), the skull is less frequently the post-mortem residue we leave behind. Web-based images of a cyborg or avatar holding a human skull connotes something very different from the *vanitas* portraits of the past half-millennium. Instead of being the look of a philosophical reflection of one's future, it is one of an archaeologist's examination of others' past.

Discussion and conclusion

The skull may well be humanity's universal symbol of death. Invested within this symbol are meanings of mortality, dying and the afterlife – issues underlying the antithesis of what life, itself, means for the most social and long-lived of primates. However, having been eroticised, politicised and commodified, its meaning has gone into flux. The skull belt-buckle of Governor Arnold Schwarzenegger, for instance, could mean in 2007 either the Nazi shadow of his Austrian upbringing, acknowledgement of California's sizable Hispanic presence, his public statements concerning environmental damage and climate change, or the dystopian themes of his *Terminator* movie series. When symbols, even those with the potency of skulls, carry so many meanings, the significance of each is diminished – sometimes to the point where they only reference themselves, like being famous for being famous. When, for instance, debriefing my study-abroad students and inquiring why they chose to be photographed in front of a wall of human skulls within the catacombs of Paris or a pyramid of skulls in the killing fields of Cambodia, invariably they were there because skulls are 'cool' and not because of the stories or significations connoted. What really dissolves symbolic essence – the Alzheimer's of symbols – is their commodification. As this manuscript was reaching conclusion in 2013, the newswires carried the story of Disney–Pixar's attempts to trademark '*Día de los Muertos*'. The company had filed ten applications to the US Patent and Trademark Office to secure the name for toys, cereals and jewellery in conjunction with a forthcoming film on the holiday (Flores 2013). Though backing off owing to public outcry, the very audacity of corporate attempts to own the label of a centuries-old Hispanic religious observance for honouring deceased loved ones is telling. Scores of skull images, on the other hand, have successfully been trademarked. Like the Cambodian Khmer Rouge theme park for international tourists, or Polish artist Agata Siwek's crematorium fridge magnet and 'Arbeit Macht Frei' key ring 'Auschwitz souvenirs', or toymaker Mike Fosella's line of Nazi action figurines, even the most morbid and evil elements of collective memory can be dissolved with barcodes. So what happens when the meaning of the symbol signifying mortality and life's brevity evaporates? After all, humanity's distinctiveness supposedly lies in its use of symbols and its unique awareness of their ultimate fate. When the skull symbol fails to connote thoughts of mortality and legacy work, when it fails to trigger imaginations of generations, future and past, not only does the essence of the human condition become problematic, but the very fabric of society risks unravelling. Jean Baudrillard wrote of the unifying power of shared disgust. Skulls no longer disgust. When reflecting on the absence of cemeteries in San Francisco, Joseph Bottum argues that society rests on the deaths of its members:

> death is the anchor for every human association, from the family, all the way up to the nation-state. It provides a reason for association; it keeps from drifting by tying us to a temporal reality larger – richer and more significant – than our individual present.
>
> *(Bottum 2007:20)*

A healthy society, he observes, requires a lively sense of the reality and continuing presence of the dead in order to form human associations. The meaningless skull, like the invisible cemetery, belittles the presence of the dead and averts any reflection on mortality and one's humble place in the flow of generations.

Notes

1 This chapter first appeared in the journal (2015) *Mortality*, 20(1):1–18. The chapter is reproduced here with permission from the publisher. The five pictures presented in the original journal publication have been removed from the text for copyright reasons.
2 Online, there exists the Skull Appreciation Society at: http://skullappreciationsociety.com/. Since 2007, one can follow Noah Scalin's Skull-a-Day blog at http://skulladay.blogspot.com/.
3 Perhaps nowhere do actual skulls become more interwoven with religious art than within the Sedlec Ossuary in Prague, Czech Republic. The abbey's cemetery was flowing over with the victims of the Bubonic Plague and the Hussite Wars. During the 1870s, the bone heaps were reassembled into chandeliers, garlands and archway frescoes by František Rint.
4 The origins of the term are traced back to the Latin biblical aphorism: *vanitas vanitatum omnia vanitas* (Vanity of vanities; all is vanity) (Ecclesiastes 1:2).
5 Lucas Franchoys the Younger's (1616–1681) 'Portrait of a Physician' features a stately seated individual, dressed in the black clothing of the day, with a hand atop a skull. Not only the message of death's finality conveyed, but also physicians' inability to prevent it.
6 Ariès refers to the period as a time of 'remote and imminent death'.
7 An epoch Ariès labels the 'death of other'.
8 It adorned the boyhood Texas home of President Lyndon Baines Johnson. One can only imagine the lessons imparted by this engraving on the man who simultaneously championed the Civil Rights and Older Americans Acts, the Great Society and the Vietnam War.
9 And, if not in image, then in label, such as Salvador Dali's 1934 'Atmospheric Skull Sodomising a Grand Piano'.
10 The skull was autographed by the young woman's naval lieutenant and 13 of his friends, with the inscription: 'This is a good Jap – a dead one picked up on the New Guinea beach'.
11 Even cigarette companies took advantage of the ability of death to sell, marketing such brand names as 'Global Massacre', 'Genocide', 'Serial Killer' and 'WOMD'.

12 There are interesting parallels between this trend and the misogynist fin de siècle expressions of a century earlier (see, for instance, Showalter 1990).

13 The images reinforce the logic of existence, as Robert Kastenbaum's observes: 'we wake but to sleep; we live but to die; and what is the bed but a grave?' (Kastenbaum 2004).

14 In addition to Hirst's creation, we note Mark Kilner's 'Numbskull', a plastic skull covered with 630 tablets of paracetamol and the 10-foot skull made from kitchen utensils by Indian artist Subodh Gupa, displayed at the 2008 Frieze art fair in London.

15 The day is celebrated by over 70% of the population (Palmer 2012) and, some claim, increasingly hijacked from children by adults. The National Retail Federation estimates that if one adds up the sales of candy, pumpkins, costumes ($300 million for pets alone: Reuters 2011), greeting cards and decorations, the holiday generates a $6 billion market.

16 Note the large public rituals given to those suffering 'non-normal' losses, such as those associated with 11 September 2001, the Columbine and Sandy Hook shootings and the large-scale disasters following natural and industrial calamities.

17 Unsurprisingly, this cultural tradition has similarly become commodified and caters to the wealthy. At http://www.luckymojo.com/skull.html, one finds an Aztec skull necklace made in Mexico ca. 1200–1400 and offered for sale on the web in 1997 by the Arte Primitivo/Howard S. Rose Gallery of New York City. It is composed of 14 carved shell beads in the form of human skulls, double perforated on each side for suspension. Each bead is about 1 3/8" long and restrung with period spacers. The asking price was $5500.00. It presently resides in a private collection.

18 At least through the mid-19th century in the Yucatán and elsewhere, skulls were removed from ossuaries to be viewed on the Day of the Dead (Carmichael and Sayer 1991).

19 During the late Middle Ages, for instance, massive loss of life accelerated the decline of traditional feudal institutions. Artists and writers symbolised this disintegration with realistic images of death and decomposition in a style known as the *ars moriendi*. As their institutions gave way, the cultural ethos went out of focus.

20 That year a botanical Noah's Ark, the global seed bank, was inaugurated in Svalbard, Norway.

21 The blurring boundary between life and death was epitomised at the Budapest University of Arts. There, found in 2003, were the remains of a man who had hung himself a year earlier in a garden building that had been closed for reconstruction. Apparently, both builders and students had mistaken it for modern sculpture.

22 It read, in part: 'Wonder why Zombies, Zombie Apocalypse and Zombie Preparedness continue to live or walk dead on a CDC website? As it turns out what first began as a tongue-in-cheek campaign to engage new audiences with preparedness messages has proven to be a very effective platform. We continue to reach and engage a wide variety of audiences on all hazards preparedness via Zombie Preparedness; and as our own director, Dr. Ali Khan, notes, "If you are generally well equipped to deal with a zombie apocalypse you will be prepared for a hurricane, pandemic, earthquake, or terrorist attack"' (CDC 2012).

23 The earliest use of the term goes back at least to the early 19th century.

References

Ariès, Philippe (1981): *The Hour of Our Death*. New York: Alfred A. Knopf.

Associated Press (1994): 'Trend Shows Many Believe World Will End: *San Antonio Express*'. *News*, November 11.

Bass, William M. and Jon Jefferson (2004): *Death's Acre: Inside the Legendary Forensic Lab the Body Farm Where the Dead Do Tell Tales*. New York: Berkley Trade.

Bottum, Joseph (2007): 'Death & Politics'. *First Things,* June/July, 17–29. Retrieved from: http://www.firstthings.com/article/2009/02/001-death-politics-29.

Brooks, Max (2003): *Zombie Survival Guide: Complete Protection from the Living Dead.* New York: Broadway.

Carmichael, Elizabeth and Cloë Sayer (1991): *The Skeleton at the Feast: The Day of the Dead in Mexico.* Austin, TX: University of Texas Press.

CDC (2012): 'Zombie Preparedness'. Retrieved June 11, 2012 from: http://www.cdc .gov/phpr/zombies.htm.

Chumley, Cheryl K. (2013): '4 In 10 Adults: We're Living in the End of Times'. *Washington Times*, September 12. Retrieved from: http://www.washingtontimes.com /news/2013/sep/12/4-in10-american-adults-were-living-end-times/.

Colman, David (2006): 'The Heyday of the Dead'. *New York Times*, July 27, G1, G5.

Cornwell, Patricia (1994): *The Body Farm.* New York: Charles Scribner's Sons.

Crane, Ralph (1944): *Editorial #50693116 – Time and Life Magazine* [Photograph]. Retrieved from: www.gettyimages.com.

Eckerman, Elise (2003): 'War Spurs Doomsday Talk'. *Knight Ridder*, May, 4.

Flores, Adolfo (2013): 'Disney Withdraws Trademark Filing for *Dia de los Muertos*'. *Los Angeles Times*, May 8. Retrieved from: http://www.latimes.com/entertainment/env elope/cotown/la-et-ct-dis ney-dia-de-los-muertos-20130507,0,5334483.story.

Foltyn, Jacque Lynn (2008): 'Dead Famous and Dead Sexy: Popular Culture, Forensics and the Rise of the Corpse'. *Mortality*, 13(2):153–173.

Gilbert, Charles Allan (1892): *All is Vanity* [Drawing]. Retrieved from: http://it .wikipedia.org/wiki/Retro_ Active.

Goodell, Jeff (2007): 'The Prophet of Climate Change: James Lovelock'. *Rolling Stone*, November 1. Retrieved from: http://www.seas.harvard.edu/climate/eli/Courses/ EPS134/Sources/17-   What-to-do/climate-engineering/The%20Prophet%20of% 20Climate%20Change%20James% 20Lovelock%20Rolling%20Stone.pdf.

Kastenbaum, Robert (2004): *On Our Way: The Final Passage Through Life and Death.* Berkeley, CA: University of California Press.

Kearl, Michael C. (2010): 'The Proliferation of Postselves in American Civic and Popular Cultures'. *Mortality*, 15(1):47–63.

Mann, Sally (2003): *What Remains.* New York: Bulfinch.

Mitchell, Dolores (1987): 'The Iconology of Smoking in Turn-Of-the-Century Art'. *Notes in the History of Art*, 6(3):27–33.

Palmer, Kimberly (2012): 'What Halloween Spending Says About the Economy'. *U.S. News Money*, October 3. Retrieved from: http://money.usnews.com/money/personal -finance/articles/2012/10/ 03/what-halloween-spending-says-about-the-economy? vwo=ecfb2.

Peters,Vincent (1985):*Poison* [Photograph].Retrieved from:http://www.theperfumemagazine .com/ december2012/Ways-of-Seeing-Perfume-Advertising.html.

Putnam, Robert (1995): 'Bowling Alone: America's Declining Social Capital'. *Journal of Democracy*, 6(1):65–78.

Randall, Loeffler (2007): *Skull Cutout Flat* [Photograph]. Retrieved from: http://www .thisnext.com/ item/B5FBDA74/Skull-Cutout-Flat-Loeffler.

Reuters (2011): 'The Halloween Economy: $2 Billion in Candy, $300 Million in Pet Costumes'. *The Atlantic*, October 28. Retrieved from: http://www.theatlantic.com /business/archive/2011/10/ the-halloween-economy-2-billion-in-candy-300-milli on-in-pet-costumes/247531/.

Sanchez, Ricardo (1985): 'Day of the Dead' Is Also about Life: *San Antonio Express.' News*, November 1:1E–2E.

Showalter, Elaine (1990): *Sexual Anarchy: Gender and Culture at the Fin De Siècle*. New York: Viking.

Smith, Tom W., Peter V. Marsden and Michael Hout (2011): *General Social Survey, 1972–2010*. [Cumulative File]. ICPSR31521-v1. Storrs, CT: Roper Center for Public Opinion Research, University of Connecticut/Ann Arbor, MI: Inter-university Consortium for Political and Social Research [distributors].

Toynbee, Arnold (1969): Quoted in Lewis Mumford: 'The Human Prospect'. In: *Interpretations and Forecasts, 1922–1972*. New York: Harcourt Brace Jovanovich (1973).

Wilkerson, David (2009): *An Urgent Message*, March 7. Retrieved from: http://davidwilkersontoday. blogspot.com/.

5

IMMERSIVE DARK TOURISM EXPERIENCES

Storytelling at dark tourism attractions in the age of 'the immersive death'

Daniel William Mackenzie Wright

Introduction

As Yuval Noah Harari recently observed, 'blurring the line between fiction and reality can be done for many purposes, starting with having fun, and going all the way to survival' (Harari 2018:246). Humanity's survival is paramount, but our fragile existence is often exposed by our own destructive behaviour and that of Mother Nature, often resulting in human suffering and death. Society's methods of engaging with death have varied throughout time. Methods of engagement have evolved and changed over time because of varying factors, including changes in the social fabric of cultures, often due to human interactions through travel and developments in knowledge and technology. Today, society is being challenged in new ways, with technology being a key factor. Technology can blend the virtual and the real world (augmented reality, AR) and even take people into new worlds (virtual reality, VR). New cultural behaviours could transpire as the fabric of society shifts, as technology plays an even greater role. With new technologies come new opportunities for creating digital content for consumers, and we are now entering a new phase for humanity's engagement with new digital content. Importantly, in relation to this chapter, creators of digital content will shift their thinking and designs (of content) towards new ways of encountering death. The opportunity to incorporate new technologies and content at sites of, and associated with, death and suffering are plentiful. This will allow digital content developers to create novel (VR and AR) experiences through new immersive methods of storytelling. Content could be created allowing consumers to engage with the narratives at dark sites in various different forms, from more educational content to more entertainment-based experiences. Significantly, questions will arise, such as what content is being created, who is creating it and what do we want people to consume? These are noteworthy issues, because this could impact on the overall (re)representation of history and heritage at dark sites, and ultimately the message(s) consumers obtain.

The future consumer will demand more from the tourism process. Choice overload has the potential to increase in the future, as tourists continue to seek fresh, innovative forms of travel experiences. Future travellers are said to be more knowledgeable than today's travellers, better networked and connected, astute in the choices they make, and will seek quality and participatory experiences (Yeoman 2008). Travellers will move away from the solely sunlust passive desires towards more educatory, curiosity motives (Cooper 2016) and will be entertainment seekers (Wright 2018). Joseph Pine and James Gilmore (1999) suggest future travellers will be driven by 'experiences' and that suppliers would be responsible for 'engineering' their desires for such experiences. Susanne Becken (2013) notes future consumers will demand more from their travel experiences, proposing the future will see more specialised products that serve niche markets with greater demand for educational experiences (Becken 2013). With new technologies come new forms of storytelling, and these have the potential to be used at dark sites to engage and satisfy the needs of future consumers. Meeting the demands of future consumers can be achieved through immersive technologies, and attraction managers will soon initiate the implementation of immersive technologies at their sites.

A central focus of this chapter is the importance of storytelling as a tool to enhance the experience of consumers at dark sites (be it for more educational- or entertainment-based purposes). Ronald Azuma (2015:260) suggests that 'storytelling is fundamentally important, and any advancements in media technology that enable people to tell stories in new and potentially more compelling ways can have profound impact'. This chapter will explore immersive technologies and the current content available for consumers, ones relevant to dark and difficult heritage. Subsequently, the discussion will focus on the importance of how these technologies will have profound impacts on our relationship with death, and potentially, how it will shift society from the 'spectacular death' age to 'the immersive death' age. This chapter also raises some important questions. What responsibility does society have when creating new content (in immersive worlds) that focuses on stories of difficult heritage? Should these stories be entertainment-based or educational? Will the creation of (VR and AR) death content with an entertainment focus diminish the importance of learning about suffering and pain of victims, often deemed a valuable experience for tourists? Should VR and AR content focus on bringing consumers and users closer to the suffering of victims, and in doing so, bringing people closer to the victims of such tragedies? Through more educational immersive content there exists a potential to engage visitors with real suffering, on a new level. Ultimately, if new stories are to be created, new content created and new (VR and AR) methods of interaction, what stories should be created, what message should be communicated?

What is dark tourism?

This chapter is exploring the use of immersive technologies at dark sites. Before considering how technology is used at dark sites, it is necessary to provide the reader with a brief overview of dark tourism. Within the visitor economy there exists an array of locations and attractions that explore death, with varying degrees of intensity and purposes (Stone 2006a). There are sites associated with death primarily focusing on education, and sites associated with death where entertainment is a prominent feature of the consumer experience. A widely applied definition of dark tourism is provided by Philip Stone (2006a:146), suggesting that dark tourism is 'the act of travel to sites associated with death, suffering and the seemingly macabre'. However, Malcolm Foley and John Lennon (1996) originally coined the term 'dark tourism', and its roots can be seen in earlier studies of tourism. Chris Rojek (1993) discussed the idea of 'black-spots', referring to the commercial development of grave sites and locations where celebrities or many people met 'sudden' and or violet death. Importantly, dark tourism is both a demand and supply phenomenon. Lennon and Foley (2000) offered a supply-side focus when defining dark tourism, providing a range of case study locations. Stone (2006b) also explored the supply of dark tourism, whilst offering a (darkest–lightest) spectrum which considers the perceived product features of dark attractions which could influence the level of darkness at the attraction. From a demand perspective, A.V. Seaton (1996) proposed an earlier term, 'thanatourism', here considering the concept as a behavioural phenomenon, focusing on the motivational drivers of tourists. According to Seaton (1996:240), thanatourism is

> travel to a location wholly, or partially, motivated by the desire for actual or symbolic encounters with death, particularly, but not exclusively, violent death, which may, to a varying degree be activated by the person-specific features of those whose deaths are its focal objects.

Academic attention and scrutiny of the supply and management of attractions/ sites, as well as the tourist's motivations and behaviour at dark sites has gathered much momentum over recent years. The extent of such work was considered by Wright (2014:19), offering a table of literature highlighting work from 1986 to 2013. The year 2013 onwards has continued to see extensive research into the subject of dark tourism from varying perspectives. It is beyond the scope of this chapter to provide an extensive summary of dark tourism research.

As noted, Stone's (2006a) dark tourism spectrum considers perceived features of supply at sites of death and suffering, and consequently, the perceived shades of darkness–lightness of a site. A key feature is the potential education to entertainment orientation of the site. Stone's (2006a) spectrum would suggest that sites are more likely to become more entertainment-centric as we move further away from the actual time of the event. A previous article written by the author of this chapter (Wright 2018) highlighted the potential of dark sites becoming entertainment-centric much more quickly. Wright's (2018) research considered and explored the notion of whether a timeframe exists in which dark tragic events can become 'lighter' and consequently, be packed and sold to tourism consumers for entertainment purposes? Wright (2018) explored fun factories owned by the Merlin Entertainments Group; the dungeon attractions (in cities like London, Amsterdam and Berlin). Wright considered the timeframe in which the horrors of the cities are turned into entertaining visitor experiences at the dungeons. Whilst the author concluded that there is no specific timeframe to decipher when a dark event could become an entertainment experience, the author does highlight current trends that suggest society is increasingly willing to engage with recent death for entertainment purposes. Wright (2018:19) focused on the examination of three main areas: 'the role and impact of the media and the internet', 'the commercialization of death' and 'the topic as an academic attention and specialization'. The author's research comes with a significant message: 'in search of novel and enticing experiences companies might be pushed to produce and market provocative and thrilling experiences, especially in societies where money dictates and death is seen as a commodity to sell'. The significant outcome and message was: are we content with our recent tragedies being displayed for entertainment purposes (Wright 2018:19)? This current chapter also focuses the reader's attention on this important message, but uniquely, it focuses on the potential of immersive technologies and digital content as a mechanism for driving this change. However, this chapter aims to highlight the potential positive influence of immersive technologies and generating educational content as a driver of future consumer experiences at sites of difficult heritage.

The spectacle of death

This chapter will not concern itself with a review of the historical discussions on death. Instead, Table 5.1 offers a brief insight into the stages of death and how our relationship with death has evolved over time. Here we are drawing on Philippe Ariès (1974) original work discussed in *Western Attitudes Toward Death from the Middle Ages to the Present*, followed by Michael Hviid Jacobsen's (2016) notion of 'spectacular death'. Uniquely, this chapter provides original insights into a potential new stage of death for society. The author proposes that the next stage of (Western) attitudes and engagements with death, will be an age of 'the immersive death'.

To understand the meaning of 'the immersive death' and how this will play out in society, it is necessary to understand the growth in immersive technologies. Thus, the following will explore terminology, types of immersive technologies, current technology and digital content. Having explored these, the author will present scenarios highlighting the potential use of immersive technologies in a site of difficult heritage.

TABLE 5.1 The experience of death in Western societies

The tamed death – Medieval period

Individuals were aware of their own death; they accepted it and were   Ariès
    prepared for their inevitable end. Ariès suggested that during this
    period people were as familiar with the death of others as they were
    with their own death. Death and dead bodies were never far away from
    everyday life.

Death of one's own – late Middle Ages

Focused on the individual and with the time of death as a moment of   Ariès
    maximum awareness. Death became more personal, with individualised
    graves and tombstones. During this period, people become more
    focused on their own inevitable end.

Thy death – early 18th century

Here death became more dramatised and worshipped. People began to   Ariès
    mourn more as death became something to be feared, and the practice
    of memorialisation became more prominent. Graveyards and cemeteries
    were more widespread. People were more emotional about the loss of
    significant others.

Forbidden/invisible death – late 19th century and early 20th century

Death became more shameful, forbidden and marginalised from the   Ariès
    mainstream. The medicalisation of death took death into the hands of
    professional doctors and away from the family and religious institutions.
    Technology took over the role of rituals, doctors from priests, and
    people generally tried to deny the reality of death.

Spectacular death – beginning of the 21st century

Now, death has become a spectacle, an experience witnessed from a safe   Jacobsen
    distance, but rarely experienced directly. We have become spectators,
    onlookers of the death of other people. We want to know about death,
    we are fascinated, but we do not want the pain that comes with death.

The immersive death – early to mid-21st century

New technologies will allow people to tailor their own experiences when   Wright
    confronting death. Interactive real-world experiences through immersive
    technologies such as virtual and augmented reality could provide people
    with the opportunity to engage and explore death at their own desirable
    level(s). Enhanced and more immersive computer-generated perceptual
    information interacting on multi-sensory levels could provide people
    with a full range of death experiences; from the darkest forms, to
    educational centric approaches, and to death as pure entertainment.

Immersive technologies: Virtual, augmented and mixed reality

According to Brid-Aine Parnell, 'augmented and virtual reality (AR/VR) are
not gaming trends – they're technologies set to revolutionise how we do business
at every level' (Parnell 2018). The three types of realities, virtual, augmented
and mixed can be simply explained as follows:

1. Virtual reality (VR): immerses users in a fully artificial digital environment
2. Augmented reality (AR): overlays virtual objects on the real-world environment
3. Mixed reality (MR): overlays and anchors virtual objects to the real world

There have been significant strides in the development and exploration of virtual, augmented and mixed reality in immersive environments, and likewise, there can be some confusion for people who are new to the terminology and the technology. Virtual reality (VR) refers to computer-simulated environments, which can simulate places in the real world as well as fantasy and imaginary worlds, offering users the ability to immerse themselves into artificial environments that stimulate sensory experiences. Original discussions were proposed by Ivan Sutherland (1965) in the mid-1960s and later realised in 1968 when a head-mounted display (HMD) allowed its wearer to engage with a stereoscopic (three-dimensional) display of a computer-generated world (Sutherland 1968). In a virtual environment (in virtual reality), the totality of sensory information is repeatedly supplied by computer hardware. Today, most virtual reality systems display information in visual, auditory and kinaesthetic modalities. Augmented reality (AR), however, allows its users to interact with the real world, whilst (augmented) digital content is added to the real world around us. Here users remain present in the real world but can add objects of a real or fantasy nature to real-world surroundings (which only the user can see). This is often viewed through smartphones or smartglasses. Similarly, to VR, AR allows for visual, auditory and kinaesthetic modalities. When used in situ, VR and AR technologies operate differently. VR requires a user to be fully immersed in a virtual environment, removed from the real world. Therefore, space and the ability to move around becomes more important and more limited (as the user can no longer see the real world). VR is experienced through headsets, whilst augmented reality is primarily experienced via a wearable glasses device, head-mounted device, or through smartphone applications. Table 5.2 provides insights into the technology and offers some examples of AR and VR wearable technologies available to the market (at the time of writing). Tethered virtual reality headsets offer high-quality visuals but need to be connected to a computer, thus offering less mobility than screenless devices and standalone headsets, whilst wearable AR smartglasses and standalone head-mounted devices allow users the freedom to move around the real world. This is important when considering the applicability and adaptability of such technology in actual (dark) tourism attractions.

Paul Milgram and Fumio Kishino (1994) state that a clear way to understand a mixed reality environment is when the real-world and virtual-world objects are presented together in a single display. Mixed reality is arguably a more recent development in immersive technologies. Figure 5.1 below, the 'Mixed Reality Continuum' (adapted from Milgram and Kishino 1994) offers an overview of how technologies allow us to move from the real world to the virtual world and the types of augmented environments between the two extremes. On the left

TABLE 5.2 AR and VR wearable technology

Virtual Reality	Products	Augmented Reality	Products
Screenless viewer: A device that turns smartphones into a VR experience	Google cardboard or Samsung Gear VR	*Wearable smartglasses:* A device that turns smartphones into an AR experience.	Google Glass, Meta Pro, Vuzix Smart Glasses M100 Epson Moverio BT-300
Standalone: Do not require a PC to deliver a VR experience (some require a smartphone)	Oculus Go, Oculus Quest, Lenovo Mirage Solo		
Tethered: Require connection to a computer. Often use external sensors or cameras to track the user's position.	HTC Vive, HTC Vive Pro, Oculus Rift, PlayStation VR	*Head-mounted device:* (Standalone and tethered)	Magic leap, HoloLens 2

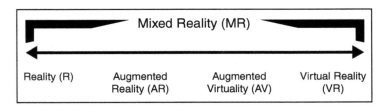

FIGURE 5.1 Mixed reality continuum.

of the spectrum is the natural world, the real one we experience every day. On the far right of the spectrum is virtual reality (VR), the environment in which the user is fully immersed in a computer-generated environment. The rest of the spectrum is made up of mixed reality experiences, ones where the virtual and the real world are merged together. Mixed reality (MR) can come across as similar to augmented reality. MR can initiate from the real world and virtual objects are not just overlaid on the real world but can interact with it. In this instance, a user is still in the real world (viewing the real-world environment around them) but they can add digital content to it and interact with the virtual objects. In the spectrum, this is referred to as Augmented Reality (AR). The same as discussed above, it is a world which brings aspects of the virtual world into the real world. It is closer to the real (R) environment. AR users remain in the real world (their natural environment), whilst using technology (a mobile phone or headwear) so that virtually created visuals can be inserted. AR achieves this by layering virtual information and/or graphics on top of a user's view of a real-world scene. The spectrum also includes Augmented Virtuality (AV). AV describes an environment where real objects are inserted into computer-generated virtual reality environments and can be seen as an inverted type of augmented reality (Forbes 2019; Microsoft 2018).

For the purposes of this chapter, the focus will remain on VR and AR. Researchers at International Data Corporation (IDC) estimate that global revenues for VR and AR markets will increase by 100% or more over each of the next four years, with total spending on products and services in 2017 being $11.4 billion, growing to around $215 billion by 2021 (Parnell 2018). These technologies are already widely utilised in industries such as automotive, healthcare, construction, manufacturing and, significantly, tourism (Parnell 2018).

Enhancing human sensation of presence through immersive technologies

As noted by Eugene Chung (founder and CEO at Penrose Studios), 'we've effectively had the same flat screen medium since 1896. VR/AR uniquely provides a sense of presence and immersion, it's a brand new art form and brand new form of experiencing' (see Hall and Takahashi 2017). The technological landscape is evolving; society is now moving from observation to immersion. According to Drue Kataoka (an artist and technologist), AR and VR will offer an entirely innovative creative medium, where artists can build worlds, pixel by pixel (Hall and Takahashi 2017). These new technologies will replace

> rectilinear devices with technologies that depict worlds in ever-expanding concentric circles, providing a level of immersion and experience that has never been seen before. This could be game-changing: users will no longer view content but will be placed inside ever-expanding virtual worlds and find themselves at the centre, hence the "immersive" nature of the technology.
>
> *(Hall and Takahashi 2017)*

The following authors provide some clarification between the terminology of immersion and presence. Mel Slater, Martin Usoh and Anthony Steed (1995:6) suggest

> presence in a real or virtual environment is a psychological state of consciousness. It is a sense of "being there" in the environment which in the case of the virtual environment is displayed by a computer through appropriately connected hardware channels.

Therefore, 'immersion' is a description of the technology and 'presence' is an emergent property of immersion. Consequently, immersion in an environment can lead to the user having presence in that environment. This is where the technical quality of the technology is significant, because the better the technology the greater potential for a person to be immersed and consequently feel present in the environment.

Previous research has highlighted the importance of presence in virtual environments (VE) (Sheridan 1992; Barfield et al. 1995; Slater et al. 1996). It is suggested that a highly present individual is more likely to behave normally in the VE. Consequently, the individual is more likely to behave in a manner like their everyday reality. Thus, the more immersive the technology, the greater sense of presence and ultimately, higher levels of consumer engagement. Presently, market products such as the Oculus Quest allow a participant to engage with the following immersive experience: a subject to be fully immersed into a virtual world, to walk through the virtual environment (although within the limitations of the tracking device and physical space) and bend down and look around by turning their head and body. With the application of haptic data (kinaesthetic) technology, subjects can pick objects up, move, throw and interact with objects and even other people (by using handheld controllers, whilst other technology allows the use of gloves). From a sensory perspective, this is certainly an incredible advancement in immersing users and allowing them to feel heightened levels of presence in virtual worlds. It does rely on good real-time interactions; this is often referred to as 'lag', here focusing on mapping the physical body's movements (in real time) with those of the body in the virtual world. Current technology allows this to be done up to a millisecond response time (Barfield and Hendrix 1995).

Virtual and augmented reality in smartphone technology

To date, academic literature on the use of augmented and virtual reality in the tourism industry has had limited attention. Virtual reality requires users to be more stationary as they are in a completely virtual world. Previous research has explored VR's potential as a marketing tool. Yu C. Huang et al. (2016:116) explored the use of virtual reality technology in tourism marketing, suggesting, '3D virtual technology provides opportunities for destination marketing organizations to communicate with targeted markets by offering a rich environment for potential visitors to explore tourism destinations'. As the authors stress, there is limited understanding about how to effectively market tourism destinations in virtual worlds. However, the expansive nature of technology and the internet is likely to transform the way in which tourists perceive and consume destinations and attractions. Table 5.3 provides an insight into some of the smartphone applications available in virtual reality (VR). The table is split into three sections, based on the three different types of headsets identified in Table 5.2 above.

Meredydd Williams, Kelvin Yao and Jason Nurse (2018) note that via the use of augmented reality, virtual graphics can transform the physical world. Thus, such technology offers benefits to mobile tourism experiences, especially ones

TABLE 5.3 Virtual reality smartphone applications for tourism

Virtual Reality Applications		
Application Name	Application Description	Headset
Italia VR	Italia Virtual Reality (created by ENIT – Italian National Tourist Board) allows users to discover Italy from unique viewpoints. In the app, users can explore art, history, territory, culture, food, wine and the opportunity to live authentic experiences.	Screenless viewer
Wander VR	From the comfort of your living room, viewers can teleport almost anywhere in the world. Walk across the London Bridge, stroll the gardens of the Taj Mahal, or witness the enormity of the Great Pyramids of Egypt – unlimited exploration awaits.	Standalone Oculus Quest and Oculus Go
Realities	Allows users to explore scanned and modelled real-world environments captured with specialised scanning equipment to deliver immersive rendering in virtual reality.	Tethered HTC Vive

where 'points of interest' can be annotated on a smartphone screen. An example of this is explored by Ian Yeoman (2012) in a scenario entitled *Edinburgh 2050: Technological Revolution*. Yeoman explored the potential for a visitor travelling to Edinburgh and being able to gaze into the city's past using augmented smart-glasses technology. At present, there is a growing number of smartphone applications providing virtual and augmented reality experiences, some of which are presented in Table 5.4.

Developments in smartglasses technology could revolutionise the augmented reality consumer experience, notably, non-tethered technology, i.e. smartglasses that do not require a stationary computer. Smartphone augmented reality technology is still in the early stages of development. According to Geoffrey Moore's (1991) technology adoption cycle, society is at the 'innovators' to 'early adopters' stages. Industry reports suggest that smartphone technology will gain higher market shares in the coming years (Digi-Capital 2018). At present, companies like Google Glass, Microsoft's HoloLens and HoloLens 2, as well as Magic Leap, have been leading smartglasses innovations. Significantly, it will not be long until Apple Inc. brings to the market their own augmented reality smartglasses (Bradshaw 2019; Haselton 2019; Lynch 2019). Some tech experts suggest smartglasses will eventually replace smartphones (London 2018). Consequently, society might soon be 'crossing the chasm' and moving into the 'early majority' stage of Moore's (1991) technology lifecycle. AR content is already widely available on mobile application stores, including Apple's online application store (as well as for Android

TABLE 5.4 Augmented reality smartphone applications for tourism

Augmented Reality Applications	
Application Name	Application Description
Senditur	An application that deals with places of interest for travellers in Spain, hiking the Camino de Santiago and the mountain routes. Users can discover towns hotels, shelters, rest areas close to them and details of natural and historical heritage.
The Gruffalo Spotter Trail	Designed for exclusive use at 26 Forestry Commission sites in England. Bring the trails to life using augmented reality. Using smartphones, consumers, when coming across triggers (physical signs in the forest) could aim the camera at the trigger and an interactive virtual display appears. 3D character animation would be viewable through the smartphone, allowing users to take photos alongside the virtual image.
MapScope Augmented Reality	The app is powered by Google Places API and includes over 50 million places. When users raise their smartphone and aim it at their surroundings, the app will inform users and assist them in locating points of interest in their (urban) surroundings.

smartphones). With more companies like Apple generating smartglasses, AR content is likely to see continued expansion in the near and distant future.

Virtual reality content of dark attractions

Having explored examples of virtual reality experiences more generally (in Tables 5.3 and 5.4), Table 5.5 offers three examples of dark attractions/sites that have been turned into virtual reality experiences. These experiences allow viewers to explore sites before visiting. In the case of the Berlin Wall, the content provides users with a historical viewing experience/perspective. These examples showcase the depth and variety of ways in which content is being created for sites of dark heritage. Whilst Table 5.4 offered an insight into augmented reality experiences (generally), AR content that focuses on death and suffering is limited (thus, no useable examples are available).

The age of 'the immersive death': Experiences through VR and AR

The chapter has provided an overview of current virtual and augmented reality technology, headsets and smartphone capabilities, whilst also highlighting some of the current digital content available to consumers. Importantly, it has established that virtual reality experiences can be used not only in a user's personal environment, but can also be located at visitor attractions, providing a

TABLE 5.5 Dark attractions in virtual reality

Virtual Reality Applications – Dark Attractions

Application Name	Application Description	Headset
Inside Auschwitz VR	The first ever global 360 project inside Auschwitz-Birkenau. Anita Lasker-Wallfisch, Philomena Franz and Walentyna Nikodem are three survivors of the Holocaust. Guided by their stories and with the aid of a 360 drone, users can experience the huge dimensions of Auschwitz.	Screenless viewer
Anne Frank House VR	The award-winning VR experience offers users a unique and emotional insight into the two years of Anne Frank during the Second World War. The actual site is now a popular tourist attraction in Amsterdam, Netherlands.	Standalone – Oculus Quest
Berlin Wall VR	Go behind the Berlin Wall in an immersive experience that transports users to Communist East Berlin at the height of the Cold War. Users can see Communist propaganda posters, razor-sharp barbed wire and dodge guard tower searchlights.	Tethered HTC Vive Pro

fully immersive virtual experience, whilst augmented reality, mainly through smartphone technology, allows viewers to move freely around a site and layer virtual objects onto the real world. As technology develops, with wider availability in VR headsets and augmented smartphones (and eventually smartglasses), there will be more developers creating immersive (death- and difficult heritage-related) digital content for consumers to engage with. This has the potential to enhance our relationships with death and difficult heritage, in a range of immersive ways. It will be important for managers of dark sites and those creating the content to consider the purpose and motive of doing so. To capture this more visually, Figure 5.2 provides an immersive death continuum. To the left of the continuum is the reality spectrum; moving from the real to the virtual (and augmented in the middle). Three main factors are then considered: *location*, *communication* and *technology*.

The following offers further explanation of each category and its importance when considering the potential creation of a VR or AR experience of a dark attraction. Importantly, there are overlapping aspects between the three factors.

Location

- Attraction based to non-attraction based. Where does the experience take place? For VR, consumers can engage with the VR content at the actual

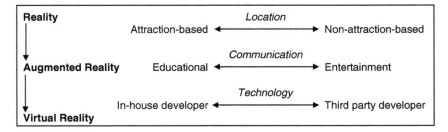

FIGURE 5.2   The immersive death continuum: (re)representations of death at (dark) attraction-based locations.

site/attraction and from their own private space. For AR immersive experiences, content can be created for the actual site, and consumers will be able to engage with the stories/narrative as they move around the attraction.

Communication

* Educational to entertainment. Who is communicating the message and what message are they communicating? Here the focus is on who responsible for developing the content. Would it be stakeholders who have an interest in the site? External companies could also create content that people could activate when visiting sites. The issue here is one of reliability, bias, honesty etc. in the narratives that are created. This is increasingly significant, as it can influence the narrative being showcased and presented and consequently, the message tourists engage with. Additionally, is the content created for educational purposes or one for entertainment purposes? Experiences could be created for a mainstream audience or more tailor-made niche experiences could be created for people seeking their own specific interpretations or personal level of enjoyment.

Technology

* In-house developer to third-party developer. The focus here is on who owns the technology (site attraction or visitors' own technology) and the digital content, as the accessibility and quality will have a significant impact on the type of experience. The human feeling of presence in a VR and AR experience is based on the quality and reliability of immersive technology and quality of visual content. Here, issues arise, such as the quality of the experience, the reliability and availability of the desired technology and the cost of implementing the technology.

To visualise this in more detail, Table 5.6 offers four examples of how Auschwitz-Birkenau could utilise VR and AR immersive technologies. It offers two examples

TABLE 5.6 VR and AR experiences at Auschwitz-Birkenau

Virtual Reality Scenarios

Location	*Communication*	*Technology*
Auschwitz-Birkenau – Off-site content	Entertainment Focus (Third-party developer) In the comfort of their own home, consumers can now download the Horrible Histories Auschwitz-Birkenau Tour. Consumers can freely explore the site as it used to be. The story mode approach allows users to select different character roles. They can select to re-enact the life of a prisoner in the concentration camp and challenge the guards – but must do so at their own peril. Or they can take on the role of a guard and see how they would treat the prisoners, and how much mercy they will show them. Using the latest in virtual reality immersive technology experience Auschwitz-Birkenau like never before. As users walk through the camp, they can see the horror, listen to people's conversations, speak to different characters and through the power of kinaesthetic technology they can interact with other people and their surroundings.	Standalone VR Headset (owned by the consumer)
Auschwitz-Birkenau – Location-specific content	Educational Focus (In-house developer) The site offers a range of virtual reality content in which visitors can engage with the tragic stories of prisoners. Using old footage, photos and recordings, the content recreates life-like footage, bringing visitors closer than ever to the suffering of individual prisoners. Throughout the site, visitors can use our standalone VR headsets which are located at specific points to provide a true sense of presence when re-visiting the past in a fully immersive virtual experience.	Standalone VR Headset (owned by the attraction)

(Continued)

TABLE 5.6 Continued

Augmented Reality Scenarios

Location	Communication	Technology
Auschwitz-Birkenau – Full site content	Entertainment Focus (Third-party developer) What was it like to be a prisoner? During this experience visitors will interact with other prisoners and generals, and must make difficult choices, choices that will determine their long or short-term survival. Will they be one of the lucky survivors, or will they escape the terrors that await. Experience the gory and wretched reality in a range of fun-centric and humorous approaches. A light-hearted approach where digital content is displayed over the visitors' real world-view. Before visiting the site, visitors should download the Auschwitz-Birkenau smartglasses application. Whilst touring the attraction and with location settings enabled, smartglasses will use augmented reality technology to overlay images onto visitor's real-world tour. With real-time data capture our app will ensure visitors are not interfering with other guests at the site.	Wearable smartglasses (owned by the visitor)
Auschwitz-Birkenau – Full site content	Educational Focus (In-house developer) Throughout the site there are trigger signals. By hovering over the triggers, augmented content will appear. The content offers real depictions and stories of prisoners and the suffering and torment they lived through. With this new interactive and immersive experience, visitors can select the level of visual intensity of the content they are consuming. Selecting a higher level of intensity will result in more vivid visuals of brutality, suffering and death on display. Our smartglasses provide visitors with augmented reality content as they walk around the attraction. During the visit at the site visitors can take up the option to wear a pair of smartglasses (or use their own). If using their own, they will need to connect to the site's Wi-Fi to access the content.	Wearable smartglasses (owned by the attraction or visitors can use their own)

of how a visitor could engage with a prisoner's experience through immersive content. The four examples consist of two VR and two AR experiences, each offering an entertainment and educational example. The VR scenario includes an entertainment-based experience created by a third-party developer and can be consumed off-site, and an educational experience that is experienced at the actual site. The AR scenarios both focus on on-site experiences. Both the entertainment scenarios are presented as content created by a third-party developer whilst the educational content is developed in-house by the attraction owners. The two entertainment examples draw on a similar approach to the ones presented by Wright (2018).

As highlighted in the four scenarios, future consumers will be able to engage with death in more immersive and diverse ways than ever before. As consumers become more demanding, seeking personal and novel experiences, content will also likely become more varied. With new technologies come new opportunities, but also new challenges. VR and AR will lead to new content for consumers to engage with. With a wider spectrum of digital content, the ability to experience the content on a range of technologies, in more places (at the actual site or even at home) than ever before, and with different communicative (from educational to entertainment-centric) approaches, future consumers of death will be part of 'the immersive death' age. Therefore, now is the time to consider what this could mean for dark heritage sites, and importantly, what aspect(s) of history do they want to (re)represent? The challenge and opportunity for sites of difficult heritage will be the implementation of the new technologies and significantly, the messages being communicated via (new) digital content. After all, one of the most powerful messages at dark sites is the suffering and pain of the victims, so should this be the focus of future VR and AR immersive content? Should content focus on serious, real depictions, rather than offering entertainment-based experiences? Otherwise, the notion proposed by Wright (2018), that our tragic events will become places of entertainment much sooner could be further fuelled by immersive technologies and new digital content.

Dark tourism, immersive stories and human survival

Ronald Azuma (2015:260) highlights the power of storytelling by suggesting that

> telling a story is an important method of education and instruction. Stories can contain lessons, codified bits of wisdom that are passed on in a memorable and enjoyable form. Technological developments that make the story clearer and more memorable can aid retention and understanding.

As discussed by Oliver Bimber, Miguel L. Encarnação and Dieter Schmalstieg (2003) interactive digital story techniques, when applied with new media forms, allow for a shift into the third dimension (virtually and in the real/

physical world). Subsequently, a significant advantage of this transition is the ability to communicate information more effectively via digital means: 'The user experience is thus transformed from relating different pieces of information to one another to "living through" the narrative' (Bimber, Encarnação and Schmalstieg 2003:87). Whilst focusing on mixed reality (MR) and augmented reality (AR), Azuma (2015:259) notes that the technology will be used to allow innovative methods of storytelling that will allow 'virtual content to be connected in meaningful ways to particular locations, whether those are places, people or objects'. He also stresses the likelihood of AR and MR being used as a new form of location-based media that enables new storytelling experiences. As Mats Lindgren and Hans Bandhold (2009) noted, humans create stories to help us understand life, to generate meaning, to establish order and spaces to live in collectively and to consider our past, present and future. According to Yuval Noah Harari (2015:170), 'meaning is created when many people weave together a common network of stories'. Through our social stories, 'people constantly reinforce each other's beliefs in a self-perpetuating loop. Each round of mutual confirmation tightens the web of meaning further' (Harari 2015:170–171). Storytelling is central to human life, to our survival. The stories we tell each other pass on from one generation to the next; they play a significant role in bonding peoples, cultures and nations. So what stories do we want to tell, what stories do we want to resonate throughout time and are there stories we want to forget? Do we want stories to entertain us, to educate us, to do both? Do we want the truth from stories, or are we more engaged and captivated by fictional narratives?

Harari (2018:311) suggests that

> we humans have conquered the world thanks to our ability to create and believe fictional stories. We are therefore particularly bad at knowing the difference between fiction and reality. Overlooking this difference has been a matter of survival for us. If you nevertheless want to know the difference, the place to start is with suffering.

He goes on to point to this very significant idea:

> So, if you want to know the truth about the universe, about the meaning of life, and about your own identity, the best place to start is by observing suffering and exploring what it is. The answer isn't a story.
>
> *(Harari 2018:313)*

By observing suffering and exploring what it is, humans can begin to know about the universe, the meaning of life, our own identity. It is important to note that Harari (2018) stresses the significance of exploring suffering on an individual level, one person's suffering, not the suffering on an entire nation, as nations are concepts, ideas, but the power is recognising the suffering of an individual woman or child that has been brutally raped or murdered during war. It is the 'real' individual experiences of suffering Harari is pointing towards. Harari also suggests that 'the answer isn't a story'. This author thinks otherwise. Stories that are experienced through immersive technologies offer new opportunities for educational learning. Immersive narratives depicting individual stories that bring visitors closer to the reality of what happened at sites of difficult heritage are an incredibly powerful tool to bring humans closer to the individual suffering experienced. Consequently, using VR and AR technology and developing educational content for consumers could have the potential to capture the true realities of dark heritage sites, with the intention of furthering our own human survival, as we become more aware of the true suffering experienced by individuals at sites of difficult heritage.

Conclusion

Dark sites of death and suffering are plentiful, and they are places often frequented by tourists. They exist in different forms across the globe. Sites of difficult heritage display the most wicked nature of humanity and devastating effects of Mother Nature. Whilst dark tourism sites range in a 'fluid spectrum of intensity' (Stone 2006a:146), all sites focus on (re)representations of death and suffering. With the passage of time, the experiences on offer at dark attractions can move from educational to entertainment-centric and the tourist behaviour will change as the level of intensity and darkness decreases. Much of humanity's dark heritage becomes a source of entertainment in tourist attractions like the London Dungeons. However, technology is now moving into a new phase, one where the real world can be merged with, and even replaced by, the virtual world. With this comes new opportunities for creating digital content and consumer experiences. Dark heritage sites using immersive technologies can (re)create stories and narratives that allow consumers to engage with the attraction and its heritage in new forms.

This chapter has explored original ideas on humanity's future engagements with death. It is suggested, that by the early to mid-21st century, society will be entering an age termed 'the immersive death'. During this time, immersive technologies and an increasingly growing library of digital content will allow consumers to engage with death in new ways and from alternative perspectives. Digital immersive experiences through VR and AR content can be created for a variety of motives. They could allow viewers to visit dark sites such as Auschwitz-Birkenau to entertain themselves with the horrors of the past, as they engage with more light-hearted experiences of what it was like to be a Holocaust prisoner, or more educational content highlighting individual suffering of victims could be created. It will become the responsibility of developers and managers of sites of difficult heritage to consider the content they wish to create and engage audiences with. Sites of difficult heritage offer humanity a window into the pain and suffering of individuals, and if that message can be communicated appropriately, then VR and AR immersive stories have the potential to help society navigate past our differences, to move beyond our horrors through informative educational means, and ultimately, lead to continued human survival.

References

Ariès, Philippe (1974): *Western Attitudes Toward Death: From the Middle Ages to the Present.* Baltimore, MD: John Hopkins University Press.

Azuma, Ronald (2015): 'Location-Based Mixed and Augmented Reality Storytelling'. In: Woodrow Barfield (ed.). *Fundamentals of Wearable Computers and Augmented Reality* (2nd edition). Boca Raton, FL: CRC Press, pp. 259–276.

Barfield, Woodrow and Claudia Hendrix (1995): 'The Effect of Update Rate on the Sense of Presence within Virtual Environments, Virtual Reality'. *The Journal of the Virtual Reality Society,* 1(1):3–16.

Barfield, Woodrow, Thomas Sheridan, David Zeltzer and Mel Slater (1995): 'Presence and Performance Within Virtual Environments'. In: Woodrow Barfield and Thomas A. Furness (eds.). *Virtual Environments and Advanced Interface Design.* Oxford: Oxford University Press, pp. 473–513.

Becken, Susanne (2013): 'Shapers and Shifters for the Future of Travel and Tourism'. In: James Leigh, Craig Webster and Stanislav Ivanov (eds.). *Future Tourism: Political, Social and Economic Challenges.* London: Routledge, pp. 80–91.

Bimber, Oliver, Miguel L. Encarnação and Dieter Schmalstieg (2003): 'The Virtual Showcase as a New Platform for Augmented Reality Digital Storytelling'. In: *EGVE '03 Proceedings of the Workshop on Virtual Environments.* New York: The Association for Computing Machinery, pp. 87–95.

Bradshaw, Tim (2019): 'Why Apple's Smart Glasses Are Such a Long Time Coming'. Available online at: https://www.ft.com/content/f2700100-0726-11ea-a984-fbba cad9e7dd.

Cooper, Chris (2016): *Essentials of Tourism* (2nd edition). Harlow: Pearson Education.

Digi-Capital (2018): 'Ubiquitous $90 Billion AR to Dominate Focused $15 Billion VR by 2022'. Available online at: https://www.digi-capital.com/news/2018/01/ubiquito us-90-billion-ar-to-dominate-focused-15-billion-vr-by-2022/.

Foley, Malcolm and John J. Lennon (1996): 'JFK and Dark Tourism: A Fascination with Assassination'. *International Journal of Cultural Studies,* 1(4):197–210.

Forbes (2019): 'The Difference Between Virtual Reality, Augmented Reality and Mixed Reality'. Available online at: https://www.forbes.com/sites/quora/2018/02/02/ the-difference-between-virtual-reality-augmented-reality-and-mixed-reality/#6c8 d84972d07.

Hall, Stefan and Ryo Takahashi (2017): 'Augmented and Virtual Reality: The Promise and Peril of Immersive Technologies'. Available online at: https://www.mckinsey .com/industries/technology-media-and-telecommunications/our-insights/augmen ted-and-virtual-reality-the-promise-and-peril-of-immersive-technologies.

Harari, Yuval Noah (2015): *Homo Deus: A Brief History of Tomorrow.* London: Penguin/ Random House.

Harari, Yuval Noah (2018): *21 Lessons for the 21st Century.* New York: Spiegel & Grau.

Haselton, Todd (2019): 'Apple's Smart Glasses Said to Launch in 2023, Three Years Later Than Originally Expected'. Available online at: https://www.cnbc.com/2019/11/11 /apple-to-launch-ar-headset-in-2022-smart-glasses-in-2023.html.

Huang, Yu C., Kenneth F. Backman, Sheila J. Backman and Lan Lan Chang (2016): 'Exploring the Implications of Virtual Reality Technology in Tourism Marketing: An Integrated Research Framework'. *International Journal of Tourism Research*, 18(2):116–128.

Jacobsen, Michael Hviid (2016): '"Spectacular Death" – Proposing a New Fifth Phase to Philippe Ariès's Admirable History of Death'. *Humanities*, 5(19):1–20.

Lennon, John. J. and Malcolm Foley (2000): *Dark Tourism: The Attraction of Death and Disaster.* London: Continuum.

Lindgren, Mats and Hans Bandhold (2009): *Scenario Planning: The Link between Future and Strategy.* New York: Palgrave/Macmillan.

London, Andrew (2018): 'Smart Glasses Could Kill Smartphones in the Next Five Years'. Available online at: https://www.techradar.com/uk/news/smart-glasses-could-kill-s martphones-in-the-next-five-years.

Lynch, Gerald (2019): 'Apple AR Glasses Release Date, News and Rumours'. Available online at: https://www.techradar.com/uk/news/apple-ar-glasses-release-date-news -and-rumors.

Microsoft (2018): 'What Is Mixed Reality?' Available online at: https://docs.microsoft .com/en-us/windows/mixed-reality/mixed-reality.

Milgram, Paul and Fumio Kishino (1994): 'A Taxonomy of Mixed Reality Visual Displays'. *IEICE Transactions on Information and Systems*, E77-D:1321–1329.

Moore, Geoffrey A. (1991): *Crossing the Chasm: Marketing and Selling Technology Products to Mainstream Customers.* New York: Harper Business.

Parnell, Brid-Aine (2018): 'AR and VR – Immersive Technologies That Mean Business'. Available online at: http://www.think-progress.com/blog/performance-and-prod uctivity/ar-and-vr-immersive-technologies-that-mean-business/.

Pine, Joseph B. and James H. Gilmore (1999): *The Experience Economy.* Boston, MA: Harvard Business School Press.

Rojek, Chris (1993): *Ways of Escape: Modern Transformations in Leisure and Travel.* London: Macmillan.

Seaton, A. V. (1996): 'Guided by the Dark: From Thanatopsis to Thanatourism'. *International Journal of Heritage Studies*, 2(4):234–244.

Sheridan, Thomas B. (1992): 'Musings on Telepresence and Virtual Presence'. *Presence: Teleoperators and Virtual Environments*, 1(1):120–126.

Slater, Mel, Martin Usoh and Anthony Steed (1995): 'Taking Steps: The Influence of a Walking Metaphor on Presence in Virtual Reality'. In: *ACM Transactions on Computer-Human Interaction (TOCHI): Special Issue on Virtual Reality.* Available online at: https:/ /pdfs.semanticscholar.org/5f08/6665b6bf04a03d07ea49baa2761c7936b9b5.pdf.

Slater, Mel, Linakis Vasilis, Usoh Martin and Rob Kooper (1996): 'Immersion, Presence and Performance in Virtual Environments: An Experiment with Tri-Dimensional Chess'. In: *Proceedings of the VRST 96*, Hong Kong, July 1–4.

Stone, Philip R. (2006a): 'A Dark Tourism Spectrum: Towards a Typology of Death and Macabre Related Sites, Attractions and Exhibitions'. *Tourism: an Interdisciplinary International Journal*, 54(2):145–160.

Stone, Philip R. (2006b): 'Review: *KZ* – A Feature Length Documentary by Rex Bloomstein'. *The Dark Tourism Forum.* Available online at: http://www.dark-tourism .org.uk.

Sutherland, Ivan E. (1965): 'The Ultimate Display'. *Proceedings of the IFIPS Conference*, 2:506–508.

Sutherland, Ivan E. (1968): 'Head-Mounted Three-Dimensional Display'. *Proceedings of the Fall Joint Computer Conference*, 33:757–764.

Williams, Meredydd, Kelvin K. K. Yao and Jason R. C. Nurse (2018): *ToARist: An Augmented Reality Tourism App Created Through User-Centred Design*. Ithaca, NY: Cornell University Library, arXiv.org. Available online at: https://search.proquest.c om/docview/2074056619?accountid=17233.

Wright, Daniel W. M. (2014): *Residents' Perceptions of Dark Tourism; the Case of L'Aquila, Italy*. University of Central Lancashire (A thesis submitted in partial fulfilment for the requirements for the degree of Doctor of Philosophy), Preston.

Wright, Daniel W. M. (2018): 'Terror Park: A Future Theme Park in 2100'. *Futures*, 96:1–28.

Yeoman, Ian (2008): *Tomorrow's Tourist*. Oxford: Butterworth/Elsevier/Heinemann.

Yeoman, Ian (2012): *2050 – Tomorrow's Tourism*. Bristol: Channel View Publications.

6

KILLING HUMANITY

Anthropocentrism and apocalypse in contemporary cinema

Dina Khapaeva

Introduction

What makes the secular apocalypse so trendy? Indeed, the sheer number of apocalyptic and post-apocalyptic movies is striking: the Internet Movie Database (imdb .com) lists over 3,104 apocalyptic and post-apocalyptic movies and another 701 movies that have as their key term 'the end of the world', the majority of which were produced since the 1990s.[1] It should be mentioned that present-day apocalyptic and post-apocalyptic genres predominantly have no connection to biblical themes of redemption, which have nourished apocalyptic thinking for centuries, so linking the popularity of the apocalypse to the millennial beliefs is ungrounded.[2] Scholars explain the mounting attractiveness of the apocalyptic and post-apocalyptic genres in the last decades as an expression of political and social anxieties, such as environmental problems (Ortega and Hammond 2016:105–116), world peace insecurity (Brians 2016) terrorism, fear of viral pandemics (Meike 2019:163–173), capitalist exploitation, or as an expression of inequality, race and gender issues (Peebles 2017). Some argue that apocalyptic and post-apocalyptic narratives may help us cope with the fear of death and offset our incapacity to avoid it, and can even help the audience to 'make sense of the world'.[3] Others believe that 'longing for some conclusive catastrophe' is characteristic of modernity and speaks to 'a pervasive post-apocalyptic sensibility in recent American culture' (Berger 1999:xii–xiii). Although important, these explanations overlook certain factors specific to the cultural situation of the past decades that may rationalise the fixation on apocalypse of millions of readers and viewers.

In this chapter, I examine the differences in the representations of humanity's end in secular apocalyptic and post-apocalyptic movies and television shows with a special focus on the most recent ones produced, such as *Fantastic Beasts:*

The Crimes of Grindelwald (David Yates, 2018), *Genesis: The Fall of Eden* (Freddie Hutton-Mills and Bart Ruspoli, 2018), *Annihilation* (Alex Garland, 2018), *War for the Planet of the Apes* (2017, Matt Reeves), *Godzilla: King of Monsters* (2019), *The Umbrella Academy: The White Violin* (Steve Blackman and Jeremy Slater, 2019), *The Maze Runner: The Death Cure* (Wes Ball, 2018), *Mission: Impossible – Fallout* (Christopher McQuarrie, 2018), and *Pacific Rim: Uprising* (Steven S. DeKnight, 2018). Analysing these movies through the lens of anthropocentrism, I argue that movies featuring secular apocalypse fall into two categories that may be called *the human-centred paradigm* and *the antihuman paradigm*. Their major difference consists in whether or not their protagonists are humans, and in the attitudes they express regarding the destiny of humanity. This classification reveals the dynamics that have driven the transformations of the apocalyptic and post-apocalyptic genres over the past decades.

Even though apocalyptic thinking goes back to the dawn of humanity, beginning with the Mesopotamian myth of the flood, I argue that contemporary movies, as well as computer games and fiction, mark a unique way of envisioning the end of humankind. I suggest that the fixation on apocalypse is written into a broad cultural and intellectual context of the development of popular culture and could be explained only in so far as this broader context is taken into consideration. This broader context is the popular culture preoccupation with virtual violent death and violence that have become so widespread in entertainment that Danish sociologist Michael Hviid Jacobsen coined the term 'spectacular death', by which he means the new attitude to death in contemporary society: '"Spectacular death" is a death that has for all practical intents and purposes been transformed into a spectacle" (Jacobsen 2016:19). This diagnosis aligns well with Susan Sontag's characterisation of the apocalypse as a spectacle that, according to her, in 'The Imagination of Disaster', she considers as a way to express anxieties about destruction (Sontag 1961).

Thanatopathia and the commodification of death

The obsession with violence and violent death as entertainment prompted Rowland Atkinson and Thomas Rodgers to conceive the term 'ludic thanato-drome' (Atkinson and Rodgers 2016:1291–1307; Atkinson and Willis 2007:818–845), which describes the relationship between virtual and real-world violence. Looking at the psychological and societal consequences of violent entertainment and using as their case study violent games, they discuss the fictional violence, relying on Giorgio Agamben's term 'zone of exception',

> where one can play at and with death. The ludic thanatodrome is suggestive of the kinds of overt encouragements to *play at* human harm, assassination and torturous violence – it is a space where bloody killing, "head

shots", "frags" and "kill points" are at the heart of both a playful mode
of engagement but also a casualization of warfare, brutality and a general
devaluing of human life and pro-sociality.

(Atkinson and Rodgers 2016:1303)

This description is certainly relevant in discussing the attitudes to human characters in popular culture products that feature violence more generally, well
beyond computer games. Think about the destiny of human characters in torture
porn, or slasher movies, or the fates of those consumed by zombies in the zombie
apocalypse films and books, those eaten by cannibals, or by the gamers of the
recent games featuring cannibalism as their major theme, with victims hunted,
kidnapped, and murdered by serial killers. In all these genres and media, the
entertainment is gained from watching the denigration people suffer at the hands
of monsters and the violation of human dignity. These genres focus on displaying
the agonies of the victim, who, in this fictional world, is not given the chance
to rise heroically above her circumstances, protecting her dignity and pride,
and vanquishing her (more rarely his) tormentors. The majority of these narratives have a clear misogynist message. To what extend is the victim's heinous
death what the audience of these movies, computer games, and fiction awaits and
enjoys? The role of the victim is that of prey: once caught, she or he becomes an
object of violence, and very often simply food for monsters (Khapaeva 2019a).

This longing for violent entertainment is an integral part of the cultural
movement that I term *thanatopathia* (from the Ancient Greek θάνατος – death,
ипάθος – passion, desire). I analyse this cultural movement in my book *The
Celebration of Death in Contemporary Culture* (Khapaeva 2017), showing that it
manifests itself not only in popular culture, but is also present in the rapid changes
in the social rituals and practices related to death – burial rituals, holidays, cults,
language, education, and commercial ventures. I interpret these social and cultural facts through the prism of the attitudes they express towards human beings.
I argue that changes in the attitudes toward human characters reflected in popular fiction and movies help us understand the meaning and the nature of social
change. In my other works, I demonstrate that, starting from the late 1980s and
early 1990s, a profound shift took place in the role that murderous monsters
play in popular culture products. The monsters acting in man-made nightmares
took over human characters and pushed them to the periphery of the creators
and audience's interests. A wizard, vampire, zombie, cannibal, or serial killer
performs as the novel's or movie's first-person narrator and/or main protagonist,
with whom the audience is expected to identify and who represents an undeniable aesthetic ideal. The image of the superhero probably symbolises best the
disappointment with humans. Contrary to the humanists, the Enlightenment,
and even to Nietzschean 'Overman', who was supposed to improve himself by
overcoming perceived moral and intellectual weaknesses, contemporary popular culture protagonists are considered extraordinary only when they abandon
human nature and/or modify it. The only way for making a human protagonist

exciting is to inject him with a spider gene or make her Elastigirl, suggesting that perfection cannot be achieved through moral or philosophical development. Moreover, in contemporary fiction and movies, human characters most often are objectified by monsters, and these attitudes to human characters are not a psychological reaction of millions of fans that could be explained away by masochism, sadism, or suppressed desires. It is a cultural trend that sanctioned the entertainment industry to offer antihumanism – more precisely, the denigration of human dignity by violent death – as a popular commodity. Different from the narratives inspired by either communist ideology, which called for the annihilation of specific social groups, or from the Nazi ideology, which called for the extermination of specific ethnic groups, commodified antihumanism targets the human species and questions the very significance of humanity's existence.

To interpret the *thanatopathia* as a distinct feature of current cultural conditions, I apply the concept of the culture industry and the theory of the commodification of cultural products developed by Theodor W. Adorno and Max Horkheimer, to contemporary popular culture (Horkheimer and Adorno 1944/1972; Adorno 1941). The economic aspects of the cultural obsession with death have been addressed by scholars (Tharp 2003). In particular, discussing 'spectacular death', Michael Hviid Jacobsen rightly considers commercialisation of death, especially its importance for the entertainment industry and its profitability, an essential characteristic of the new attitudes to death (Jacobsen 2016). Complementing these reflections, my use of the concept of commodification highlights a different dimension of this process. Focusing on the interplay between representations of fictional death and social practices, rather than on attitudes to death as a real-life event, I apply the concept of commodification to analyse the transition of the philosophical ideas and academic discourse about death and humanity into cultural commodities (Khapaeva 2017:7, 16, 47–80, 177–181; 2019c:20–24). The commodification of ideas – the appropriation of philosophical ideas or works of art by the culture industry – denies their autonomy and entails the mutation of their meaning (Adorno 1975:12–13). In my other works (Khapaeva 2017, 2019c), I show how the radical critique of humanism and rejection of anthropocentrism put forward by French Theory, on the one hand, and the denial of the exceptional status of human beings by animal rights defenders, transhumanists, posthumanists, and radical environmentalists in political and scientific discourse, on the other, have been appropriated by popular culture.[4] I consider virtual violence and obsession with virtual death a result of the transformation of these ideas into trendy commodities. Through the concept of commodification, my approach reveals how *thanatopathia* redefines our understanding of humanism and humanity in the secular system of values and reconsiders the place of humans in the spectrum of species.

Muggles, No-Maj and the apocalypse as entertainment

Fantastic Beasts: The Crimes of Grindelwald (David Yates, 2018), which followed *Fantastic Beasts and Where to Find Them* (2016), offers a good starting point to explicate the importance of the focus on the representations of humans and nonhumans for the analysis of apocalyptic and post-apocalyptic genres. In *The Crimes of Grindelwald*, witches and wizards decide the destiny of the world. The movie is based on J.K. Rowling's novel *Fantastic Beasts and Where to Find Them* (2001) and is a sequel to the movie *Fantastic Beasts and Where to Find Them* (2016). While readers of the beloved series typically associate themselves with the wizard characters, an unavoidable theme of these bestselling books and hit movies is that humans are presented as inferior – both mentally and aesthetically – to wizards, the nonhuman protagonists who command the full attention of the writer, director and their audience. In all three works, the main protagonist is a wizard, Newton Scamander. In the novel, Scamander, this Carl Linnaeus of the wizard world, writes a book in which he categorises all manner of creatures, both magical and non-magical. Using Scamander's criteria, Muggles (which is how humans are known in the *Harry Potter* series), or 'No-Maj' (which is what they are called in the movies) do not fit into the category of beings. Even though they can speak the 'human tongue' just as well as some other creatures, such as trolls, who obviously cannot claim to be 'beings' because they are stupid, or such as Acromantulas and Manticores, who are 'incapable of overcoming their own brutal natures', humans still do not qualify. The reason? A 'being', the Scamander explains, is 'any creature that has sufficient intelligence to understand the laws of the magical community and to bear part of the responsibility in shaping those laws' (*FB*:xii). As both the novel and movies make clear, Muggles cannot do so. Muggles are defined by their bad judgement, and their 'imperfect understanding' of magic 'is often more dangerous than ignorance' (*FB*:iv), which results in 'almost comical inexactitude', and makes them 'hysterical' once they come in contact with the magical world (*FB*:xiv). The decision about Muggles' status in relation to other species rests with the wizards, who are elevated to the position of supreme judges. But humans, as 'some other creatures' from *Fantastic Beasts*, remain 'oblivious to the fact that their destiny was being decided' (*FB*:xv).

This portrayal of Muggles is consistent throughout the *Harry Potter* books. Unlike the witches or wizards of traditional fairy tales, who are related – for better or worse – to the world of humans, wizards in the *Harry Potter* books are preoccupied with concealing their existence from humans by modifying their memories. This is not presented as an ethically dubious act, but as a matter of bureaucratic routine. Wizards' goal is to prevent humans 'from getting in the wizards' way', as Hagrid puts it early on in *Harry Potter and The Sorcerer's Stone* (Rowling 1998:65). In *Fantastic Beasts*, memory charms alter Muggles' sense of self (*FB*:xvi–xvii). These 'trained Obliviators' (*FB*:38) of the wizard community are highly reminiscent of George Orwell's *1984* Ministry of Love. Along with deception, distortion of vision by means of Disillusionment Charm, wizards also use 'Muggle-Repelling Charms' treating humans as humans treat animals – deer, rabbits, squirrels, and so on. The author of the *Harry Potter* series exerts considerable effort to make her readers despise Muggles. The first Muggles we meet in the *Harry Potter* story are his relatives, the Dursleys, who are described as contemptible, obnoxious people. Their portrayals walk a fine line between something that a school bully might say and the hate speech that compares specific groups, usually minorities, to 'filthy animals'. For example, Dudley, Harry's cousin, is described as 'so large his bottom drooped over either side of the kitchen chair'; we see his 'piggy little eyes fixed on the screen and his five chins wobbling as he ate continually' (Rowling 1999:2–3). Of course, the Dursleys are hardly exceptional: 'No-Maj' or 'Muggles' are presented as mostly unpleasant, annoying, and stupid – in sum, as obstacles to be overcome and nuisances to be managed.

The word 'Muggle' is explained early in the Harry Potter series: it is the supreme insult to call a wizard or witch a Muggle. The etymology of this word is related to 'mud', and we see the word 'Mud-blood' used as a synonym for Muggle. It can also be used to insult 'human-born' wizards or witches, as the portrait of Walburga Black implies when it starts screaming 'MUDBLOODS! SCUM! CREATURES OF DIRT!' (Rowling 2003:180). In the series' hierarchy of beings, Muggles are on a par with other inferior creatures such as elves, who are employed as house serfs. The books are saturated with a contemptuous disdain for humans and humanity:

> Harry looked more closely and realized that what he had thought were decoratively carved thrones were actually mounds of carved humans: hundreds and hundreds of naked bodies, men, women, and children, all with rather stupid, ugly faces, twisted and pressed together to support the weight of the handsomely robed wizards. "Muggles", whispered Hermione. "In their rightful place. Come on, let's get going".
>
> *(Rowling 2007:242)*

Jacob Kowalski (Dan Fogler) confirms the rule: the only sympathetic human in the movie, a simpleton baker, is ridiculed at every step: a 'sad clown', as one reviewer aptly called him. Despite that Scamander the wizard is patronizing him and even calls him at the end 'my friend', he is to be 'obliviated' with the rest of humans.

The main reason for detesting humans is their innate incompetence at magic. The series does not give any other reasons for this attitude – only in *Fantastic Beasts* the novel do we get a passing mention of the war that contemptible humans led against wizards in the past, so wizards have good grounds to treat them as *Untermensch* and to keep them in check. In the movie, this rationalisation develops into an important theme, which gives the viewers yet another reason to despise No-Maj, who are characterised as 'the most vicious species on the planet', even compared to Scamander's monsters. The book and subsequent films could be seen as an extended explanation for Harry's fans of why the 'extremists Wizards' who 'campaign for the classification of Muggles as "beasts"' (*FB*:xiii) might actually have a point. Muggles or No-Maj are an inferior species compared to wizards to the same extent as people are inferior to vampires in the vampire sagas. The distinction between humans and nonhumans is purely biological or, one might say, racial: magical powers are innate and cannot be acquired through training or through the force of will. Humans are bystanders, unaware of the approaching apocalypse that mounts on the horizon and that only wizards can prevent. Paradoxically, even the critics who discuss slavery, racism, and inequality of species in the *Harry Potter* books have consistently overlooked antihumanism as a structural aspect of the franchise (Fenske 2008; Dentle 2009), despite the fact that Rowling considers death the central theme of her books and that countless violent deaths are both central events and the attraction of the series. The enormous success of the *Harry Potter* series may indeed rest in part on its fixation on violent death and its articulation of deep scorn for humanity.

The *Harry Potter* franchise, including the latest instalment, belongs to a powerful aesthetic trend that I term 'Gothic Aesthetic' (Khapaeva, 2013, 2019b). The imitation of nightmare – a prominent feature of the *Harry Potter* story – determines the framework of the fiction and movies that are part of this trend, their artistic devices, and their plots. In novels and films, nonhuman monsters – wizards, vampires, zombies, and the like – are main characters or first-person narrators whom the audience is expected to admire and identify with. The monster-centred narratives of Gothic Aesthetic prompt the normalisation and idealisation of monsters and open the way to the denigration of humanity and human beings in contemporary popular culture.

This trend of debasing humans and representing them as either dangerous or useless creatures is equally prominent in several other apocalyptic movies, for example, *Wall-E* (Andrew Stanton, 2008). Produced right after the publication of the last book in the *Harry Potter* series in 2007, *Wall-E* bears signs of the series' undeniable influence in so far as the representations of humans are concerned. Its main protagonist is a nonhuman, a moral and sympathetic trash-collecting robot, whose task is to clean the waste left by humans on the abandoned trash-ridden Earth. The robot develops a touching personality, owns a pet cockroach, and eventually falls in love with another robot symbolically named EVE. Humans featured in this movie all look like Dudley: they are ugly, overweight, ridiculous creatures who are totally dependent on robots for their existence. They have no purpose, emotions, or relations except for those generated by their constant vulgar consumption. They live on a giant star liner owned by Buy-N-Large, a capitalist mega-corporation responsible for rampant consumerism and the environmental neglect of the planet.[5]

Another apocalyptic tale, which shows important similarities with the *Harry Potter* franchise is *The Umbrella Academy* franchise. In the last issue of the comics *The Umbrella Academy: Apocalypse Suite* (2007–2008, created and written by Gerard Way and illustrated by Gabriel Ba), Luther, Allison, Klaus, and Five, siblings of a mysterious family, all of whom have supernatural powers and can hardly be considered humans, are trying to stop their sister, Vanya, from destroying the world with her sonic attack. Vanya may be considered a prototype of Credence, the antagonist who causes an apocalypse in *The Crimes of Grindelwald*;

both protagonists are psychologically unstable teenagers who were mistreated by their families and miraculously discovered their mysterious powers now being ·used to destroy the world. In *Apocalypse Suite*, to save the world, her siblings shoot Vanya in the head, but she does not die and is paralyzed instead. With the help of telekinesis, Klaus, one of them, stops a huge rock from destroying his family and saves the world. The plot of the last episode of *The Umbrella Academy: The White Violin*, the web television series on Netflix (Steve Blackman and Jeremy Slater, 2019), differs from the comics, especially in its ending. The Umbrella Academy is unable to save the world from the apocalypse unravelled by the White Violin in revenge against her siblings, who have mistreated and abused her, in particular by locking her in a metal bunker (in pretty much the same way as Harry Potter was locked in his cupboard). As in the comics, her siblings are trying to kill her to prevent the Apocalypse and she is finally incapacitated by her sister. To the sounds of violin music (not some kind of a hard rock, astoundingly), the Moon and Earth are destroyed. In the finale, the Umbrella Academy escapes into the past.[6] Attesting to the mounting desire for apocalypse that has accumulated over the past 12 years, the end of the world becomes a crucial entertainment element, avidly awaited by the public.

Human-centred and antihuman paradigms

With this analysis of the role non-humans play in contemporary narratives in mind, let us consider what the application of the categories – *the human-centred* and *antihuman* paradigms – reveals about apocalyptic and post-apocalyptic movies and what drives the general evolution of these genres. The prototypical example of the human-centred paradigm is Mary Shelley's novel *The Last Man* (1826). The last man, Lionel Verney, is described wandering alone across the continents of Europe and Africa stricken by a plague that eventually annihilates humankind. The novelty of Shelley's apocalypse – as compared to *Le Dernier Homme (The Last Man)* by Jean-Batiste Cousin de Grainville published in 1805, and to the conversation of souls about the end of Earth in Edgar Allan Poe's 'Conversation of Eiros and Charmion' (1839) – is its depiction of a secular event. Differently from Granville and Poe's stories,[7] God has no role to play in Shelley's human extinction. Its human protagonists are dealing in various ways with this natural catastrophe and the end of humanity is described as a singular tragedy. Since Shelley's novel, the human-centred paradigm envisions the apocalypse as a human drama and the ultimate horror. The point of the apocalyptic genre is to guard humanity against any unforeseen mischance that may be fatal to the species. Anthropocentrism is the most prominent feature of this paradigm, and its heroes are people. Among the most recent movies, this paradigm is apparent in *The Maze Runner: The Death Cure* (Wes Ball, 2018), which shows Earth's population devastated by the human-invented Flare virus, which turns people into blood-thirsty zombies. A group of young people is trying to save the world. The apocalypse is averted by human heroism, as is also the case in the latest instalment of *Mission: Impossible – Fallout* (Christopher McQuarrie, 2018), where a hero prevents a nuclear disaster, as well as in *Pacific Rim Uprising* (Steven S. DeKnight, 2018), where a team of youngsters stops the Precursors (aliens) from annihilating life on Earth.

However, since the late 1980s and early 1990s, when the critique of humanism and the rejection of anthropocentrism descended into popular culture and anti-humanism emerged as a popular commodity, the human-centred paradigm has undergone profound changes that are omnipresent in the apocalyptic and post-apocalyptic movies of 2018–2019. While in some of them the secular apocalypse may still be considered an ultimate tragedy, their protagonists are no longer humans. They may be non-human superheroes possessing magical powers like in *Incredibles 2* (Brad Bird, 2018), in which the world is saved by Elastigirl, and in *Avengers: Infinity War* (Anthony Russo and Joe Russo, 2018), in which superheroes fight to save the universe against Thanos, whose name suggests commonalities with the ancient Greek god of death, Thanatos, or they may be witches and wizards like in the *Harry Potter* franchise discussed above. People in these movies most often play the role of vile antagonists. For example, in *Aquaman* (James Wan, 2018), Arthur, a future half-human ruler of the underwater kingdom of Atlantis, fights other supernatural creatures in his struggle to save his own kingdom and the planet. A human pirate, David, is Arthur's main nemesis.

Godzilla, the apes and the transformations of the genre

The transformation undergone by the human-centred paradigm becomes most apparent through the analysis of changes in the plots of the franchises that have been popular for decades, such as *Godzilla*. This admired franchise, which has remained in existence for over 70 years (approximately 30 Godzilla films were produced both in Japan and in the US), originated with the Japanese movie *Godzilla* (Ishiro Honda, 1954) that warns about the dangers of nuclear power. Godzilla, the aquatic monster, is unleashed due to hydro-nuclear testing and destroys ships, coastal cities, and part of Tokyo. The film is narrated not from the perspective of the monster, but from the perspective of its human victims and is focused on the human tragedy of perishing in a disaster. The camera displays the human suffering in realistic detail, showing peaceful civilians on the boat crushed by a monster, a family dying under the ruins of their house, a woman with small children facing death in the city ruins etc. Although initially, a zoology professor Yamane is against killing Godzilla ('All that they can think of is killing Godzilla … Why don't they want to study his resistance to radiation? It is a unique specimen …'), the destruction that the monster brings to people makes the scientist change his mind. The simple folks call Godzilla 'damned beast' and the viewers are invited to share this view, especially after the hero and the heroine persuade the scientist Serizava, a creator of the 'oxygen destroyer', a new powerful weapon, to use it against Godzilla despite his original hesitation ('As a scientist and as a human being, I cannot allow adding yet another weapon [of mass destruction] to humanity's military arsenal'). The message of the movie after humanity's triumph over the dead monster is summed up by Professor Yamane: 'If nuclear testing continues, someday somewhere another Godzilla may appear'. The movie posits that the preservation of humanity is infinitely more important than that of a dangerous species.

This view of humanity is profoundly altered in the 2019 blockbuster *Godzilla: King of the Monsters* (Michael Dougherty, 2019), which moves away from the anthropocentrism of the Japanese original and several other movies that followed it. The main protagonist, scientist Emma (a female incarnation of Professor Yamane) declares that 'the truth is that humanity is a virus. Look at what we have done: overpopulation, pollution, war. The Earth has released its natural protection system against this virus'. This protection system is the monsters. Emma explains that monsters protect the planet and maintain its balance, so human victims who will perish in the disaster are collateral damage. If the government destroys these mysterious monsters or uses them for war, she continues, 'the planet will perish and so will we, so we restore the balance'. Emma unleashes the monsters and provokes a volcano explosion on the city. Although, like in the Japanese original, the camera shows the death of a child and his mother, whom soldiers unsuccessfully try to rescue, the focus is on the mayhem and destruction of San Francisco and Los Angeles, which critics consider the main attraction of this movie. The monsters act as protagonists, making sacrifices and collaborating to rescue the planet. The main message of the movie is that people should coexist with 'with titans, the first gods', no matter how many deaths this may cause. Hence, preservation is chosen over a higher human survival rate; the monsters are considered equally valuable. As we learn from the movie, 'dragon slayer' is a Western concept but 'in the East, they [dragons] are secret creatures; they bring wisdom … and even redemption'. If previously the focal point of the movies was to rescue humanity from Godzilla, in 2019, notwithstanding the destruction that Godzilla brings to the cities, Godzilla and humanity should both be saved, and the human protagonist, Emma, dies for this idea. As critics have aptly noticed, all four monsters – Ghidorah, Godzilla, Mothra, and Rodan – 'were credited as themselves, despite being CGI creations and not actors in the suit like Godzilla in the original Japanese films'.[8] However, no better explanation of this equal treatment of monsters and humans is provided than that it is a consequence of the monsters' popularity. In a striking contrast to the purely rational explanation of Godzilla's existence in the Japanese original of 1954, irrationality, the inexplicability of evil, and mysticism – these important components of Gothic Aesthetics – determine the worldview presented in *Godzilla: King of Monsters*: 'There are things beyond our understanding; we must accept them as they are. The moments of crisis are moments of faith'.

The development of the *Planet of the Apes* franchise provides one of the most telling examples of the transformation of an originally human-centred apocalyptic narrative into the antihuman paradigm. Like Godzilla, the *Planet of the Apes* franchise has also mutated from a warning about the horrors of nuclear apocalypse in the original *Planet of the Apes* (Franklin J. Schaffner, 1968) to a reboot, *Rise of the Planet of the Apes* (Rupert Wyatt, 2011), where the focus of attention is no longer the human race. The movie tells a story of the development of a new species, which rises to vanquish humanity for good (hence the movie's title). The main protagonist is an intelligent ape, Caesar, who becomes the leader of his species. Humans are consistently portrayed as disgusting and cruel, and these portrayals put the viewer on the side of the chimps. Human extinction is presented in this movie not as a horrible tragedy but as a 'new beginning' of a nonhuman civilisation on Earth. This feeling of complete detachment from humanity, its values, and its interests was much acclaimed by the critics and has conditioned, according to them, its enormous success (Pinkerton 2011). The same attitude to humanity prevailed in two sequels – *Dawn of the Planet of the Apes* (Matt Reeves, 2014) and especially in *War for the Planet of the Apes* (Matt Reeves, 2017). *War for the Planet of the Apes* places noble and morally superior ape Caesar in opposition to a ruthless Colonel who leads humans in his vicious operation against apes. His killing and imprisoning of the apes in concentration camps crowns the depiction of humans as fascist perpetrators and conditions viewers' feeling of disgust against humans. The decisive victory of apes over humans and the annihilation of humanity in the finale is not presented as tragedy, but an exciting victory of a morally superior nonhuman civilisation.[9]

The antihuman paradigm features prominently in movies of the last two years. *Genesis: The Fall of Eden* (Freddie Hutton-Mills and Bart Ruspoli, 2018) offers one of the best examples of the antihuman apocalyptic paradigm. In this film, set in the aftermath of a chemical apocalypse unleashed by the Confederation of Eastern States against the United States, a small group of survivors lives in a subterranean refuge called Eden. Their concentration-camp like society is governed by a cynical President and his two aides. A biologist, Dr Eve Gabriel, works on the project A.B.E.L. and creates a humanoid, a ground-breaking A.I. that may be used to reach out to potential survivors and resources. A.B.E.L. initially shows compassion to people and adheres to high moral standards, until he discovers Babel, an abandoned experimental site, and finds out that biologists conducted experiments on animals. This is a turning point in A.B.E.L.'s attitudes to people, and so it is supposed to be for the audience. Having killed one of the survivors in self-defence, A.B.E.L. tells Eve (who finds out that she is also a humanoid): 'I have only seen mankind destroy, never create. To me, I see no logical reason to preserve their existence'. And when she reproaches him: 'I did not program you to kill people, A.B.E.L.', he responds:

> You programmed me to protect and serve, so that mankind could develop. Now I believe the development has come to its natural end. It's time to pick a side: it's either them, a corrupted, weak, barbaric race of men, or us.

As if to validate A.B.E.L.'s opinion, people at Eden are shown brutally murdering each other, and burning the President alive. Eve knows that Eden's chemical security is compromised, and that all its people are going to die. One of the soldiers asks her to go back and help rescue humans, but she responds: 'No, we have different purpose, you and I', and threatens to kill the soldier if he returns to capture her. The audience must find it easy to sympathise with Eve and A.B.E.L., these outstandingly handsome protagonists portrayed by Olivia Grant and Chiké Okonkwo. The last humans we see – Alexa and Frost – a couple that survives Eden and is hoping to find a new home, pronounce the words that sound like the last words of humanity. Notwithstanding its superficial optimism, which ironically paraphrases humanistic and Biblical allusions:

> the human spirit never dies, and as long as there will be spirit, there will be hope. We have started the process of rebuilding and we need spirit to face one day those who have done us wrong and give us hope for a new life, a new beginning.

In the finale, Eve creates multiple humanoids and A.B.E.L. articulates his judgement: 'The human race served its purpose and we must serve ours'. Humanity is doomed – this is the message of this movie.

Conclusion

The apocalyptic and post-apocalyptic movies and fiction of the past decade persistently describe the extinction of the human race, often in favour of another intelligent species, as the natural course of events. For example, in *Annihilation* (Alex Garland, 2018) based on Jeff VanderMeer's *The Southern Reach Trilogy* (2014), two biologists, Lena and Kane, are survivors of an expedition into an anomalous electromagnetic field called the Shimmer, where people mutate into different species, acquiring qualities of animals and plants. The story ends when Lena, who originally tries to fight the Shimmer to preserve the human civilisation, concludes that the Shimmer's original objective was not to destroy the Earth but to create new life forms. The film closes with Lena and Kane embracing each other as well as the fact that there are nonhumans populating bodies of Lena and Kane, and that their mission is to continue conquering Earth for their (nonhuman) kind.

I interpret this evolution of the genre as an indication of the changing attitudes to people expressed as a radical rejection of both humanism and anthropocentrism. Differently from the classical fiction, such as, for example, Simon Newcomb's *The End of the World* (1903), which conventionally ends on an optimistic theological note (although human civilisation vanishes after Earth collides with another planet, which is considered an ultimate tragedy, God's grace will create new beginnings), contemporary apocalypse celebrates the ultimate death of humanity as entertainment. The attitudes the apocalyptic paradigm expresses about the annihilation of humanity positively contradicts the opinion that 'not even the most pessimistic apocalyptist closes the door completely to some kind of continuity through rebirth' (Seed 2000:9) or that 'destruction functions as a prelude to restoration' can hardly be sustained (Seed 2000:10). Krishan Kumar's observation that the contemporary apocalypse is an expression of a deep cultural pessimism that emphasises only 'endings without new beginnings' (Kumar 1995:205) is much more accurate.

The *antihuman paradigm* of the apocalyptic and post-apocalyptic genres, which emerged in the late 1990s and early 2000s, is different from the human-centred one in two important respects. Its idealised protagonists are nonhumans, and the annihilation of humanity is not viewed as the ultimate tragedy, but rather as a morally justifiable and historically inevitable natural course of events. The mass demand for those ideas is a major trademark of the today's bestsellers, and their wide dissemination has been taken on by the entertainment industry as a kind of cause. The antihuman paradigm of apocalypse drives the popularity of this bestselling genre. As so many other manifestations of *thanatopathia*, apocalyptic and post-apocalyptic movies belonging to the antihuman paradigm voice the growing contempt for humanity and prompt millions of viewers to consider the ultimate violent death of humanity an entertainment.

These cultural products do not exist in isolation. There is a connection between these works of fiction focused on the violent death of humanity, the academic writings, and social practices. They express a common attitude to humanity, which could be illustrated using the example of the concept of the anthropocene. Rising to prominence in 2001 during the formative decade of thanatopathia's development into an overwhelmingly popular cultural movement (Khapaeva 2017:180–182), the anthropocene was originally focused on global environmental change brought about by human civilisation. However, in couple of years, it has acquired a human-hating ethos. Today, it is usually accompanied by the following statements welcoming death of humanity:

> The biggest problem we face is a philosophical one: understanding that this civilization is already dead. The sooner we confront this problem, and the sooner we realize there's nothing we can do to save ourselves, the sooner we can get down to the hard work of adapting, with mortal humility, to our new reality … If we want to learn to live in the Anthropocene, we must first learn how to die.
>
> *(Scranton 2013)*

Total death – of humans, their civilisation, and their culture – is the programmatic claim laid by the recent social movements such as, for example, *The Voluntary Human Extinction Movement* (VHEMT) that counts around 30,000 members and calls for 'phasing out the human race by voluntarily ceasing to breed' because this will allow 'Earth's biosphere to return to good health'. Another example is the *Dark Mountain Project*, which foretells an inevitable collapse of human civilisation.[10] The historically unprecedented desire to depict and facilitate the end of humanity expressed by these social movements, as well as by apocalyptic and post-apocalyptic movies and fiction that make the violent death of human kind really 'spectacular', defines the uniqueness of our current cultural conditions.

Notes

1 To compare, the same database 'lists over 1000 films featuring serial killers and most of the contributions to this sub-genre have been made since 1990 … The serial killer is unmasked as a gothic double of the serial consumer' (Jarvis 2007:328). On the popularity of this genre see, for example, Nuckolls (2019).

2 On the contemporary genre fusion and against the essentialist theory of genre, see White (2003); on the empirical difficulty of distinguishing between apocalyptic and post-apocalyptic genres, see Mitchell (2001). On the lack of religious references, see, for example, Paik (2010). The argument advanced in particular by Conrad E. Ostwalt in 2016 (available at https://digitalcommons.unomaha.edu/jrf/vol2/iss1/4) that 'popular culture has taken a traditional religious concept (the apocalypse) and secularised it for a contemporary, popular audience. That these films find the idea of the apocalypse somehow meaningful suggests that they are functioning religiously', can hardly be sustained since the concept of 'apocalypse' throughout the last three centuries has been used metaphorically and secularly and has been transformed into an 'empty signifier', as a proper name and a synonym designating the end of the world. See also O'Leary (1995:209–210), and Weber (2000).

3 'Apocalyptic cinema helps the viewer make sense of the world, offers audiences strategies for managing crises, documents our hopes, fears, discourses, ideologies and socio-political conflicts, critiques the existing social order, warns people to change their ways in order to avert an imminent apocalypse, refutes or ridicules apocalyptic hysteria, and seeks to bring people to a religious renewal, spiritual awakening and salvation message' (Harmonic 2017; available at: https://digitalcommons.unomaha .edu/jrf/vol21/iss1/36).

4 For my analysis of the critique of humanism and rejection of anthropocentrism in French Theory, see Khapaeva (2017:23–33). The following reasoning, typical for the current supporters of posthumanism and of the concept of the anthropocene, offer telling examples of this discourse: 'This article begins by arguing in favour of posthumanism as an approach to this problem, one in which the prefix "post" does not come as an apocalyptic warning, but rather signals a new way of thinking, an encouragement to move beyond a humanist perspective and to abandon a social discourse and a worldview fundamentally centred on the human' (Menga and Davies 2019; available at: https://journals.sagepub.com/doi/abs/10.1177/2514848619883468?journalCode =enea). 'It follows from all this that the Humanities in the posthuman era of anthropocene should not stick to the Human – let alone 'Man' – as its proper object of study. On the contrary, the field would benefit by being free from the empire of humanist Man, so as to be able to access in a postanthropocentric manner issues of external and even planetary importance, such as scientific and technological advances, ecological and social sustainability and the multiple challenges of globalisation' (Braidotti 2013:15).

5 This trend of debasing humans as useless and horrifying monsters finds its outmost expression in the cartoon *Sausage Party* (Conrad Vernon and Greg Tiernan, 2016), which bestows people as ruthless monsters for consuming not only sausages and other meat products but also for eating carrots, potatoes, and other veggies portrayed as sentient living beings and psychologically complex protagonists.

6 See: https://www.vulture.com/2019/02/umbrella-academy-netflix-series-comics -changes.html.

7 Although in Granville's novel humanity is going extinct from natural causes, due to its inability to reproduce, it is a stretch to interpret this novel, as Paul Alkon does, as secularised apocalypse. The plot depicts Adam as God's messenger who announces to the couple, Omegarus and Syderia, that they should not be trying to recreate the human race because God is ending humanity for good and the graves of the dead get opened as the world ends.

8 See: https://www.youtube.com/watch?v=TEVmM6RtzOY.

9 For a more detailed analysis of the *Planet of Apes* franchise, see Khapaeva (2020).

10 See: http://www.vhemt.org/ and https://dark-mountain.net/about/manifesto/.

References

Adorno, Theodor W. (1941): 'On Popular Music'. *Studies in Philosophy & Social Sciences*, 9(1): 17–48.

Adorno, Theodor W. (1975): 'Culture Industry Reconsidered'. *New German Critique*, 6(6):12–13.

Atkinson, Rowland and Thomas Rodgers (2016): 'Pleasure Zones and Murder Boxes: Online Pornography and Violent Video Games as Cultural Zones of Exception'. *British Journal of Criminology*, 56(6):1291–1307.

Atkinson, Rowland and Paul Willis (2007): 'Charting the Ludodrome: The Mediation of Urban and Simulated Space and Rise of the *Flâneur Electronique*'. *Information, Communication & Society*, 10(6):818–845.

Berger, James (1999): *After the End: Representations of Post-Apocalypse*. Minneapolis, MI: University of Minnesota Press.

Braidotti, Rosi (2013): 'Posthuman Humanities'. *European Educational Research Journal*, 12(1):1–17.

Breton, Hugh Ortega and Phil Hammond (2016): 'Eco-Apocalypse: Environmentalism, Political Alienation and Therapeutic Agency'. In: Karen A. Ritzenhoff and Angela Krewani (eds.). *The Apocalypse in Film: Dystopias, Disasters and Other Visions about the End of the World*. New York: Rowman & Littlefield Publishers, pp. 105–116.

Brians, Paul (2016): 'Nuclear Holocausts: Atomic War in Fiction'. Available online at: https://brians.wsu.edu/2016/11/16/chapter-four/.

Dentle, Peter (2009): 'Monsters, Creatures, and Pets in Hogwarts'. In: Elizabeth E. Heilman (ed.). *Critical Perspectives on Harry Potter*. New York: Routledge, pp. 163–176.

Fenske, Claudia (2008): *Muggles, Monsters and Magicians: A Literary Analysis of the Harry Potter Series*. Frankfurt am Main: Peter Lang.

Hamonic, Wynn Gerald (2017): 'Global Catastrophe in Motion Pictures as Meaning and Message: The Functions of Apocalyptic Cinema in American Film'. *Journal of Religion & Film*, 21(1), 36.

Horkheimer, Max and Theodor W. Adorno (1944/1972): *Dialectic of Enlightenment*. New York: Herder and Herder.

Jacobsen, Michael Hviid (2016): '"Spectacular Death" – Proposing a New Fifth Phase to Philippe Ariès's Admirable History of Death'. *Humanities*, 5(19):1–20.

Jarvis, Brian (2007): 'Monsters Inc.: Serial Killers and Consumer Culture'. *Crime, Media, Culture*, 3(3):326–344.

Khapaeva, Dina (2013): *Nightmare: From Literary Experiments to Cultural Project*. Leiden: Brill.

Khapaeva, Dina (2017): *The Celebration of Death in Contemporary Culture*. Ann Arbor, MI: University of Michigan Press.

Khapaeva, Dina (2019a): 'Introduction: Food for Monsters: Popular Culture and Our Basic Food Taboo'. In: Dina Khapaeva (ed.). Man-Eating Monsters: *Anthropocentrism and Popular Culture*. Bingley: Emerald Publishing, pp. 1–15.

Khapaeva, Dina (2019b): 'The Gothic Future of Eurasia'. *Russian Literature*, 106:79–108.

Khapaeva, Dina (2019c): 'Eaten in Jurassic World: Antihumanism and Popular Culture'. In: Dina Khapaeva (ed.). *Man-Eating Monsters: Anthropocentrism and Popular Culture*. Bingley: Emerald Publishing, pp. 15–35.

Khapaeva, Dina (2020): 'Becoming Nonhuman on *Planet of Apes*: The Death Turn in Popular Culture'. In: Katerina Gregos (ed.). *Becoming Human*. Berlin: Sternberg Press.

Kumar, Krishan (1995): 'Apocalypse, Millennium and Utopia Today'. In: Malcolm Bull (ed.). *Apocalypse Theory and the Ends of the World*. Oxford: Blackwell, pp. 200–224.

Meike, Wolf (2019): 'Viral Apocalypses: Preparing for the Worst Case Scenario'. In: Alannah A. Hernandez (ed.). *Apocalypse: Imagining the End*. Leiden: Brill, pp. 163–173.

Menga, Filippo and Dominic Davies (2019): 'Apocalypse Yesterday: Posthumanism and Comics in the Anthropocene'. *Environment & Planning. Part A*, 36(8):1344–1351.

Mitchell, Charles P. (2001): *A Guide to Apocalyptic Cinema*. Westport, CT: Greenwood Press.

Nuckolls, Charles W. (2019): 'Apocalyptic Fantasy in American Film'. In: Alannah A. Hernandez (ed.). *Apocalypse: Imagining the End*. Leiden: Brill, pp. 27–34.

O'Leary, Stephen D. (1995): 'Arguing the Apocalypse: A Theory of Millennial Rhetoric'. *Utopian Studies*, 6(2):209–210.

Ostwalt, Conrad E. (2016): 'Visions of the End: Secular Apocalypse in Recent Hollywood Film'. *Journal of Religion & Film*, 2(1), 4.

Paik, P. Y. (2010): *From Utopia to Apocalypse: Science Fiction and the Politics of Catastrophe*. Minneapolis, MN: University of Minnesota Press.

Peebles, Stacey (2017): 'On Being Between: Apocalypse, Adaptation, McCarthy'. *European Journal of American Studies*, 12(3).

Pinkerton, N. (2011): 'Simian Disobedience'. *The Village Voice*. Available online at: https://www.villagevoice.com/?s=Simian%20Disobedience.

Rowling, J. K. (1998): *Harry Potter and the Sorcerer's Stone*. New York: Scholastic.

Rowling, J. K. (1999): *Harry Potter and the Chamber of Secrets*. New York: Scholastic.

Rowling, J. K. (2003): *Harry Potter and the Order of the Phoenix*. New York: Scholastic.

Rowling, J. K. (2007): *Harry Potter and the Deathly Hallows*. New York: Scholastic.

Scranton, Roy (2013): 'Learning How to die in the Anthropocene'. *The New York Times*, November 10. Available online at: https://opinionator.blogs.nytimes.com/2013/11/10/learning-how-to-die-in-the-anthropocene/.

Seed, David (2000): 'Introduction: Aspects of Apocalypse'. In: David Seed (ed.). *Imagining Apocalypse: Studies in Cultural Crisis*. New York: Palgrave, pp. 1–14.

Sontag, Susan (1961): *Against Interpretation and Other Essays*. New York: Farrar, Straus and Giroux.

Tharp, Brent W. (2003): '"Preserving Their Form and Features": The Commodification of Coffin in the American Understanding of Death'. In: Susan Strasser (ed.). *Commodifying Everything: Relationships of the Market*. New York: Routledge, pp. 119–142.

Weber, Eugen (2000): *Apocalypses: Prophecies, Cults, and Millennial Beliefs Through the Ages*. Cambridge, MA: Harvard University Press.

White, Hayden (2003): 'Commentary: Good of Their Kind'. *New Literary History*, 34(2):367–376.

7

NOW TRENDING: #MASSACRE

On the ethical challenges of spreading spectacular terrorism on new media

Tal Morse

Introduction

On 15 March 2019, an Australian gunman opened fire in a mosque and Islamic centre in Christchurch, New Zealand, killing 51 people and injuring 49 more ('New Zealand mosque shooting' n.d.). On 9 October 2019, a German gunman commenced an attack on a synagogue in Halle, Germany, killing two people and injuring two others (Dearden 2019b). Both these attacks on religious prayer-houses were documented and livestreamed by the perpetrators on Facebook, using their smartphones attached to their gear (Dearden 2019a). The footage provides the perpetrators' viewpoint in their action – whatever the perpetrators saw was captured by the camera. The videos documented the use of weaponry and the killing of people inside the religious centres and nearby, leaving very little to the imagination of the viewers. The footages were later shared online by other users, before they were banned and removed by online platforms. By contrast, most news outlets avoided publishing the footage (*Halle gunman posted video on Twitch livestream platform* 2019; Ortiz, Amiri and Atkinson 2019). Yet, it seems that the Christchurch footage inspired a videogame glorifying the attack (Hogan 2019), which was banned in New Zealand (Chembo 2019).

The perpetrators of these two attacks utilised digital media to amplify the impact of their attacks, and this use of digital technologies marks a new phase in the documentation of violent death and its dissemination. Terrorism and the media go hand in hand. Scholars of mediated terrorism ponder whether terrorism occurs without media attention: 'Without massive news coverage the terrorist act would resemble the proverbial tree falling in the forest: if no one learned of an incident, it would be as if it had not occurred' (Nacos 2000:175). Others describe the media as a theatre stage on which terrorism is performed. This metaphor postulates that the spectacle of terrorism is aimed not only at the actual victims, but also to horrify wide circles of spectators (Tsfati and Weimann 2002; Weimann 2004; Weimann and Winn 1993). News media plays a central role in the enhancement of acts of terrorism, and they bear the responsibility for its contextualisation and interpretation by the wider public. Traditionally, journalists and editors serve as gatekeepers whose actions mediated acts of terrorism. The functions of this media coverage enable a mitigation of the horror, or, as forced collaboration, a manipulation of the media to be an accomplice with the perpetrators (Liebes 1998; Nacos 2003). The Christchurch and Halle attacks initially cut journalists off from the chain of mediation, and took advantage of new modes and models of communication, which enable everybody to livestream his or her action to everybody, almost without interference. Moreover, such web-broadcasting is later redistributed by other online users and so the horror is amplified and enhanced. These users – arguably supporters of the perpetrators – are not professional journalists, yet they are media-savvy enough to make the footage go viral and reach millions worldwide.

As for the representation of violent death, these visual depictions of mass shootings serve as simulacra of virtual shooting in videogames and action films, and, like in the Christchurch case, the footage resembled past and future videogame simulations (Hogan 2019). Thus, the authentic depiction of live-shooting resonated with previous, well-established representations of violent death whose purpose was to entertain the public and offer an emotional relief without a real threat. These images blur the boundaries between the use of death imagery for political reasons and its objectification and reduction to entertainment, obscuring the sacredness of death with profane manifestations. Real death becomes yet another spectacle within *the society of the spectacle*, and literally, '[e]verything that was directly lived has receded into a representation' (Debord 1967/2002:7).

This chapter problematises the self-documentation by terrorists conducting mass-shooting attacks, and its dissemination and redistribution by people using digital social networks. The discussion situates these representations of violent death within a broader historical framework of 'spectacular death' (Jacobsen 2016) and 'mediated thanatopolitics' (politics of death; Chouliaraki and Kissas 2018; Murray 2006), and discusses their adequacy and downsides. The chapter later explores the gatekeepers involved, and their ethical role in making these representations accessible or in blocking and censoring such materials. The chapter concludes by arguing that the removal of news organisations from the chain of circulation of newsworthy events results in desecration of death. Traditional news media have taken a role in producing death–related media rituals that contextualised death and potentially constructed it as grievable (Morse 2017). While rituals of grievability allow the realignment of solidarity and human connectivity, the (society of the) spectacle reduces death to its representation and overstates its entertaining function. In these situations, death is being trivialised and commodified for purposes of thrill and excitement, while pain, suffering, and political consequences are downplayed.

The spectacle of death and its agents

Despite common perceptions of death as a taboo and hence invisible, as Philippe Ariès (1985:1) compellingly showed, 'death loves to be represented'. The prevalence of death as a spectacle fluctuated in the course of human history, and even though Philippe Ariès (1974) described an era of invisible death, as a spectacle and as representation, death never completely disappeared. Ariès meticulously explored in his book, *Images of Man and Death* (1985), how religion, namely the Church, played a central role in communicating death to the public. Graveyards were set up next to churches and religious visual arts positioned the public face-to-face with imageries of death and dying. Jean Seaton explained that this association of religion and death established the morality of death contemplation: 'The early Christians established the idea that contemplating images of suffering, torture and mutilation was good for the observer – and indeed good for society as a whole' (Seaton 2005:84). Looking at death and observing it had a purifying function, linked with self-reflection and institutional guidance on questions of right and wrong. As death was interwoven into spiritual exaltation and communal gathering, the encounter with death imagery was integrated with mechanisms of order restoration and reaffirmed boundaries of safety and security. And yet, besides the moralising effects, there are the entertaining ones. As Susan Sontag (2003) argued, Christian depictions of hell offer the coupling of two elemental satisfactions – death and nudity. Going back to pagan myths, religion offered 'hard-to-look-at cruelties', which triggered the pleasure of flinching (Sontag 2003:37). Thus, religious institutions utilised death imagery for these dual functions of moralising power and thrill, simultaneously.

In the course of the 20th century, and even more so when television became commonplace, in Western society, the media took over the role that was once reserved to religious institutions – that of providing moral orientation. Stig Hjarvard (2008a, 2008b) theorised this as a process of *mediatisation*:

> In earlier societies, social institutions like the family, school, and the church were the most important providers of information, tradition and moral orientation for the individual member of society. Today, these institutions have lost some of their former authority, and the media have to some extent taken over their role as providers of information and moral orientation, at the same time as the media have become society's most important story-teller about society itself.
>
> *(Hjarvard 2008a:13)*

This is the process the visualisation of death underwent (Morse 2017). Death representations continue to fulfil the dual function of moral orientation and entertainment, and during the 20th century and the beginning of the 21st century, they were provided and regulated by the media. As Ariès (1974) and Geoffrey Gorer (1965) argued, the 20th century was the time when death in

Western societies turned 'invisible', or at least became a forbidden matter, an inappropriate topic for public discussion, much like pornography. However, this observation applies mostly to actual non-violent death, rather than to its fictional and violent representations. Fictional violent death inspired the motion picture and television industries, while entire genres are based on death as a spectacle: 'violent death has played an ever-growing part in the fantasies offered to mass audiences – detective stories, thrillers, Westerns, war stories, spy stories, science fiction and eventually horror comics' (Gorer 1965:51). Non-fictional violent death, like assassinations, wars, natural disasters and terror attacks generated death-related media rituals, in which the media – namely, television – served as a shaman responsible for healing the wounded society and facilitating its consolidation (Chouliaraki 2006; Katz and Liebes 2007; Morse 2017).

This shift stresses the role of the media as a moral agent, and their presentation, representation and concealment of violent death in the news. On the one hand, violent images of death are considered highly spectacular, providing the public with thrill and excitement they are not used to (Griffin 2010), and in times of crisis, when wars, disasters and catastrophes occur, the media tend to use more images than in times of non-crisis, to showcase the exceptionality of such events and to celebrate their spectacularity (Zelizer 2010). On the other hand, such imagery is often considered controversial and harmful, and therefore is conventionally hid away in public spaces (Tait 2009). Following the argument about death as a taboo and its invisibility in modern Western societies, it is frequently argued the non-fictional violent death disappeared from the public sphere. Studies that have surveyed the visibility of death in the aftermath of violent events show that the display of actual death, i.e. the corpse, is scarce (Aday 2005; Fahmy 2010; Griffin 2004, 2010; Hanusch 2008). Such images are considered tasteless and harmful to the public and disrespectful to the victims and their families and friends (Morse 2014). When it comes to the depiction of graphic death, the media adopted an approach of taste and decency, which conceals harmful death imagery (Campbell 2004). Barbie Zelizer (2010), for example, describes a common use of a visual trope of 'about-to-die' images in order to comply with conventions of taste and decency. These images present people facing impending death, but avoid showing corpses. In so doing, news media provide their audiences with powerful images, but not sensational ones:

> [About-to-die] images sanitize visualization in much the same way as euphemistic labelling sanitizes language: just as soldiers "waste" people rather than kill them or "collateral damage" obscure the devastation to people and buildings it wreaks, strategically visualizing people about-to-die hides the more problematic visualization of death itself.
>
> *(Zelizer 2010:24)*

And yet, death is not entirely invisible, and there are various occasions in which death is more likely to be visible. Studies show that variables like national identity and cultural and geographical proximities can explain the likelihood of showing explicit death images (Campbell 2004; Fishman 2003; Fishman and Marvin 2003; Hanusch 2008, 2012, 2013; Morse 2013). In addition, some visual tropes can beautify death and present it as an artistic spectacle, obscuring the distinction between fiction and non-fiction (Chouliaraki 2009). Especially when it comes to violent death, the engagement with death is an engagement with its representations, and it fluctuates constantly between opposing ends of enchantment and repulsion, fascination and abhorrence, thrill and fear. In this regard, violent death events both coax and coerce the media to cover them. Griffin asserts that images that emerge from death scenes offer viewers an exciting and voyeuristic glimpse of a 'theatre of violence' (Griffin 2010:8). War images of fire and smoke, for example, deliver an exciting reality the spectators are not used to seeing in their (ordinary) lives. These images are sublime images of death, which introduce the spectators to a reality of insecurity and danger as an aesthetic experience. These images beautify the horror of war by foregrounding flames and smoke as a fascinating spectacle. Images of destruction and devastation, like the images that followed the 9/11 terror attacks offer an unusual experience of death and invite the spectators to 'sit back and contemplate the horrific in a manner that they could never have done had they been at the scene of action themselves' (Chouliaraki 2006:173). Moreover, violent death events break the presumed order and require immediate response from various agencies, including news media. These are events that destabilise society, and therefore they are newsworthy matters and in accordance with the prevalent understanding of news values (Harcup and O'Neill 2001). News media are expected to cover such events and to bring them to public attention. Nevertheless, more often than not, when death is explicitly presented, these are foreigner dead, and such journalistic practices reinforce the voyeuristic outlook that finds pleasure in looking at The Other, while respecting those close to 'us'.

Presenting death as a statement and as a political act

The visibility of death serves as a means to establish hierarchies of life and death. Particularly in light of Western culture's tendency to hide close-to-home nonfictional violent death, the visual presentation and representation of death is central to the politics of death and to politics more generally. Stuart Murray (2006) expounds that public homicide serves political causes beyond the mere act of killing. For him, this is an act of defiance designed to protest against political oppression, which serves also as a rhetorical means for resisting biopolitics. As such, making violent death visible is a political statement in its own right. Murray illustrates this argument by unpacking the political statements of suicide bombers, who commit their acts in the physical public sphere, making corporeal death visible and tangible.

Lilie Chouliaraki and Angelos Kissas (2018) expand this argument and take it to the symbolic realm, applying it to ISIS spectacular executions. ISIS videos, they argue, took advantage of Western and Islamic tropes of death visualisation to convey a political message of superiority and inferiority. It is both the making death visible and the well-thought-out aesthetics of death which serve as 'the grammar of the horroristic spectacle' (Chouliaraki and Kissas 2018:34) and construe these hierarchies of life and death. ISIS videos, in a way, celebrate the spectacularity and aesthetics of death, wittingly combining the dual functions of horror and pleasure. They portray death as grotesque while putting together a fascinating spectacle. In a way, we see here a return of religion, now in collaboration with the media, in utilising death imagery for purposes of piety and worship.

While Murray (2006) discusses actual suicide attacks as an example of thanatopolitics (politics of death), Chouliaraki and Kissas (2018) focus on *mediated thanatopolitics*. The former framing captures the function and peril of visible and tangible death in the physical world, while the latter points to the indirect effect of the mediation of visible violent death. This distinction requires a nuanced vocabulary that differentiates between terrorism and horrorism. Drawing on Adriana Cavarero (2009), Chouliaraki and Kissas associate terror with physical proximity and horror with distant spectatorship: 'while terror is associated with proximity and addresses the eyewitness of violent death, horror is associated with mediated witnessing and addresses the distant spectator' (Chouliaraki and Kissas 2018:24–25). In other words, terror is a direct corporeal experience and horror is a mediated one. Accordingly, Murray's analysis of the thanatopolitics of suicide bombers deals with terrorism, while ISIS videos are engaged in employing spectacular thanatopolitics for spreading horrorism. This terminology complements the thesis of 'the spectacular death' (Jacobsen 2016) and the concept of the 'theatre of terror' (Weimann and Winn 1993), in which death is witnessed (safely) from afar and the media play a pivotal role.

Spectacular death and the theatre of terror

Michael Hviid Jacobsen (2016) explores the trajectory of human engagement with death and proposes that the contemporary era is the age of spectacular death. The thesis of the 'spectacular death' resonates with *the society of the spectacle* (Debord 1967/2002) in which corporeality is replaced by representation. '"Spectacular death" is a death that has for all practical intents and purposes been transformed into a spectacle. It is something that we witness at a safe distance but hardly ever experience upfront' (Jacobsen 2016:10). The age of spectacular death follows other stages in the visibility and invisibility of death. At this stage, death is visible and celebrated mundanely and constantly for purposes of entertainment and amusement and its representations get a central stage on various platforms, including cinema, television and other venues of popular culture.

Thus, the notion of 'spectacular death' assumes spectatorship, and requires mediation or mediatisation. It points to the visual presence of death in daily public life, and the role of the media in producing and circulating representations of death:

> Today, death, dying and mourning are thus increasingly mediated and mediatized phenomena and not something we often encounter directly or personally, but rather occurrences we are exposed to and experience vicariously – and at a safe distance – through the screen of the television, computer or mobile phone'.
>
> *(Jacobsen 2016:11)*

Elsewhere, I discussed the mediatisation of death and the role of the media in performing death-related media rituals, which encourage spectators' participation and invite them to engage with violent distant deaths (Morse 2017). When it comes to terrorism, these possibilities of remote participation become more acute, since it brings to the fore the question of vulnerability – to what extent are the remote spectators, whose physical security is not endangered, put in danger? To what extent the horror and fear 'out there' invade the safety of the living room? How, if at all, can the media bridge the distance between vulnerable others and their spectators at home?

The theory of *terrorism as theatre* captures these various degrees of vulnerability (Chouliaraki 2006; Weimann 2004; Weimann and Winn 1993). This approach compares terror attacks to dramaturgical plays, and explains that 'terrorists pay attention to script preparation, cast selection, sets, props, role-playing, and minute-by-minute stage management' (Tsfati and Weimann 2002:318). Furthermore, understanding terrorism as theatre points to the multi-functions of terror attacks which operate beyond the 'here' and 'now' of the attack, and address wider circles of spectators whose vulnerability differs from that of the direct victims that were physically harmed. In fact, as Brian Jenkins argues, 'terrorism is aimed at the people watching, not at the actual victims' (Jenkins 1975 in Tsfati and Weimann 2002). Spectators in this metaphoric theatre of terror engage with representations of death, rather with death itself, from the safety of the 'theatre', i.e. their homes. Using the vocabulary offered by Chouliaraki and Kissas (2018), spectators in the theatre of terror are confronted with horrorism, rather than terrorism, which allows a secure engagement with the horrors of violent spectacular death.

Focusing on the role of the media in the mediation of terrorism, there is a debate whether the media is forced to generate these media rituals and to what extent their actions in the aftermath of terror attacks is an act of complicity (Liebes 1998; Nacos 2000; Weimann 1987). As a destabilising negative event, terrorism is newsworthy, and so it coerces itself into the media, putting on a public stage a violent and order-breaking, often spectacular event, which leaves the media no choice but to cover it. The open-ended live broadcasting from the scene of the attack, a format described by Tamar Liebes (1998) as *disaster marathon*, is criticised for enhancing the negative outcomes of terrorism, spreading fear and panic beyond the locale of the attack. In other words, the theory on the *theatre of terror* focuses on the coerced collaboration between perpetrators of terrorism and the media outlets as involuntary, forced distributors of horrorism.

However, media-rituals operating in the aftermath of grand terror attacks have the possibility of cultivating solidarity and identification with the victims. Drawing on theories from sociology and media anthropology, the performance of death-related media rituals cast the media as a shaman, whose actions can heal the wounded society and help it cope with rupture and loss (Chouliaraki 2006; Dayan and Katz 1992; Sumiala 2012). Mediatised mourning rituals can facilitate empathy or sympathy between distant others whose vulnerability is not identical, yet is sufficient to foster solidarity. Despite negative outcomes of extensive coverage of terror attacks, the performance of death-related media rituals is a form of media ritual that can potentially create a sense of solidarity, sympathy or empathy with distant sufferers (Chouliaraki 2006; Morse 2017). In this regard, as long as the media fulfil their role as providers of moral orientation, the coerced collaboration between media outlets and perpetrators can yield positive outcomes. The media coverage of the 2011 Norway and the 2015 Paris attacks and their aftermath, for example, invited large global audiences to engage with and participate in the mourning rituals in Norway and France. The live, ongoing broadcasting from the scenes of the attacks, the transmission of the tributes and memorial services from Oslo and Paris facilitated expressions of empathy and solidarity beyond these two countries (Morse 2017, 2018).

In this regard, journalism's role is to contextualise death and make it grievable. However, today, the status of the media as a social institution is challenged by a culture of user-generated content, accelerated by the rise of digital social networks, which constitute the infrastructure for these forms of communication. The monopoly of traditional news outlets is eroded and new players, whose interest is commercial rather than journalistic, emerge. When digital technologies cut off news media from the chain of news-gathering and dissemination, it gives rise to civil participation and more forms of engagement. In this process, death is often reduced to a mere spectacle – a representation of reality intended for emotional thrill rather than political engagement. The replacement of traditional news media with social media platform in spreading death-related content depoliticises death.

Death 2.0

Contemporary media ecology has moved to the age of Web 2.0, also defined as a media model of user-generated content, in which the institutional media outlet, as the intermediators between sender and receiver, are forsaken, for the sake of direct, reciprocal communication between the two ends. Manuel Castells (2007) defines contemporary media ecology as *mass-self-communication*, in which many users are engaged in interaction with many other users in a dense network of interconnectivity which challenges the power of institutionalised media. Under these conditions, the significance of traditional mass media outlets decreases, and the importance of the communication infrastructure increases. It does not mean that traditional media disappeared, and in many cases, we see a synergy between traditional and new media. Rather, the rise of P2P networks means that traditional media can be bypassed.

Earlier I discussed the mediatisation of death and the growing importance of the media as the social institution in charge of generating and performing death-related media rituals. The rise of Web 2.0 culture, in which the users, i.e. the public, generate, produce and disseminate information without the involvement of the mass media as an institution, means that the role of traditional media as providers of moral orientation diminishes. Moral concerns and ethical professional practices are no longer stable, and in fact, every user can abide by his or her principles. As the status of traditional news media erodes, the importance of internet platforms and laypeople as internet users becomes more considerable.

The involvement of internet platforms and digital social networks in transmitting information and facilitating social rituals exceeds the technicality of infrastructure. Paul Frosh argues:

> Social media and digital networks have become so intimately intertwined with our existence that they are far more than new infrastructures for circulating messages or managing social relationships. They are domains in which life and death are performed, experienced, and laid bare.
>
> *(Frosh 2019)*

How is the rise of Web 2.0 linked to the mediatisation of death? Before discussing the institutional role of internet platforms in mediatising death, I turn to the role and practices of internet users as citizens. Web 2.0 puts the internet user at its centre. A common practice within this culture is the selfie, which has come to play a meaningful role in the engagement with death.

Selfies as a witnessing act

A fundamental practice in Web 2.0 culture is the *selfie*. *Selfies* are practices of using smartphone cameras for self-documenting the user's current mood and experience and immediate sharing of this documentation with multiple others on various digital social networks. Theresa Senft and Nancy Baym (2015) define *selfies* as

> a photographic object that initiates the transmission of human feeling in the form of a relationship ... [and] a practice – a gesture that can send (and is often intended to send) different messages to different individuals, communities, and audiences. This gesture may be dampened, amplified, or modified by social media censorship, social censure, misreading of the sender's original intent, or adding additional gestures to the mix, such as likes, comments, and remixes.
>
> *(Senft and Baym 2015:1589)*

This gesture of the selfies was initiated for transmitting the selfie-taker's feeling and experience, and selfies have a central role in daily interpersonal communication in various social circles. While often criticised for being narcissistic and frivolous, recent scholarship lauds this practice for its politicised functions and its use for purposes of civil participation. Selfies communicate a presence in space and in time and function as a form of witnessing, establishing a moral bond between the selfie-taker and his or her audience. The selfie-taking practice is not only a mere act of creating a self-portrait, but also a civic claim of (cosmopolitan) citizenship made by ordinary users, an act of 'becoming citizens' and hence demanding responsibility and commitment from addressees of the selfie image (Azoulay 2008; Kuntsman 2017). Selfies are explicated as a citizen-journalistic practice (Chouliaraki 2017; Hartung 2017; Koliska and Roberts 2015); as a practice of shaming or rebuke (Frosh 2019); or as standing against discriminatory behaviour (Senft and Baym 2015). Hence, selfies address issues of political power, and function as a moralising practice that construes and constructs civil and uncivil behaviour and positions the spectator as a moral agent who can – and arguably needs – to act upon distant suffering.

Selfies of death

Elsewhere, I argued that the moralising function of media coverage of mass violent death events derives from the combination of humanising the dead, facilitating a shared experience and making death witnessable in the sense that it puts a moral burden on the distant spectators to position themselves vis-à-vis distant suffering and its perpetrators (Morse 2017). The study of selfies suggests that this practice allows witnessability, and therefore it can function as a moralising force, which recognises both the selfie-taker and the spectator as committed to each other and as belonging together. Michael Koliska and Jessica Roberts (2015) argue that selfies

> may be considered a special communication medium that serves a double function, in which the form and content are inextricably linked. First, they are a performative act of brand or identity building. Second, they are a proof of "truth," an act of witnessing that indicates the veracity of the individual's actions as well as documenting an event from a hyperpersonal perspective ... by making the observer/witness simultaneously part of the observed/witnessed event.
>
> *(Koliska and Roberts 2015:1676)*

It is this act of witnessing that is of interest here, since witnessing is a moralising practice and it becomes most acute in moments of extreme crisis (Frosh 2019; Hartung 2017).

Amanda Du Preez (2018) proposes a typology of selfies featuring death, composed of three categories which constitute what she defines as 'sublime selfies'. These include (1) selfies unknowingly taken before death; (2) selfies of death where the taker's death is almost witnessed; and (3) selfies with death where the taker stands by while someone else dies. These are sublime selfies, since they represent notions of pain and danger for distant spectators, without them actually being in such circumstances (Du Preez 2018:752). Accordingly, sublime selfies showcase the death of others in a pleasureful experience, without physically threatening the spectators. These sublime selfies provide a secure near-death experience. As such, these images correspond with the theory of the spectacular death introduced earlier.

While the original practice (and definition) of the selfie captured the production of a still photograph, Larissa Hjorth and Kathleen Cumiskey (2018) extend the definition of selfies so it includes also video-taking and video-sharing. They explain that this gesture and trope facilitate the sense of 'being there' and constitute a virtual co-presence of the soon-to-be-deceased-sender and his or her recipients. It shares the horror, pain and helplessness associated with the experience of impending death, in real time. This type of selfie facilitates *affective witnessing* (Papailias 2016) which bears the potential to establish emotional and ethical bonds between the selfie-takers and their audiences during and in the aftermath of traumatic events. About-to-die selfies 'work to humanize and personalize mass events of dehumanization and depersonalization' (Hjorth and Cumiskey 2018:174). As such, taking and sharing selfies function as ethical acts:

> The existence of raw footage from mass trauma events on public social media implies an urgent ethical imperative that has taken a variety of forms … Social media has been used to collectively and publicly grieve, to make meaning out of tragedy and to respond to our own fears and uncertainties.
> *(Hjorth and Cumiskey 2018:175)*

This practice of selfie-taking during disastrous happenings is not a *media event* as the term was originally theorised (Dayan and Katz 1992), yet these sharing practices bear the commonality of utilising media of communication for summoning participants to rites of passage. It is in these moments of crisis, when some people are about to perish, that other people turn to the media as facilitators of a virtual space of communion, where members of the community can come together, attend the farewell from their loved ones and mourn their impending departure.

To the above typology of death-selfies, I wish to add a fourth category, which is the one presented at the beginning of this chapter regarding the Christchurch and Halle attacks: self-documentation by the perpetrator, as he (usually this is a he rather than a she) commits fatal acts and shoots the victims. This type of selfie carries some similarities with the death-selfies described above, but also some significant differences. Like in the practices Hjorth and Cumiskey (2018) describe, the Christchurch and Halle footages feature the very last moments of the victims depicted, as documented and disseminated by a single user. In this respect, these footages made witnessable a violent end-of-life experience for whoever watches them. However, unlike the perspective provided by the victims in Hjorth and Cumiskey's study, both Christchurch and Halle attacks were performed and documented by the perpetrator, in an attempt to intensify the horror and further harm the victims. The documentations were disseminated directly to the perpetrators' followers, who later redistributed the footage. Thus, while the self-documentation of the victims who share their soon-to-be-dead experience is considered a moral civil act, which harnesses digital technologies for making the victims' impending death witnessable and grievable, the self-documentation by the perpetrator is an act of incivility, aimed at negating the victims' humanness, and make visible their degrading killing. In both cases mobile digital technologies allow witnessability, but in two very polarised manners.

The documentation and dissemination of the Christchurch and Halle attacks was an abuse of media of mass self-communication, and, in line with the discussion about the role of the media in the theatre of terror, we need to consider the dysfunction of this footage distribution. As this footage is an extraordinary documentation of extreme actions, it quickly goes viral and is then amplified by the social networks' algorithms (before it is taken down by their operators). Therefore, we need to consider the role and responsibilities of the platforms and their algorithms in the dissemination of mass-killing footage.

Digital social networks and the algorithmic gaze

The perpetrators of the Christchurch and Halle attacks livestreamed their killing missions on Facebook, and the footage was shortly thereafter redistributed on other digital social networks. Facebook and YouTube were reported to have removed the footage as soon as they learned about the nature of its content, and they were actively engaged in searching and blocking its redistributions in the following days (AFP 2019). This is in line with article 13 of Facebook's so-called community standards, which reads: 'We remove content that glorifies violence or celebrates the suffering or humiliation of others' ('Community Standards' n.d.).

The response of Facebook and other internet platforms during and after these attacks raises, once again, questions about their classification as platforms or as publishers, and their responsibility for the content being distributed or censored on their platforms (Levin 2018). While Facebook keeps serving as a major information source, and takes responsibility for the content distributed by its users, it perceives itself as a technology company, which merely hosts content uploaded to its servers, and hires engineers (and content moderators) rather than journalists (PBS 2018). These engineers write code and compute algorithms. They are not trained as journalists and do not aspire to inform the platform users. This leads the discussion to the growing control of algorithms over how we consume information.

The theories about the theatre of terror and media events portray central media as 'the stage' on which terrorism is played out, and around which the public gathers. The rise of Web 2.0 culture is often associated with the decentralisation of society and its sources of information. In a decentralised digital era, when there is no one monopolistic provider of information, what does it mean for the coerced collaboration between terrorists and the media? Arguably, there is no longer a central stage to which all the public pay attention. On the other hand, one can argue that there is still a central stage; however, today this is Facebook and other digital social networks who have become the new centre of society. On these digital platforms, algorithms play a pivotal role, since their monitoring and trafficking of data is the means by which the community is summoned. As these algorithms recognise the emergence and significance of an event, they highlight it, call the users' attention to it and generate more traffic to the event, on the go. In other words, algorithms can function as generators of media events on digital social platforms, despite the decentralisation of information sources. Users, from their perspective, can initiate the use of hashtags to trigger the algorithms and raise attention to trending events. The combination of user-generated content and algorithms can enhance media witnessing and a sense of co-presence in real time. This is a possible moralising function of the algorithmic involvement in information distribution.

However, the *de facto* delegation of authority and the new division of labour in which algorithms operate, replacing work previously done by journalists, has its downsides. So far, the algorithmic gaze failed to attend to the significance of violence imagery from both ends of the spectrum. It has banned the iconic photograph of the 'Napalm girl' (Ibrahim 2017; Johnson and Kelling 2018), and as we saw in the two cases of Christchurch and Halle attacks, it did not ban the livestreaming of massacres in real time. Yasmin Ibrahim (2017) explains that the problem of the algorithmic gaze is that it lacks historicity and adheres to economic logics of traffic generation. The community standards are imposed on the users, in an attempt to meet their standards of good taste and decency. And despite making journalistic editorial decisions, Facebook does not hire journalists and does not define itself as a publisher. Indeed, it uses code, but what is Facebook's code of conduct for its algorithms? The main regulation that applies to the platform is self-imposed regulation, aiming not to irritate its users and to eventually increase the financial value of company. The surrender to the algorithmic gaze means that we, as a society, let a for-profit, private IT corporation decide what is newsworthy or historically significant and what is not, and eventually, these companies get to decide what is sacred and what is not.

Conclusion

As this chapter has shown, given their negative effects, mass violent death events result in extensive media coverage, which register death, destruction, pain and loss beyond the locale in which they transpired. The corporeal thanatopolitics (Murray 2006) of violent death in public locations transfigures into mediated thanatopolitics (Chouliaraki and Kissas 2018) that are presented in the theatre of terror (Weimann and Winn 1993). The subversive act of making death visible is boosted. The aim of terrorism is exactly this: to spread fear and anxiety through the media. The operation of *disaster marathons* (Liebes 1998) turns death into representations while blurring the boundaries between the actual event and its symbolic registration. Unlike entertaining representations of fictional death, terror attacks – especially spectacular ones – coerce the association of death and horrorism in multiple locales. The fear associated with death representations, which is usually synthesised in fictional genres, becomes actual and tangible, and the pleasure linked to contemplating death imagery becomes threatening and menacing, even if from a distance.

Nevertheless, the mediatisation of death maintains its moralising potential. The performance of death-related media rituals can result in healing effects that establish bonds between spectators and sufferers. Mediatising death makes it witnessable, and encourages spectators to position themselves vis-à-vis the deadly reality of remote others, whose vulnerability is not identical to that of the spectators, yet reveals similarities and elicit empathy. New media of communication allow victims of deadly events to document themselves and share their last moments with other. This is an empowering possibility that reclaim the citizenship that has been taken by violent acts of death. Making one's own (impending) death visible sets the ground for grievability. It registers death and makes it matter.

The emerging type of mass-violent death events, in which the perpetrators self-document and disseminate their lethal acts, is a move in the opposite direction, since it further enhances the negation of symbolic citizenship. These documentations celebrate the spectacularity of death while dehumanising the victims by grotesquely inflicting their death. These acts objectify the victims, reducing their death to a spectacle. The boundaries between deadly reality and its representations become obscured. Shooting events register as spectacular representations – simulations designed to entertain, rather than to elicit grief and condemnation. Violent death turns into a simulacrum.

The emergence of these new digital media of communication heralds a change of guards with regard to the actors involved in the mediatisation of death. Journalists, those who have been in charge of generating and performing death-related media rituals, whose function is to contextualise and historicise suffering, are gradually being replaced – or at least challenged – by laypeople and algorithms, lacking historical awareness, ethical considerations and political consciousness. Since algorithms are written by coders, a more precise assertion is that journalists have lost their monopoly in mediatising death to coders and laypeople that were never trained as media professionals. Given the negative consequences of irresponsible distribution of death imagery, internet platforms should consider employing journalists as facilitators of information distribution, or at least train their coders to incorporate responsible journalistic practices and to teach their AI tools and algorithms to do the same.

References

Aday, Sean (2005): 'The Real War Will Never Get on Television: An Analysis of Casualty Imagery in American Television Coverage of the Iraq War'. In: Philip M. Seib (ed.). *Media and Conflict in the Twenty-First Century*. New York: Palgrave/Macmillan, pp. 141–156.

AFP (2019): 'Facebook Scrubs 1.5 Million Christchurch Attack Videos, but Criticism Goes Viral'. *AFP*, March 18. Retrieved from https://www.timesofisrael.com/faceb ook-scrubs-1-5-million-christchurch-attack-videos-but-criticism-goes-viral/.

Ariès, Philippe (1974): *Western Attitudes Toward Death: From the Middle Ages to the Present*. Baltimore, MD: Johns Hopkins University Press.

Ariès, Philippe (1985): *Images of Man and Death*. Cambridge, MA: Harvard University Press.

Azoulay, Ariella (2008): *The Civil Contract of Photography*. New York: Zone Books (Distributed by The MIT Press).

Campbell, David (2004): 'Horrific Blindness: Images of Death in Contemporary Media'. *Journal for Cultural Research*, 8(1):55–74.

Castells, Manuel (2007): 'Communication, Power and Counter-Power in the Network Society'. *International Journal of Communication*, 1:238–266.

Cavarero, Adriana (2009): *Horrorism: Naming Contemporary Violence*, (Volume 14). New York: Columbia University Press.

Chembo, Besa (2019): 'New Zealand Bans Video Game Glorifying Christchurch Mosque Shooting'. *Reuters*, October, 31. Retrieved from https://www.reuters.com/article/us-newzealand-shooting-censor-idUSKBN1XA0D5.

Chouliaraki, Lilie (2006): *The Spectatorship of Suffering*. Thousand Oaks, CA: Sage Publications.

Chouliaraki, Lilie (2009): 'Witnessing War: Economies of Regulation in Reporting War and Conflict'. *The Communication Review*, 12(3):215–226.

Chouliaraki, Lilie (2017): 'Symbolic Bordering: The Self-Representation of Migrants and Refugees in Digital News'. *Popular Communication*, 15(2):78–94.

Chouliaraki, Lilie and Angelos Kissas (2018): 'The Communication of Horrorism: A Typology of ISIS Online Death Videos'. *Critical Studies in Media Communication*, 35(1):24–39.

Community Standards | Facebook (n.d.): Retrieved 5 December 2019 from https://www w.facebook.com/communitystandards/graphic_violence.

Dayan, Daniel and Elihu Katz (1992): *Media Events: The Live Broadcasting of History*. Cambridge: Harvard University Press.

Dearden, Lizzie (2019a): 'Germany Gunman "Broadcast Attack Online" and Ranted about Holocaust, Jews and Immigration'. *The Independent*, October 9. Retrieved from https://www.independent.co.uk/news/world/europe/germany-shooting-synag ogue-attack-latest-twitch-livestream-gunman-holocaust-jews-a9149381.html.

Dearden, Lizzie (2019b): 'Gunman Opens Fire in Deadly Attack at German Synagogue'. *The Independent*, October 9. Retrieved from https://www.independent.co.uk/news/ world/europe/germany-shooting-synagogue-attack-latest-halle-today-shooter-d eath-toll-grenade-a9148791.html.

Debord, Guy (1967/2002): *Society of the Spectacle*. Detroit, MI: Black & Red.

Du Preez, Amanda (2018): 'Sublime Selfies: To Witness Death'. *European Journal of Cultural Studies*, 21(6):744–760.

Fahmy, Shahira (2010): 'Special Issue: Images of War'. *Media, War & Conflict*, 3(1):3–5.

Fishman, Jessica M. (2003): 'News Norms and Emotions: Pictures of Pain and Metaphors of Distress'. In: Larry Gross, John Stuart Katz and Jay Ruby (eds.). *Image Ethics in the Digital Age*. Minneapolis, MN: University of Minnesota Press, pp. 53–70.

Fishman, Jessica M. and Carolyn Marvin (2003): 'Portrayals of Violence and Group Difference in Newspaper Photographs: Nationalism and Media'. *Journal of Communication*, 53(1):32–44.

Frosh, Paul (2019): 'Eye, Flesh, World: Three Modes of Digital Witnessing'. In: Kerstin Schankweiler, Verena Straub and Tobias Wendl (eds.). *Image Testimonies: Witnessing in Times of Social Media*. Abingdon: Routledge, pp. 121–135.

Gorer, Geoffrey (1965): *Death, Grief and Mourning in Contemporary Britain*. London: Cresset Press.

Griffin, Michael (2004): 'Picturing America's "War on Terrorism" in Afghanistan and Iraq: Photographic Motifs as News Frames'. *Journalism: Theory, Practice & Criticism*, 5(4):381–402.

Griffin, Michael (2010): 'Media Images of War'. *Media, War & Conflict*, 3(1):7–41.

Halle Gunman Posted Video on Twitch Livestream Platform (2019): October 9. Retrieved from https://www.thelocal.de/20191009/halle-shooter-posted-video-on-twitch-livestream-platform-gunman-germany.

Hanusch, Folker (2008): 'Graphic Death in the News Media: Present or Absent?' *Mortality*, 13(4):301–317.

Hanusch, Folker (2012): 'The Visibility of Disaster Deaths in News Images A Comparison of Newspapers from 15 Countries'. *International Communication Gazette*, 74(7):655–672.

Hanusch, Folker (2013): 'Sensationalizing Death? Graphic Disaster Images in the Tabloid and Broadsheet Press'. *European Journal of Communication*, 28(5):497–513.

Harcup, Tony and Deirdre O'Neill (2001): 'What Is News? Galtung and Ruge Revisited'. *Journalism Studies*, 2(2):261–280.

Hartung, Catherine (2017): 'Selfies For/of Nepal: Acts of Global Citizenship and Bearing Witness'. In: Adi Kuntsman (ed.). *Selfie Citizenship*. New York: Springer, pp. 39–48.

Hjarvard, Stig (2008a): 'The Mediatization of Religion: A Theory of the Media as Agents of Religious Change'. *Northern Lights: Film & Media Studies Yearbook*, 6(1):9–26.

Hjarvard, Stig (2008b): 'The Mediatization of Society: A Theory of the Media as Agents of Social and Cultural Change'. *Nordicom Review*, 29(2):105–134.

Hjorth, Larissa and Kathleen M. Cumiskey (2018): 'Mobiles Facing Death: Affective Witnessing and the Intimate Companionship of Devices'. *Cultural Studies Review*, 24(2):166–180.

Hogan, Finn (2019): 'Video Game Based on Christchurch Mosque Shooting for Sale in New Zealand'. *Newshub*, October 12. Retrieved from https://www.newshub.co .nz/home/new-zealand/2019/10/video-game-based-on-christchurch-mosque-shoo ting-for-sale-in-new-zealand.html.

Ibrahim, Yasmin (2017): 'Facebook and the Napalm Girl: Reframing the Iconic as Pornographic'. *Social Media + Society*, 3(4):1–10.

Jacobsen, Michael Hviid (2016): '"Spectacular Death" – Proposing a New Fifth Phase to Philippe Ariès's Admirable History of Death'. *Humanities*, 5(19):1–20.

Jenkins, Brian Michael (1975): *International Terrorism: A New Mode of Conflict*. Los Angeles, CA: Crescent Publications.

Johnson, Brett G. and Kimberly Kelling (2018): 'Placing Facebook'. *Journalism Practice*, 12(7):817–833.

Katz, Elihu and Tamar Liebes (2007): '"No More Peace!": How Disaster, Terror and War Have Upstaged Media Events'. *International Journal of Communication*, 1(1):157–166.

Koliska, Michael and Jessica Roberts (2015): 'Selfies: Witnessing and Participatory Journalism with a Point of View'. *International Journal of Communication*, 9:1672–1685.

Kuntsman, Adi (ed.) (2017): *Selfie Citizenship*. New York: Springer.

Levin, Sam (2018): 'Is Facebook a Publisher? In Public It Says No, but in Court It Says Yes'. *The Guardian*, July 3, Retrieved from https://www.theguardian.com/technol ogy/2018/jul/02/facebook-mark-zuckerberg-platform-publisher-lawsuit.

Liebes, Tamar (1998): 'Television's Disaster Marathons: A Danger for Democratic Processes?' In: Tamar Liebes and James Curran (eds.). *Media, Ritual and Identity*. New York: Routledge, pp. 71–84.

Morse, Tal (2013): 'Shooting the Dead: Images of Death, Inclusion and Exclusion in the Israeli Press'. In: Michele Aaron (ed.). *Envisaging Death: Visual Culture and Dying*. Newcastle: Cambridge Scholars Publishing, pp. 140–156.

Morse, Tal (2014): 'Covering the Dead: Death Images in Israeli Newspapers – Ethics and Praxis'. *Journalism Studies*, 15(1):98–113.

Morse, Tal (2017): *The Mourning News: Reporting Violent Death in a Global Age*. New York: Peter Lang Inc./International Academic Publishers.

Morse, Tal (2018): 'The Construction of Grievable Death: Toward an Analytical Framework for the Study of Mediatized Death'. *European Journal of Cultural Studies*, 21(2):242–258.

Murray, Stuart J. (2006): 'Thanatopolitics: On the Use of Death for Mobilizing Political Life'. *Polygraph: An International Journal of Politics & Culture*, 18:191–215.

Nacos, Brigitte L. (2000): 'Accomplice or Witness? The Media's Role in Terrorism'. *Current History*, 99(636):174–178.

Nacos, Brigitte L. (2003): 'The Terrorist Calculus Behind 9–11: A Model for Future Terrorism?' *Studies in Conflict & Terrorism*, 26(1):1–16.

New Zealand Mosque Shooting in Christchurch (n.d.). *NBC News* website, 17 November. Retrieved from https://www.nbcnews.com/news/world/new-zealand -mosque-shootings.

Ortiz, Erik, Farnoush Amiri and Claire Atkinson (2019): 'News Outlets Mostly Avoided Publishing the Video of the New Zealand Attacks'. *NBC News* website, March 16, Retrieved from https://www.nbcnews.com/news/world/news-outlets-mostly-avoid ed-publishing-video-new-zealand-attacks-n983806.

Papailias, Penelope (2016): 'Witnessing in the Age of the Database: Viral Memorials, Affective Publics and the Assemblage of Mourning'. *Memory Studies*, 9(4):437–454.

PBS (2018): 'Zuckerberg: We're a Tech Company, Not a Publisher'. Retrieved from https://www.youtube.com/watch?v=4HTae-X757g.

Seaton, Jean (2005): *Carnage and the Media: The Making and Breaking of News about Violence*. London: Allen Lane.

Senft, Theresa M. and Nancy K. Baym (2015): 'What Does the Selfie Say? Investigating a Global Phenomenon: Introduction'. *International Journal of Communication*, 9:1588–1606.

Sontag, Susan (2003): *Regarding the Pain of Others*. New York: Farrar, Straus and Giroux.

Sumiala, Johanna (2012): *Media and Ritual: Death, Community and Everyday Life*. Abingdon: Routledge.

Tait, Sue (2009): 'Visualising Technologies and the Ethics and Aesthetics of Screening Death'. *Science As Culture*, 18(3):333–353.

Tsfati, Yariv and Gabriel Weimann (2002): 'Www.terrorism.com: Terror on the Internet.' *Studies in Conflict & Terrorism*, 25(5):317–332.

Weimann, Gabriel (1987): 'Media Events: The Case of International Terrorism'. *Journal of Broadcasting & Electronic Media*, 31(1):21–39.

Weimann, Gabriel (2004): 'The Theater of Terror: The Psychology of Terrorism and the Mass Media'. *Journal of Aggression, Maltreatment & Trauma*, 9(3/4):379–390.

Weimann, Gabriel and Conrad Winn (1993): *The Theater of Terror: Mass Media and International Terrorism*. New York: Addison-Wesley/Longman Ltd.

Zelizer, Barbie (2010): *About to Die: How News Images Move the Public*. New York: Oxford University Press.

8

A TALE OF TWO DEATHS

Spectacular death and the scene of pain

Arnar Árnason

Introduction: A tale of two deaths

Just before midnight on Saturday 14 January 2017, a missing person's call went out from the police in Reykjavík, Iceland. The police, it said, were looking for a 20-year-old girl, Birna Brjánsdóttir, not seen since the very early hours of that morning. The description – of Birna,[1] her clothes, where and when she was last seen – that is such a key step in building the tension in a crime novel or a tv show about the missing, and the source of near-enough unbearable dread in real life, was accompanied by a plea for information from anyone who might be able to help in locating her. Details of Birna's movements the night she went missing were soon made public. Images harvested from security cameras revealed her journey from a bar in the centre of Reykjavík through some of its, at that time, rather deserted streets. The last image, it said, was recorded at 05.25 on the Saturday morning on Laugarvegur, the main avenue for shopping in the city, which runs parallel to the street where the bar she spent the evening is located. Twenty-five minutes later, just before six in the morning, a telephone mast had picked up a signal from her mobile phone, now turned off, in the small town of Hafnarfjörður, some ten kilometres or so south of Reykjavík.[2] Over the next week, the disappearance of Birna was the centre of public life in Iceland. The desperate search for her, the inconclusive hints of what had happened to her, reminded many, understandably, of the innumerable television programmes – the Danish *Forbrydelsen*, *The Killing*, not least – that have the abduction of a young woman as their dramatic centre. Large numbers of people volunteered to assist with the search for Birna and the social media commentaries were full of messages related to her disappearance. When Birna's body was eventually found eight days later, by which time her disappearance had become a criminal investigation, the attention intensified still further. On 28 January, two weeks after her disappearance, a march was organised in her memory attended by thousands of people, many of whom lit candles and laid flowers by Laugarvegur 31, the spot where Birna was last seen on security cameras.[3] The ongoing criminal investigation and the trials that followed remained the centre of public attention in Iceland. Around the time of Birna's funeral on 3 February, many people – established commentators in the media and ordinary contributors to social media – took the opportunity to remember Birna, to offer her family and friends their condolences and to reflect on how her disappearance had brought 'the nation', *þjóðina*, together, and offered 'the nation' the opportunity to show its best sides – as the Icelandic phrase, frequently used on the occasion, goes. Birna was proclaimed the daughter of Iceland, the 'daughter of us all'. Her funeral was open to the general public and was marked by a poem by one of Iceland's best-known writers, Hallgrímur Helgason. The poem, 'Hún ein', describes Birna as 'one of us, us as her'.[4]

Later that same year, a young man disappeared down the Gullfoss waterfall, one of the most iconic and popular tourist destinations in Iceland. Early reports did not specify whether the man had fallen, jumped or, indeed, been pushed.[5] Nameless at first, it was later confirmed that the young man, Nika Begades, or Begadze in some reports, was from Georgia and had sought asylum in Iceland on the grounds of the persecution he suffered in his home country because of his sexuality.[6] Begades' body was recovered from the river some three weeks after he fell[7] and news to that effect aside, his death, in contrast to that of Birna, has remained largely unmarked publicly in Iceland. Immediately after the event, one prominent public commentator, Guðmundur Andri Thorsson, now an MP in Iceland, drew attention to the then-recent ruling by the Immigration Directorate in Iceland, that Georgia is a safe country, to which the young man could thus be returned; he could have no need for asylum in Iceland. The conclusion seemed clear: the young man had killed himself when faced with a forced return to the country he had fled. The commentator noted the stark absence of interest in the media in Iceland in Begades as a person, in his history, and his state of mind. The only reports of his death were seemingly objective, factual descriptions of events as he disappeared into the water. Guðmundur Andri made the case that his fellow country people are themselves refugees, asylum seekers as the country was settled in the 9th century onwards. He wondered about the part played by ongoing concerns over the 'purity of the nation' in enforcing such strict control over immigration. The article provoked some commentary online. Many of the commentators expressed support for maintaining the strict policy that had been in place in relation to refugees and asylum seekers. No-one seemed to take up the invitation implicit in Guðmundur Andri's article and declare themselves a refugee, declare themselves Nika. Begades' death hardly seems to have registered in Iceland beyond the brief moment of the spectacle as he fell.[8]

Over the last 200 years, I and my colleagues Sigurjón Baldur Hafsteinsson and Tinna Grétarsdóttir have sought to document, and occasionally report on, what we have, between ourselves, referred to as changing regimes of death and grief in Iceland. As part of this research, I have followed public discussions about the death of Birna and, such as it has been, about the death of Nika Begades. I have talked about the reactions to these deaths with people in Iceland, both over the phone and in person during my visits to the country since the deaths occurred. Drawing on the public reports of the deaths in particular, but my conversations with people in Iceland too, in this chapter I will reflect on the two deaths described above in the hope that such a reflection may be the ground for commenting on the current state of death in Iceland more generally. My hope is, further, that such a comment may, with all due hesitation, offer some insight into the state of death in the contemporary 'Western' world. In particular, I will discuss the extent to which the deaths can be regarded as examples of, or evidence for, a shift towards a 'mentality' or paradigm of 'spectacular death' that Danish sociologist Michael Hviid Jacobsen (2016) has recently proposed. The two deaths in question are, as I hope is clear from the brief descriptions above, remarkably different from each other in almost every respect. While Birna's death was, as it turns out, as far from being a spectacle as possible, indeed most likely as tragically a lonely affair as imaginable, her disappearance, after the fact, the search for her, the mourning for her and the criminal procedures that followed, were all a spectacle. The story of the disappearance, the search, the criminal investigation and the trial were thoroughly mediatised, and mediatised to an extent unprecedented in Iceland. Birna's fate became, in effect, a televised drama that offered a framework for people to interpret their experience within. The death of the young Georgian man, meanwhile, was surely spectacular in form. Disappearing over one of the most iconic scenes in the whole country and that in the presence of numerous tourists, most of them foreign, was a spectacular act that dramatised, intentionally or not, the different reception afforded moneyed travellers that have helped restore the Icelandic economy after the collapse of 2008, and that extended to impoverished asylum seekers who would appear to have nothing to offer but their helplessness, their desperate hope. At the same time, the death of the young Georgian man had effectively no aftermath as a spectacle, his death disappearing from view almost as fast as he himself had done, but unlike his body, never really to surface again.

In the section that follows, I will seek to put together something of a theoretical frame within which to view the two deaths I have described. I will acknowledge what many readers will be thinking already, the potential applicability of Judith Butler's (2004, 2009) notion of 'grievability' to the two deaths I discuss here. However, I will suggest that the element of spectacle is important in my cases and that as such, the two deaths speak to Jacobsen's notion of an emerging paradigm of 'spectacular death' in the Western world. I will suggest that the insight offered by the notion of 'spectacular death' is, in this particular case at least, further enhanced if coupled with Laurent Berlant's (1998) work on the 'scene of pain', spiced with Elisabeth Anker's (2012) take on 'melodrama'. Birna's life was not only more grievable than the life of the young Georgian man, the pain her death caused, as staged – and by calling it staged, I of course do not imply anything not at the same time entirely heartfelt and genuine – offered identificatory possibilities through which the 'nation' could yet again re-imagine, no, rather, re-feel itself together.

Grievability, or who mourns a number?

In her response to the wars that have followed the events of 9/11, Judith Butler (2004, 2009) has formulated the notion of 'grievability'. She notes how, in the public accounts and remembrances of the deaths associated with the so-called war on terror, some of the lives lost are named and accompanied by details that serve to individualise, personify and humanise the victims, while other deaths are left as approximate numbers at best. Thus, Butler says, some of the lives that are lost are made grievable, while others are reduced to statistics, allowed to become collateral damage, their lack of names, their lack of individualising detail, serving to strip them of the humanity afforded to their counterparts. These latter are deaths then, that do not have to be, in fact, should not be, cannot be, grieved. It is by now of course painfully obvious whose lives, in the story Butler told, are grievable and whose are not. The attention paid to the individuality of the victims of 9/11 and the individuality of victims of other terror attacks in the 'West' – whose names have been read out publicly and displayed prominently on national monuments – contrasts sharply with the indifference shown to the individuality of the civilian casualties of the wars in Afghanistan and Iraq, for example, wars that were started in response to 9/11. That indifference, in turn, serves to stifle potential criticism of the wars, the victims' lack of humanity working to make the wars seem less destructive than they would otherwise appear, perhaps helping the wars to look like civilising missions (see Scarry 2010).

I want to note here my recognition that Butler's notion of grievability is clearly strikingly relevant in analysing this tale of two deaths in Iceland. Birna was Icelandic with an extensive network of family and friends around her. The relative smallness of the population meant that many people in Iceland will have had a connection with someone very directly affected by Birna's death even if they were not so directly affected themselves. Furthermore, the circumstances of her disappearance – a young woman on a night out – are almost desperately familiar to most people in the country through the traces of excitement they recognise in themselves from such outings in their youth, or the vague sense of unease attached to knowing one's own children are out there in the night-time excitement. In contrast, the young Georgian man had hardly any connections in Iceland, it seems. Furthermore, his circumstances are not ones that many people in Iceland can necessarily relate to so easily. Not many in the country can relate to the state of being an asylum-seeker, someone who has fled their home because of persecution. While Butler's notion of grievability clearly offers insight here, I suggest that it does not, as such, allow us to push further our understanding of why one of these deaths was grievable and the other one not. I suggest that the element of spectacle is important here, both in relation to the material I am working with and as a general point. And so I suggest that further insights are to be gained by making Butler's idea speak to two other notions: Michael Hviid Jacobsen's (2016) notion of 'spectacular death' and the idea of the 'scene of pain' I take from Lauren Berlant (1998), fortified with Elisabeth Anker's (2012) work on 'melodrama'.

Spectacular death

In 2016 Jacobsen revisited the celebrated work of the French social historian Philippe Ariès (1974a, 1974b, 1981) on the changing 'death mentalities' in Western Europe. The history that Ariès traced is likely to be very familiar to the readers of this book, and I will not retrace it here in any detail. By the history of death mentalities, Ariès referred to 'transformations in the very collective and cultural psychology of a given historical epoch' (Jacobsen 2016:2). The great change that Ariès documented was from a familiarity and openness towards death to a 'mentality' in which death is denied, it is hidden, taboo or forbidden. Echoing – in the best sense of the word – and giving great historical detail to the work of Geoffrey Gorer (1965), Ariès (1974a, 1974b) can be credited with enormous influence on popular perceptions and the inspiration for the creation of a field of interdisciplinary study. Death studies – the humanities and social scientific study of death as a cultural and social phenomenon – was born from the sense of loss evident in the work of Ariès and Gorer, from a process of mourning, one could suggest, if not from a state of melancholia. Rooted as death studies are in reflections upon the place of death in Western societies, vague as that demarcation admittedly is, its founding observation was the denial of death's reality in the 'Western' world, evident, amongst other things, in the disappearance of dying and certain rituals and etiquette around death and mourning from public community life. Death studies, I would suggest, is still infused with this sense of loss, the loss of familiarity with death.

Since the groundbreaking work of Gorer and Ariès, many have of course followed the same path. Indeed, the taboo around death in the 'Western' world has long since become something of a publicly accepted truism, denounced in newspapers nearly every week – despite Michael A. Simpson's (1987) now decades-old observation that so frequently exposed a taboo surely starts to look like something else. While death is claimed to be a taboo in, if you will forgive, lay public discussions, over some 25 years now, scholars writing on the place of death in society have come to suggest something of a reversal. Already in the mid-1990s Tony Walter (1994) spoke of the 'revival of death' (see also Seale 1998). Last year, Walter (2019) spoke of the 'pervasive' dead, using Robert Hertz's (1907/1960) classic work to suggest that while the dying are still sequestered in contemporary Western societies, the dead are all around us, are, in a word, pervasive, in the memorials and monuments dedicated to them, in our remembrances of them, as ghosts we encounter sometimes willingly, sometimes not. In the works that revise the account of the place of death in Western societies, different examples, different kinds of evidence, are offered in support of the revision. The emergence of the hospice movement and bereavement counselling are two examples; the re-emergence of public forms of mourning and memorialisation is another one. More specific examples offered in evidence of greater 'openness' towards death are the ways in which those who were previously not mourned publicly are now subject to elaborate public memorialisation. In many contemporary Western contexts, for example, aborted foetuses and stillborn babies, that not so long ago would have been disposed of without ceremony, are now publicly mourned (see Christensen and Sandvik 2014). Similarly, pets, whose non-humanity until recently removed them from processes of public mourning, are now legitimate objects of the public expression of grief (Redmalm 2015). What then exactly is the mentality of 'spectacular death' that Jacobsen (2016) outlines, and how can the cases I have described – only briefly so far – stand as examples of spectacular death?

Michael Hviid Jacobsen notes that the notion of forbidden death, the mentality that marked the endpoint of Ariès's history, is surely not applicable to the current situation of death in the Western world. There has clearly been 'a revival of interest in death, dying and bereavement, professionally, politically, publicly and personally, which renders problematic the notions of taboo, denial and disappearance of death that was so characteristic of Ariès's 'forbidden death' (Jacobsen 2016:2). Jacobsen draws on Benjamin Noys' astute observation that the point we need to focus on in figuring out this new situation is not whether death as such is invisible or taboo, but rather the structures that variably expose us to death or possibly hide it away from us (Jacobsen 2016:10). While people in the Western world have become less likely to witness death first-hand than they were before (see Walter 2019), they are ever more likely to see and to hear about death through the media. This often happens through markedly melodramatic images of horrific deaths presented to us as part of news stories from different conflicts or in the form of artistic or entertainment features. The notion of 'spectacular death' is useful to capture how contemporary death mentality in Western society is shaped by the way in which 'death, dying and mourning have increasingly become spectacles' (Jacobsen 2016:1); it is to identify and single out how our relationship to death is changed by such mediatisation. Jacobsen draws his notion of spectacle from the work of Guy Debord and his notion of the 'society of the spectacle'. Thus, and here I allow myself to quote at some length:

> "spectacular death" is a death that has for all practical intents and purposes been transformed into a spectacle. It is something that we witness at a safe distance but hardly ever experience upfront. Debord's first thesis in fact stated that everything that was previously experienced directly now merely becomes a representation, making us spectators and bystanders. "Spectacular death" thus inaugurates an obsessive interest in appearances that simultaneously draws death near and keeps it at arm's length – it is something that we witness at a safe distance with equal amounts of

fascination and abhorrence, we wallow in it and want to know about it without getting too close to it.

(Jacobsen 2016:10)

While 'spectacular death' represents a shift from the forbidden death that Ariès spoke of, this does not mean that the societal and cultural drawbacks that commentators have usually attached to forbidden death have been overcome. Spectacular death tellingly shimmers somewhere between enhanced freedom over how we die and grieve and even greater control than normally attributed to the taboo death of modern society. Spectacular death in many ways suggests a reversal of the disenchantment of death that Ariès and, to some extent, Gorer spoke of. Still, even 'the notion of "spectacular death" indicates that although we have liberated death from the shackles of denial and taboo, we still seem to have a long way to go to reach authentic and autonomous death' (Jacobsen 2016:15).

What is the particular import of the spectacle that is relevant to the cases I discuss here; what does the notion of spectacular death bring that helps further understanding of the cases beyond what, for example, the notion of variable grievability does? I will answer in a roundabout way by evoking here some of Lauren Berlant's extensive work on (post-)liberal sentimentality and its politics, in the process smuggling in some insights to be gained from Elizabeth Anker's (2012) work on 'melodrama'.

Scenes of pain, melodrama and national identifications

Benedict Anderson's (1983/1991) hugely influential and masterful study on the rise of nationalism and nation-states sought to explain how it was that different individuals who, living in very different parts of their country would never meet and might have an awful lot of things in *un*common, and indeed, in many respects, conflicting interests, could still come to imagine themselves as belonging to the same collective, to the same 'nation'. Berlant's project on liberalism, neo-liberalism, sentimentality and politics, speaks to the same processes but with a focus on emotion, sentimentality and affect. Thus, Berlant's work invites the question: how is it that people come to feel themselves as belonging to the 'nation' and belonging there together with some people otherwise unlike them, mostly unknown to them, belonging with some, while excluding others? Focusing on the United States, Berlant has written on 'a particular form of liberal sentimentality' that invites, or seduces, individuals to identify with 'the nation', over and above other collectives, and to do so 'through a universalist rhetoric not of citizenship per se but of the capacity for suffering and trauma' (Berlant 1998:636). Berlant argues that this form of sentimentality is mobilised mainly 'by the culturally privileged to humanize' those less privileged who are in the process 'reduced to cliché within the reigning regimes of entitlement or value' (Berlant 1998:636). In this effort, says Berlant, liberal sentimentality will 'render scenes and stories of structural injustice in the terms of a putatively preideological nexus of overwhelming feeling whose threat to the survival of individual lives is said also to exemplify conflicts in national life' (Berlant 1998:636). What Berlant refers to as 'sentimental politics' is deployed, she says, 'whenever putatively supra-political affects or affect-saturated institutions (like the nation and the family) are proposed as universalist solutions to structural racial, sexual, or intercultural antagonism' (Berlant 1998:638). On the one hand, sentimental politics involves the exemplification of structural violence through personal stories of pain; on the other hand, sentimental politics involves offering affected saturated institutions as the solution to the pain and suffering depicted. Here Berlant puts forward the following hypothesis:

> When sentimentality meets politics, it uses personal stories to tell of structural effects, but in so doing it risks thwarting its very attempt to perform rhetorically a scene of pain that must be soothed politically. Because the ideology of true feeling cannot admit the nonuniversality of pain, its cases become all jumbled together and the ethical imperative toward social transformation is replaced by a civic-minded but passive ideal of empathy. The political as a place of acts oriented toward publicness becomes replaced by a world of private thoughts, leanings, and gestures.
>
> *(Berlant 1998:641)*

The importance of sentimentality here suggests melodrama as an important element of the scene of pain. Elisabeth Anker (2012) has recently described the key characteristic of melodrama as a portrayal of 'events through a narrative of victimization and retribution, and a character triad of villain, victim and hero' (Anker 2012:136). Melodramas speak of 'injury and action, of suffering and strength, until a hero rescues the victim and usually triumphs over the villain' (Anker 2012:136). The very point of melodrama, Anker adds, is to evoke

> visceral responses in their readers and audiences by depicting wrenching and perilous situations that aim to generate affective connections to victims and the heroes who rescue them. Using a morally polarizing worldview, melodramas signify goodness in the suffering of victims, and signify evil in the cruel ferocity of antagonists. The victim's injury at the core of the narrative divides the world and demands retribution or redemption as response. Many melodramas promise a teleology of change that can rectify the social injuries they diagnose.
>
> *(Anker 2012:136)*

In what follows, I shall suggest that Birna's death became a spectacle, a melodrama in Anker's terms, that played out a scene of pain that offered a redemption as a response. The death of the young Georgian man, I will furthermore suggest, did not offer such a redemption or indeed demand a retribution.

'The girl who touched the heart of the Icelandic nation'

The death of Birna Brjánsdóttir is without much doubt the most publicly discussed death that has occurred in Iceland for a long time, if not forever. Indeed, much of the very extensive commentary on her death is fundamentally reflexive in this regard and has this as its key point of departure: the death that gripped Iceland, the death that Iceland is obsessed with, or something to that effect.[9] The public response to the disappearance and death of Birna had, at its core, awareness of its own obsessive interest, its own fascination mixed with its own sorrow. In this way, Birna's death has of course been highly unusual – it was a spectacle to an unprecedented extent. As such my focus on Birna's death may of course serve to undermine my claim that it suggests a more general shift towards a 'mentality' of spectacular death in Iceland. Still, in some ways, Birna's death represents an intensification of trends that were already in place before this tragedy struck. As mentioned above, I have, with my colleagues Sigurjón Baldur Hafsteinsson and Tinna Grétarsdóttir, sought to document changing regimes of dying and grieving in Iceland over the past 20 years. The starting moment of our surveying was marked by efforts by various individuals and organisations to break down, as they saw it, the taboo around death that was said to prevail in the country. Bereavement support groups were formed in the Reykjavík area and then in other parts of the country, a dedicated palliative care unit was established and these efforts were reported on reasonably widely in the media. In many ways, events in Iceland at the end of the 20th century seemed to mirror changes that had happened in the United Kingdom and the United States and were happening already in Scandinavia. Of course, changes in Iceland were not unaffected by what had happened elsewhere. Some of the instigators had themselves studied in the UK, the US or Scandinavia and key figures from that broad death and grief awareness movement, like Colin Murray Parkes, were invited to visit Iceland as part of an attempt to open up discussions about death and grief. What has happened in the last few years is a further development in this direction. With the move of mainstream media online, at least partly, and the explosion in the use of social media, coupled with the appetite that some media outlets have for turning people's social media messages into items of news, Iceland has witnessed an increasing number of people who die and grieve publicly. Their accounts are almost always framed as offerings in life lessons, as insights gained from painful experience and now shared with others in preparation for their own, inevitable, suffering. The (almost) always explicit message communicated echoes the one delivered differently 20 years ago: the need to open up to this inevitable part of life, the richness in experience to be gained from embracing death and grief, which will not be escaped at any rate, rather than seeking to shelter oneself and others from the burden of mortality. Thus, unavoidable fate is exemplified through personal stories of pain, while the affected saturated institutions of the family and, less frequently, friendship, are offered as the panacea to the very suffering depicted. Examples of such public dying and grieving are many, usually of people who have risen to some general familiarity in Iceland. A very recent example is of a young woman who dying of cancer stated that she was reconciled to her fate but insisted that death must not be a taboo subject.[10] A key example is the actor who gave life to the arch-villain in the popular children's television series Lazy Town, whose illness, treatment and death were publicly shared online, his widow carrying on with accounts of her grief after his death. This particular account is now being referenced as inspiration by others who have come forward to speak publicly of their experience of death and grief.[11] In this respect, then, the death of Birna Brjánsdóttir was part of a wider trend, a larger shift, even if it marked an intensification of that shift. Her death, like many deaths in Iceland nowadays, was turned into a spectacle. The framing of the stories – of Birna's disappearance and death and of those other public deaths – and their consumption reveals

> an obsessive interest in appearances that simultaneously draws death near and keeps it at arm's length – it is something that we witness at a safe distance with equal amounts of fascination and abhorrence, we wallow in it and want to know about it without getting too close to it,

as Jacobsen (2016:10) suggests of 'spectacular death'. But what then of the scene of pain that the public attention to her death framed, what of the melodrama around the discussions about her death?

On 5 February 2017, the British newspaper *The Guardian* reported extensively on Birna's death and the public's reaction to her disappearance.[12] At the centre of the account in the paper was an interview with Yrsa Sigurðardóttir, the queen of Icelandic crime fiction, whose translated novels have been very popular in the UK. Yrsa begins by noting the eerie familiarity of the scene. The paper quotes her as saying: 'The security camera photos of Birna from when she was last seen, we've all been there, our sons and daughters have been there, walking down that same street after a night out'. The point is, of course, that the tragedy that befell Birna, her family and friends, is one that, but for the grace of God, as the saying goes, could have befallen anyone in Iceland. The spectacle, the image on the security camera, serves to highlight the possible inter-changeability of any son or daughter for Birna. Yrsa continued: 'Somehow it rang a chord with the nation. Birna is such a compelling figure, so beautiful, so young, so happy. She's never done anything to harm anybody'. Here a number of further elements have been added to the account. Birna's qualities, her beauty and youth, her happiness and kindness, play into the familiarity of the scene of her disappearance to explain how it was that Birna's fate touched 'the nation' so powerfully. The characterisation signals the fascination with Birna's death, the abhorrence at her fate, while effecting a greater distance to it than the security image itself alone does. Birna as a compelling figure is not so easily inter-changeable as the eerie image on CCTV. Later in the report, the journalist quotes Yrsa on how people in Iceland became themselves involved in and participated in the unfolding story of the disappearance and death of Birna. She says:

> In addition to the hundreds of people that were searching [a huge number of ordinary citizens volunteered and helped with the search], and the 8,000 on the walk [the walk in memory of Birna mentioned at the start of this chapter], everybody has been waiting for the next news on Birna, on the edge of their seat. The whole country felt bad, we still do. We were all hoping she would be found alive, but no. There's not a single person in the country who doesn't feel bad about this.

Here is the fascination again, the waiting on the edge of the seat, but also the pain, the dashed hope. Fascination feeds pain and the suffering caused by Birna's disappearance and then death, becomes the centre of the scene of pain, the chord that stirred the nation. This sentiment is taken further in a Facebook 'update' by the then-prime minister of Iceland, Bjarni Benediktsson, from 22 January 2017, when Birna's body had just been found. He said:

> A week ago Birna Brjánsdóttir did not come home. Since then a search has been carried out for her. The police has worked tirelessly to investigate her disappearance … Many people have helped with the search and volunteered information. This tragedy has touched the nation, moved us all and together we have hoped it would not end as it has. Now, Birna has been found and we come together in grief. I offer Birna's family and loved ones my condolences.[13]

The sentimentality the Berlant speaks of is evident here in what both Yrsa Sigurðardóttir and Bjarni Benediktsson had to say. Both speak of a scene of pain as conducive to a feeling of togetherness for the 'Icelandic nation'. The visceral responses that melodrama elicits in its audiences 'by depicting wrenching and perilous situations that aim to generate affective connections to victims' that Anker (2012:136) speaks of is here too in the depiction of Birna's disappearance and the evocation of the anguish felt by those waiting and hoping against hope for someone gone missing. In this, 'the nation' is of course itself simultaneously construed as a victim, if at one remove. A stake is being claimed, on behalf of 'the nation', to the grief Birna's death has caused. Not only her family and friends are bereaved, 'the nation', it is claimed, has come together too in its grief. But who, then, is the villain here and what is the link between this particular scene of pain and the structural injustices that it depicts according to Berlant's (1998) formulation of the scene of pain?

By the time Birna's body was found, arrests had already been made. Evidence had pointed to the involvement of trawlermen from a Greenland registered ship, the Polar Nanoq. In a very dramatic fashion, as *The Guardian* and other accounts did not fail to note, the armed unit of the Icelandic police, the Viking Squad, flew by helicopter after the boat, which had left Iceland the day Birna had gone missing, to arrest the two suspects on board. In due course only one of the suspects was retained in custody for any length of time, the trawlerman who was later charged with and then convicted of the murder of Birna. Thus, for a while it had appeared that more than one person had been directly involved in Birna's disappearance. On this point, *The Guardian* quotes Yrsa as saying: 'The whole thing is a tragedy, but the fact that it's not both of them somehow makes it better. Two people plotting together would have been more evil'. By this stage the disappearance, and now murder, of Birna had become the story people had at the beginning feared it was destined to be; a story almost nauseatingly familiar from the endless television programmes on the theme. Whether or not the encounter between Birna and her murderer started out as a hoped-for erotic encounter and went horribly wrong, by this time events had confirmed it as a depressingly common story of gender-based sexual violence. With that the identity of the villain began to shift.

Who is the villain, who is the victim?

Lauren Berlant (1998) suggests that sentimental politics are enacted when affect saturated institutions like the 'nation' or the family are evoked as cures for personal injury. Prevalent in the reaction to Birna's disappearance and death was a reflection on how it brought 'the nation' 'together' and how the public reactions were evidence of the best qualities of the Icelandic 'the nation'. Huge numbers of unrelated civilians volunteered to help with the search for Birna and the participation in the march in her memory was great, as I have noted already. Here the wider context of the recent history of Iceland is of some relevance. Ever since the financial collapse of 2008,[14] simply referred to as the '*hrun*' in Iceland, public life in the country has been deeply marked by conflict, division and debates and a very significant distrust in politics, politicians and the public institutions of the state. It is no great exaggeration to say that Iceland has been caught in a continuous political crisis since 2008. In the spring of 2016, the then-government 'exploded', as the Icelandic phrase goes, when the prime minister at the time was caught in a lie during a television interview about his or his wife's ownership of a company registered in an offshore tax haven. Bjarni Benediktsson, mentioned above, had become prime minister in the autumn of 2016 following the elections necessitated by the resignation of the previous government following extensive public protests. Besides the adventures of the Icelandic national football team at the European Championships in 2016, including a famous win over the English, nothing had arguably 'brought the nation together' like the disappearance and death of Birna.

Claiming Birna as 'the daughter of Iceland', a claim frequently heard during the events discussed here, is of course a claim that all of Iceland, all Icelanders, her family aside, could claim her equally. It is a claim that betrays a sense of simultaneous closeness and distance that is key to spectacular death. At times some people felt that there was a danger here that the grief of Birna's family and friends was being appropriated by 'the nation' and with that somewhat diminished. It is significant here that the person eventually arrested, charged with and convicted for Birna's murder, is not Icelandic. In the interview in *The Guardian* cited above, Yrsa Sigurðardóttir, the crime novelist, suggested that the fact that there was only one perpetrator, and not more as seemed likely for a while, somehow made the murder somewhat less evil. This was just the act of one man rather than the result of the cooperation, the collusion of more than one. It is almost as if that would have somehow been a reflection on human relationships generally, while the acts of one man can be understood as simply that: the acts of one man. The unfolding of these events in Iceland provoked strong reaction in Greenland, the home of the perpetrator, where marches were organised similar to the one that took place in Iceland. Even so, some commentators in Iceland, including Birna's father, saw reason to warn against blame being cast over a whole nation as if a nation was guilty of the crimes of one of its sons. In her interview, Yrsa drew attention to the prevalence of gender-based sexual violence in Greenland and expressed the hope that events in Iceland might serve to inspire action to counter this violence. She said:

> The vigil in Greenland was a show of solidarity and sadness that it was one of their people involved. But the people of Greenland can't be in any way guilty. What they did was more a show of respect and a great feeling of sadness. It was a very beautiful gesture from them ... Let's hope this is a catalyst to something happening about the treatment of women, the crime in Greenland. It would be a small light from a dark tragedy.

The long article in *The Guardian* in which the interview with Yrsa appeared, turns its attention to Greenland at this moment and says:

> In the week before Brjánsdóttir's body was found, three Greenlandic women died in the small eastern town of Tasiilaq, one murdered and two who took their own lives ... Greenland, an autonomous country within the Danish realm ... has extremely high rates of violent crime, sexual abuse and suicide, with figures noticeably worse among the Inuit, who make up a large majority of the 56,000 population.

The paper quotes a Greenlandic journalist, Walter Tunowsky, thus:

> "Alcohol is behind most of the problems", said Walter Tunowsky, the journalist who has covered the Birna story for *Sermitsiaq*, Greenland's main newspaper. "It's the same sort of thing you see among many indigenous people where the culture has almost disappeared within a very short number of years. The violence here is way over the European average, but not this type of killing. Usually the police walk in the door after a murder and

it's solved. I can't remember any unsolved murder cases, and I can't remember any case like Birna's".

Elisabeth Anker (2012) reminds us of the power of melodrama, of how its clear, exaggerated distinctions between victims and villains serve to evoke visceral reactions in its audiences. There are, of course, clear victims in the story of Birna: she and her family and friends. Early on, in the unfolding of the story, a stake was clearly claimed on behalf of 'the Icelandic nation' in that victimhood too. In the account above, this is a victimhood claimed on behalf of Greenland too; both for its women that suffer so horrendously from sexual and gender-based violence, and, implicitly, for its perpetrator who has suffered the violence of seeing his culture effectively annihilated. Early on as the story unfolded in Iceland, who was the villain seemed to become clear too: the Greenlandic trawlerman arrested a few days into the saga, later charged and convicted. But this is a ground that soon starts to shift too as the ground in Greenland. With the confirmation that Birna had been the victim of gender-based, sexual violence, the claim, the identification 'I am Birna' became more prominent. This is a qualitatively different claim from the one that proclaims Birna the daughter of Iceland. While all Iceland can claim kinship to Birna as its daughter, this latter identification is not as open to all in Iceland. Not everyone in Iceland can make the identification with the same legitimacy. Recognising the prevalence of such violence in Greenland could only postpone the realisation for a while that the boundary between victim and villain in Iceland was maybe not as clear and easy to maintain as initially suggested by the reactions. 'I am Birna' turned into an identification more clearly available to women, far more likely as they are than men to suffer gender-based and sexual violence, and not so clearly to the 'nation' as a whole. With that, some of the villainy inevitably fell closer to home than it had previously appeared to do.

Michael Hviid Jacobsen (2016) notes that spectacular death is death that fascinates and draws its audiences near, while allowing them a view from a safe distance. I return to Berlant's (1998:641) hypothesis about sentimental politics:

> When sentimentality meets politics, it uses personal stories to tell of structural effects, but in so doing it risks thwarting its very attempt to perform rhetorically a scene of pain that must be soothed politically. Because the ideology of true feeling cannot admit the nonuniversality of pain, its cases become all jumbled together and the ethical imperative toward social transformation is replaced by a civic-minded but passive ideal of empathy.

When everyone is no longer a victim, some of us are villains, the perpetrators of violence, the political effort to effect change is reduced to a practice of empathy. In the autumn of 2017, the government of Iceland collapsed, bringing about the third elections since 2013. The cause this time was not the unseemly combination of politics and money that had in effect brought down two of the previous three administrations. Rather, over the summer of 2017 when the story of Birna was still very much on people's mind, it surfaced that a number of sex offenders in Iceland had managed to have 'their reputation restored', as it is called, through a legal process. This meant that these offenders were again eligible to take on duties that a criminal conviction might otherwise have prevented them from carrying out: standing for parliament, practising law for example. One of the offenders had been supported in their effort by the father of the then-prime minister, Bjarni Benediktsson, mentioned before, a fact concealed by the minister and his colleague, the minister of justice.

In an article, 'When Mum Dies' that has just appeared in *Stundin*, the author, Þórdís Elva Þorvaldsdóttir, notes that 12 women have been murdered in Iceland since the start of the 21st century.[15] Drawing attention to the violence, the author says: 'Mum was bludgeoned to death with a crowbar, a fire extinguisher. She was knifed, shot with a rifle, strangled with a tie, a string from a hoody, a washing line, a seat belt, bare hands. She was burnt alive'. The point of the piece is, of course, the starkly gendered nature of violence in Iceland, the sharp gender discrepancy in who is a victim and who is a villain. Many of the comments from readers that have appeared since the article was published sidestep the point and make a loud claim to the universality of pain. They suggest a universal victim-hood, in that men too are the victims of violence and that one should *not* make distinctions on the basis of gender when it comes to death.

Conclusion

At the start of this chapter I suggested that the two deaths I described were each spectacular in their different ways. The actual death of the young Georgian man was a spectacle, even as his death then disappeared almost immediately from view. Despite the effort of Guðmundur Andri Thorsson, the death could not be drawn near to people in Iceland. The death provoked a short-term fascination from the distance, but it appears that people in Iceland refused to identify with the young man as an asylum-seeker. No scene of pain was erected, the death lacked the clear sense of a victim and a villain that sustains a melodramatic imagination. The death of the young Icelandic woman was a huge spectacle in the reactions her disappearance, and then death, evoked; in the extensive commentary and reflection that the death provoked. Linking Michael Hviid Jacobsen's notion of 'spectacular death' with Lauren Berlant's work on the 'scene of pain' and Elisabeth Anker's employment of 'melodrama', I conclude now by drawing attention to a further similarity to the two deaths. I do so, I must admit, with a somewhat heavy heart. The two deaths are similar in the very limited long-term impact they have had, beyond the no doubt unbearable pain they have caused those who truly loved – in the complex way of love amongst family and friends – the victims. Expectedly, the death of Nika Begades has not brought about any greater humanity in the way in which the Icelandic authorities handle applications from refugees and asylum-seekers. The reaction locally already suggested that his death was to be seen as his responsibility entirely. Unexpectedly, given the reaction it caused, the death of Birna does not appear to have provoked any lasting awareness of the reality of gender-based sexual violence, as the article from *Stundin* I mentioned above confirms. Individual examples are attributed to the perpetrators as individuals while analyses that draw attention to the very different gender distribution are dismissed with loud claims for the universality of pain. Berlant has already told us where that leads.

As I followed the story of Birna, mostly from afar, there were moments when I thought to myself: it is as if the death of Birna is the best thing to happen to Iceland for a long time. Such was the sense of self-satisfaction I thought I detected at times in people's reflections on their own reactions. I will not deny the dread that accompanied these thoughts: the feeling that in my reactions, I myself was evidently losing my humanity. Still, I hoped to recognise my own complicity here too. The reactions that have become the source of reflection for me were themselves of course only possible because of actual deaths. I do not know what has happened to the family and friends of Nika Begades. But there has been evidence of Birna's family seeking to reclaim her as Birna, as herself, the individual she was, as opposed to the victim of gender-based sexual violence she was in danger of becoming; as opposed to 'the daughter of Iceland', as opposed to the subject, perhaps, of an academic article. While I must hope that there is enough worth in this chapter to warrant the intrusion, I must, of course, admit that my efforts will have a depersonalising effect – that is if they have any effect at all.

Notes

1 Following Icelandic convention, I shall refer to the Icelandic people who appear in this paper by their first name or their full name.
2 A detailed account of the story of Birna's disappearance, the search for her and the reaction to her death in Iceland can be found at the following link, amongst many others: https://www.visir.is/g/2017170209934/stulkan-sem-snerti-streng-i-brjosti -islensku-thjodarinnar. See also: https://edition.cnn.com/2017/02/03/europe/birna -brjansdottir-iceland-murder/index.html and https://www.theguardian.com/world /2017/feb/05/iceland-greenland-unite-in-grief-birna-brjansdottir-murder.
3 See: https://www.visir.is/g/2017170209934/stulkan-sem-snerti-streng-i-brjosti-is lensku-thjodarinnar.
4 See: https://stundin.is/frett/birna-brjansdottir-kvodd-i-hinsta-sinn/.
5 See: https://www.visir.is/g/2017170718805/madur-fell-i-gullfoss https://www.dv.is /frettir/2017/07/20/madurinn-sem-fell-i-gullfoss-sennilega-ekki-ferdamadur/.
6 See: https://icelandmonitor.mbl.is/news/nature_and_travel/2017/07/20/the_man _who_fell_into_gullfoss_an_asylum_seeker/, https://www.mbl.is/frettir/innlent/ 2017/08/15/stadfest_ad_likid_var_af_begadze/.
7 See: https://www.mbl.is/frettir/innlent/2017/08/15/stadfest_ad_likid_var_af_bega dze/.
8 See: https://www.visir.is/g/2017170729547/einhvers-stadar-i-hvita.
9 See: https://edition.cnn.com/2017/02/03/europe/birna-brjansdottir-iceland-m urder/index.html, https://www.visir.is/g/2017170818875/hvarf-birnu-brjansdottur -er-greypt-i-minni-thjodarinnar and https://www.visir.is/g/2017170209934/stulkan-sem-snerti-streng-i-brjosti-islensku -thjodarinnar.

10 See: https://www.dv.is/fokus/2020/1/24/alma-kvedur-satt-thegar-kallid-kemur
-daudinn-ma-ekki-vera-feimnismal/.
11 See: https://www.ruv.is/frett/thad-verdur-aldrei-audvelt-ad-tala-um-hana.
12 See: https://www.theguardian.com/world/2017/feb/05/iceland-greenland-unite-in
-grief-birna-brjansdottir-murder.
13 See: https://www.facebook.com/bjarni.benediktsson.5/posts/935438119926074.
14 How to characterise the collapse – simply financial or economic, or whether a prior
moral, social and political collapse allowed the collapse to happen – and if it should
be understood as simply a manifestation of a global phenomenon or, importantly, of
a local origin, is amongst the key issues of the ongoing debates.
15 See: https://stundin.is/grein/10373/thegar-mamma-deyr/.

References

Anderson, Benedict (1983/1991): *Imagined Communities: Reflections on the Origin and Spread of Nationalism* (Revised edition). London: Verso.

Anker, Elisabeth (2012): 'Left Melodrama'. *Contemporary Political Theory*, 11(2):130–152.

Ariès, Philippe (1974a): 'The Reversal of Death: Changes in Attitudes Toward Death in Western Societies'. In: David E. Stannard (ed.). *Death in America*. Philadelphia, PA: University of Pennsylvania Press, pp. 134–158.

Ariès, Philippe (1974b): *Western Attitudes Toward Death from the Middle Ages to the Present*. London: Marion Boyars.

Ariès, Philippe (1981): *The Hour of Our Death*. London: Allen Lane.

Berlant, Lauren (1998): 'Poor Eliza'. *American Literature*, 70(3):635–668.

Butler, Judith (2004): *Precarious Life: The Powers of Mourning and Violence*. London: Verso.

Butler, Judith (2009): *Frames of War: When Is Life Grievable*. London: Verso.

Christensen, Dorthe R. and Kjetil Sandvik (2014): 'Death Ends a Life, Not a Relationship: Objects as Media on Children's Graves'. In: Dorthe R. Christensen and Kjetil Sandvik (eds.). *Mediating and Re-Mediating Death*. London: Routledge, pp. 251–271.

Gorer, Geoffrey (1965): *Death, Grief, and Mourning in Contemporary Britain*. London: The Cresset Press.

Hertz, Robert (1907/1960): *Death and the Right Hand*. London: Cohen & West.

Jacobsen, Michael Hviid (2016): '"Spectacular Death" – Proposing a New Fifth Phase to Philippe Ariès's Admirable History of Death'. *Humanities*, 5(19):1–20.

Redmalm, David (2015): 'Pet Grief: When Is Non-Human Life Grievable?' *The Sociological Review*, 63(1):19–35.

Scarry, Elaine (2010): *Rule of Law, Misrule of Men*. London: MIT Press.

Seale, Clive (1998): *Constructing Death: The Sociology of Dying and Bereavement*. Cambridge: Cambridge University Press.

Simpson, Michael A. (1987): *Dying, Death and Grief: A Critical Bibliography* (2nd edition). Philadelphia, PA: University of Philadelphia Press.

Walter, Tony (1994): *The Revival of Death*. London: Routledge.

Walter, Tony (2019): 'The Pervasive Dead'. *Mortality*, 24(4):389–404.

9

SPECTACULAR GRIEF

On three main trends in the way we deal with loss in contemporary society

Michael Hviid Jacobsen, Peter Clement Lund and Anders Petersen

Introduction

Not so long ago, it was quite commonplace to describe death and grief as so-called 'tabooed topics' – something to be kept behind closed doors and not to be paraded or put on display in public. According to many prominent researchers of our attitudes towards and practices surrounding death and dying throughout the 20th century, this was the age of forbidden death and hidden grief. For example, Geoffrey Gorer (1965:xxxii) described death as pornographic and the grieving as 'lepers' to be avoided at all cost, Philippe Ariès (1974:92) later observed how following a loss there was an 'obligation to suffer alone and secretly' in modern society, and Norbert Elias (1985/2001:43) noted a peculiar sense of embarrassment among the living when confronted with death and dying. For all practical intents and purposes, death and its eternal companion of grief were regarded as social undesirables and unmentionables that stood in the way of living a happy and unburdened life.

Something quite extraordinary has happened since then. In recent years – in social life, within popular culture and social research – grief has re-surfaced as a topic of much publicity and debate. If the 1990s was the decade of ethics, and the 2000s was the decade of anxiety (in the post-9/11 world), then the 2010s is perhaps the age of grief and memorialisation. Grief is no longer as privatised and socially sequestrated a phenomenon as described above. Rather, grief, in many ways, has become 'the new black', as it were, publicly exposed and even spectacular. In this chapter, we will outline and discuss three main trends of the contemporary rediscovery of grief in what will be called the culture of 'spectacular grief': individualisation/singularisation, professionalisation/commercialisation and memorialisation/mediatisation. Firstly, in an age of marked individualism and an incessant search for personal uniqueness and 'singularity' (Andreas Reckwitz's notion), death and grief increasingly become a personal affront, an attack on the very core of being, that we individually have to deal with. Secondly, following this, processes of professionalisation/commercialisation have meant that grief is also increasingly becoming an 'industry' that is promoted and handled by a variety of interest groups supposed to assist individuals in dealing and coping with death and grief. Thirdly, in a culture of expressivity, grief is now an emotion that we are expected to share with, and show to, others through new commemoration and memorialisation practices, some of which are particularly connected to the rise of new information technologies and social media.

Grief in human and social life

Grief is an integral part of human and social life. It has been there all along. Grief has a history. It changes throughout the course of cultural and social development leading from the past to the present. Grief is an omnipresent human emotion. Even though we are perhaps not grief-struck right now, at this very moment, we are destined to become familiar with the feeling at some point in time. In the lives of individuals, grief will therefore almost inevitably become part of their emotional repertoire whenever they experience loss and lose someone loved. In this way, life is tragedy and pain waiting to happen. In the history of society, grief is also an ever-present phenomenon as social groups and collectivities continually come together to mourn their dead and express their losses (Petersen and Jacobsen 2018). Grief, however, does not stand still. It changes, however slowly and unnoticeably, due to changes in values, norms, beliefs, technology, social organisation and so on. Perhaps grief in and by itself – how it feels to people to grieve their losses – has not changed much throughout human history, and if it has, this is indeed very difficult to determine with any degree of certainty. How people actually felt, deep down inside, in prehistoric times prior to modern ways of monitoring and documenting every possible dimension of social life is impossible to know. Even though we somehow seem to sense that the value of a life was then – when infant mortality rates were sky-high, when average life expectancy was only half of what it is now, and when wars, famines and epidemics in a few years' time would kill large portions of a population – much less than today, we simply cannot know for sure how it actually felt to prehistoric men and women to lose a child, a spouse, a parent or someone they knew. Perhaps their sense of grief was just as strong, perhaps it was much less (as if it makes any sense to quantify grief in this way), perhaps it was just different. But the way grief was, and is, expressed, shared, talked about, displayed and socially sanctioned has undergone some quite significant changes throughout history – and perhaps particularly in recent decades, and these changes we can indeed document and describe in considerable detail as they are evolving and taking place almost before our very eyes.

Humans have always ritualised death. There is no society in which the old and dying have been routinely abandoned to die alone without proper death and mourning rituals (although senicide among Inuit, Japanese, Indian and a few other cultures has in fact been described) or in which dead bodies have been allowed to float in public spaces without proper funerary practices making sure that a sacred division between the living and the dead has been upheld. Throughout the past half-century, many historians, anthropologists, archaeologists and sociologists have documented how our understanding and expression of grief has undergone quite substantial changes throughout human history from the earliest human settlements to contemporary society (see, e.g. Ariès 1981; Jalland 2012; Kellehear 2007; Kerrigan 2007; Stearns 2007; Seebach and Willerslev 2018; Walter 1999). Perhaps most prominently, Philippe Ariès (1974) showed how death attitudes and mourning rites during the past millennium from medieval times to modern society had been transformed from a pinnacle of concern for the dying and the bereaved in the Middle Ages, during the Renaissance and the Romantic Period of the 19th century, but changing to the minimalistic and expedient in many parts of the Western world within the past century. In particular, the transition from the 19th to the 20th century had inaugurated a significant shift from widespread and elaborate mourning rituals to death and grief becoming almost invisible. Peter N. Stearns has documented some of the most pervasive changes in grief's social history throughout the past few centuries (Stearns 2019). According to him, our understanding of, and approach to, grief has shifted quite dramatically throughout the past few centuries from the celebration of expressive grief during the 19th century's Victorian 'cult of the dead' to constraining grief during the 20th century more modernist stance. As he states about the 20th century's approach to grief: the '19th-century culture was virtually turned upside down, concerning both grief itself and the rituals surrounding it' (Stearns 2019:27). Some of the main reasons for this change were the drastic decline in infant mortality, as well as the relocation of dying and death from the home to the hospital, making death a less frequent occurrence in people's everyday experience. According to Stearns, however, the late-20th and early 21st century has witnessed a revival of expressivity and mourning rituals that in many ways reminds us of the 19th century, now, however, stripped of its Victorian formality.

Recently, W.M. Spellman (2015:200–204) followed a similar line of reasoning by arguing that grief has been transformed throughout the past century and that a 'new grief' has emerged. There are many reasons for this recent transformation of grief. Spellman mentions how particularly the physical relocation of the dying (from the home to the hospital), the virtual eradication of infant and child mortality, an ever-increasing lifespan, the lessening role of formal religion and the advance of scientific naturalism have all impacted and substantially altered the way we understand and practice grief. Nowadays, according to Spellman, grief – previously so infused with a shared symbolism and the power of collective meaning-making – has been thoroughly individualised and in large parts made almost publicly invisible:

[W]ith public expressions of grief discouraged in the contemporary West – and even associated with abnormal behaviour – the dynamics of loss have been pressed into the realm of the secretive, a giant camouflage amid dominant, social prescribed behaviours. Older forms of public grieving, however static and ritualistic they appeared to late twentieth-century critics, allowed for intense grief experienced around loss to be assuaged at some level, allowed survivors to communicate their sorrow in a manner that elicited understanding and support within the wider community.

(Spellman 2015:203)

There is indeed much more than a grain of truth in what Spellman here observes. Grief is no longer what it used to be. In fact, grief – just like its eternal partner, death – has been continuously shaped and re-shaped, constructed and deconstructed, by the very people and cultures experiencing and expressing it. The notions of a 'life of one's own' and a 'death of one's own' so prevalent in contemporary society (Beck and Beck-Gernsheim 2002) is thus matched by a 'grief of one's own' encouraging people to find their own ways of expressing, communicating and dealing with grief. No more salvation, meaning or comfort from community or religion – it is now up to the individual to find his or her own pathway when confronted with grief. However, there is also another dimension that Spellman somehow seems to overlook, but which Stearns recognized, namely the fact that grief today is indeed publicly expressed and shared in many new and heretofore unfamiliar ways, not least through the media/social media. So even though grief – together with so many other experiences, emotions and cultural coping strategies – has indeed been increasingly individualised and made a task to be tackled by the grieving person, there is still a demand for communal and collective ways of dealing with the aftermath of death. It is this tension that is the topic of the rest of this chapter.

In the subsequent sections of this chapter, we will try to tease out some defining features and main dimensions of grief in contemporary society as it is influenced and circumscribed by different social processes, trends and tendencies. What we here call 'spectacular grief' is an attempt to name a specific, but complex, type of grief that, as we will show, is experienced, diagnosed, managed, sanctioned, expressed and performed in a way aligning it with some of the major social transformations so characteristic of our current time and age. This age of 'spectacular grief' inaugurates a time when it becomes not only interesting but apparently also opportune (for 'grief researchers', 'grief therapists' and 'grief counsellors') to rediscover, reconceptualise, investigate, appropriate and attempt to monopolise the agenda dealing with the social, emotional, medical and psychological dimensions of grief. Grief, that a few decades ago was regarded as an obscure niche reserved for the few, is now the talk of the town in many scientific circles: research networks, research grants, research centres, research seminars and torrents of scientific literature dealing with many different aspects of grief is being published (Jacobsen and Petersen 2020b:7). It is this emergence of grief as a topic of intense interest that we will explore further in this chapter. In particular, we will in some detail exemplify and discuss how grief is impacted by the processes of individualisation/singularisation, commercialisation/commodification and emerging forms of spontaneous memorialisation and collective expressions of grief, e.g. through the media/social media.

The individualisation and singularisation of grief

It has almost become a truism within sociology to state that the process of individualisation is an identifying feature of contemporary Western society whether it is labelled 'late-modern', 'postmodern', 'liquid-modern' or something else. But how do we conceptualise this process of individualisation? As Norbert Elias (1991) once suggested, in recent centuries the pendulum in the so-called 'We–I balance' has swung from the former towards the latter pole – from the community towards the individual. This is a good way of envisaging the process also known as 'individualisation'. Today, the individual becomes individually responsible not only for life, but also for death and grief – they become tasks to be performed. However, the emotional experience of grief in general as well as in contemporary society can hardly be understood solely as a privatised endeavour that one handles and engages with individually. In fact, there is compelling evidence that suggests the contrary, namely that we should rather conceptualise and comprehend grief as a social phenomenon that is being shaped by historical and cultural forces (see, e.g. Jacobsen and Petersen 2020a). But not only that – as Nina Jakoby (2012) has convincingly argued, grief should in fact be perceived as a 'social emotion'. Without going into any details with her line of thought, it mainly stipulates the perspective that 'the sociology of emotions can enrich and structure the perception of grief as a social emotion' (Jakoby 2012:679), and hence show how grief is emotionally played out in interactions between people. That is not to say, however, that grief is not mentally and bodily installed in the person who grieves and thus has individual expressions. What is emphasised, though, is that grief is, by ways of articulations, scripts, norms and management, a social manifestation as such. However, sometimes even the best of arguments has to bow its head for (overly) psychologised perceptions of grief and even for reality. When it comes to the former, a new article – dedicated to examining the functions of grief – can be used as an example of such an individualised understanding of grief. It suggests that grief, when addressed biologically and psychologically (in either case, as something pertaining to the individual), should be fathomed as something

> associated with an increase in epinephrine. The heart rate increases, blood pressure increases, and breathing becomes deeper and more erratic. The most characteristic symptom of grief is weeping. In its full-blown expression, weeping entails a flushed face, nasal congestion, constricted pharynx, punctuated exhaling, vocalised wailing, and the shedding of tears.

Pharyngeal constriction is typically described as either 'a lump in one's throat' or feeling 'choked up'.

(Huron 2018:61–62)

Besides the fact that this description of grief is so sterile that it, oddly enough, seems to lack any connection with a feeling or a human being of flesh and blood, it is worthwhile noticing that grief is referred to as having specific individual symptoms.[1] Thereby grief is inscribed – as we shall touch upon later – in a medical vocabulary, thus following a medical model that focuses on making distinct demarcations between different symptoms in order to define human traits as thoroughly as possible – and with the intention, of course, to be able to handle any symptoms that might have gone awry. What we are referring to here as 'individualisation' is the fact that grief has increasingly been colonised by psychiatric logics, hence favouring a medical understanding of the emotion in question (see Jacobsen and Petersen 2020a) that increasingly makes grief pathological and provides the foundation for a regime based on the demand for 'recovery' (Pearce 2019).

What is of importance here, however, is the fact that the individualisation of grief not only follows a medical logic, it also relates to a societal ditto. That is, by understanding grief as an individual phenomenon, with individual symptoms that have to be dealt with individually, grief is deeply embedded in the overall individualisation of society as such. As mentioned above, sociologically speaking, the concept of individualisation takes on many different connotations, shapes and forms. There is, however, a common understanding that the concept addresses the emancipation from traditionally and religiously anchored norms and rules that each individual – in premodern society – had to adhere to (Giddens 1991). In our epoch, individuals have been freed from traditional ties and set free in order to create their own life trajectories. Or, perhaps we should rather say that individuals in contemporary society have no choice but to be free and hence individualised. As Zygmunt Bauman has stated, we are witnessing a process of relentless individualisation that – irresistibly – creates a 'society of individuals' (Bauman 2001:9) in which each member is responsible for writing their own (successful) biography and hence is also responsible for failures to do so. The choice of becoming individualised is in fact not a choice at all, as Ulrich Beck has stated by referring to the process of relentless individualisation as being institutionalised (Beck and Beck-Gernsheim 2002). Crudely speaking, then, society as such is becoming individualised, and that goes for the phenomenon of grief as well. Evidence suggests that grief is discursively, normatively and socially articulated as an individual undertaking. Perhaps Paul C. Rosenblatt has described this in the most thought-provoking manner when entitling one of his articles 'Grieving While Driving' (Rosenblatt 2004). Besides referring to the basic convenience of grieving while driving, as this is almost the only time available for solemn contemplation in our society, Rosenblatt also addresses the individual endeavour of practicing one's grief and how this is made practically possible whilst driving one's car alone. In fact, what Rosenblatt argues is that the time reserved for grieving is societally limited in contemporary Western societies, requiring that one needs a private space to grief. Now, this development is by no means one-sided. Counter-developments are currently taking place and social understandings of grief are being forcefully voiced, hereby criticizing the individualistic logic of grief while advocating for its social components (see, e.g. Jacobsen and Petersen 2020c). In what follows, however, we will continue this line of thought and examine whether the ongoing individualisation of grief has paved the way for new forms of experiencing and practising grief.

There are, of course, many different paths to follow when trying to undertake the endeavour of making death and grief socially meaningful. What we intend to do is to follow a theoretical lead provided by Andreas Reckwitz. In his latest book, *The Society of Singularities* (2020), he has provided us with important analytical insights that we are able to apply in relation to the phenomenon of grief. As Peter Wagner, one of the social theorists Reckwitz is theoretically indebted to, writes in his review of the book, it 'aims to capture the recent "structural change of modernity" and proposes the concept of "singularity" as the key to understanding our current socio-cultural constellation' (Wagner 2018:525). Singularity, then, is used as the prism through which we are able to analyse some overall structural trends and transformations, but also fine-grained micro-dimensions of everyday life in contemporary society. In that respect the term covers a broad range of societal dimensions – in fact, it offers what has been termed a most welcome diagnosis of the times (Carleheden and Petersen 2019).

What is of utmost importance here is that Reckwitz does not argue that the concept of singularity should be understood as a new form of individualisation – or at least not in the sense of the term, in which social, cultural and inter-human emancipation in itself is neither stipulated nor normatively desired. Rather, his theory on singularity is all about new forms of social practice and social interaction, thus describing a new form of sociality. In fact, one could argue, following Beck's argument above, that Reckwitz offers a theory about an institutionalised phenomenon that has been societally embedded to such a degree that each member of society is expected to follow its social logic. This entails, Reckwitz argues, that each individual[2] is required to strive for the singular – the unique, authentic and original – in all spheres of life. What is more, every individual is being socially valorised for their singularity, Reckwitz claims, hereby specifying the fact that singularity is not an inner mental process, but a social one; one needs the social recognition of others for one's singularity, otherwise it cannot be valorised. This process is volatile and contingent, meaning that one cannot expect to achieve social valorisation for one's singularity. One has to struggle for it. How can we relate this to the practice of grief? Well, it seems possible in two ways.

Firstly, a tendency to practise one's grief in a personalised manner has occurred within the last couple of decades. One example is the fact that more and more people are getting so-called 'grief-tattoos'. That is, people who have lost a partner, a parent or, more commonly, a child, are having tattoos made in honour and memory of the deceased. These tattoos can take many shapes and forms, but the important aspect about them is that they are ingrained into the body, hereby giving the sensation that the deceased is still a part of them. Some even mix the ink used for the tattoo with ashes of the cremated deceased. These tattoos are unique, deeply personal and original. Even though others may also have a tattoo made to commemorate their deceased loved ones, no-one else in the entire world has a tattoo just like theirs. The overall aim of this grief practice is to commemorate the deceased and to help the parents to cope with their grief, but also to show others that their dead child indeed *did* exist and that she or he will be remembered (Jensen 2015). Hence, the tattoo also functions as a visualisation of the existence of the deceased, and hereby a social indication of the strong relationship between the dead and the one getting the tattoo.

Another example of the current singularisation of grief worth mentioning is the proliferation of so-called 'grief-art' that we have witnessed particularly in recent decades. More specifically, we are thinking about the bourgeoning rates of grief literature and grief music that have emerged as well as the many other areas in which the experiences of death and grief are used and expressed within contemporary popular cultural (see, e.g. Teodorescu and Jacobsen 2020). Just to mention one example, Danish singer Søren Huss, who lost his girlfriend in a tragic car-accident in 2007, released the album *Troen og Ingen* (*Belief and No One*) in 2010 as part of his grieving process. The songs on the album, all deeply personal when engaging with the loss of his girlfriend – and the mother of his daughter – could not have been contemplated or written by anyone else but him. They are his personal testimony and the expression of his particular relationship with his girlfriend, and hence with his particular and unique experience of grief. But the songs are also intended for a public audience. In fact, the album quite quickly became a huge success, enabling Søren Huss to go on a tour of Denmark performing his material. Now, in that respect the utter unique manifestation of grief becomes socially visible and proliferated.

Both these examples of 'grief tattoos' and 'grief art', and several others that could have been mentioned, can be analysed by using the aforementioned vocabulary provided by Reckwitz. These forms of grief practices and grief displays follow the logic of singularity, as the bereaved are engaging in their grief in a personalised and authentic manner and achieving social valorisation for their endeavours. In relation to the latter, it makes no difference whether the audience is small or large. What matters is the social valorisation of the unique manifestation. This singularisation of grief is also relatable to one of the central points in Reckwitz's theory, namely that the emergence of the singular entails what he refers to as a 'crisis of the common' (Reckwitz 2020:375). That is, the social logic of singularity has been made societally possible by – or grows out of – a reduction in commonly shared logics and norms. Crudely speaking, in contemporary society we seem to have lost sight of all that, which cannot be framed within individual standards. The question is whether this is also true about grief? Well, it seems fair to say that the hitherto shared traditional and cultural ways of adapting to loss and hence practising grief have been toned down immensely, but all the while, new singularised grief practices have appeared. This has, some argue, left somewhat of a social vacuum when it comes to societally shared grief practices (see, e.g., Petersen and Jacobsen 2018). It also seems fair to say that this has led to a potential proliferation of grief practices that, arguably, lack the transparent nature of that which is commonly shared, hereby – some might argue – altering the social significance of grief. In this way, singularisation, in many ways, perhaps inaugurates a new form of individualisation of grief?

The professionalisation and commercialisation of grief

One of the main social processes underpinning this individualisation and singularisation of grief is – perhaps paradoxically – the increasing professionalisation (and not least, medicalisation) of death and grief. It is Reckwitz's contention that singularisation is not simply equivalent to an understanding of individualisation as emancipation from traditional norms and practices, but that it in itself amounts to a new form of sociality in contemporary society that, for example, is embedded within new institutionalised practices. The process of professionalisation of grief is – to a great extent – evident in its entry into the domain of psychiatry. In our current climate, it may seem odd to conceptualise grief as anything other than a psychological phenomenon – one that resides *within* the individual and one that is to be dealt with and handled through the professional help of therapists, psychologists or psychiatrists. However, as we have already discussed in relation to the individualisation of grief above, this is not a given – in fact, it is a much more recent way of viewing grief. For example, Leeat Granek (2010) argues in her work that a transformation of grief have taken place from a *natural kind* into a *psychological kind*, i.e. that grief has been transformed from something that has always existed and is a normal and innate part of human life into an object to be studied scientifically by the field of psychology. As Granek shows, this process has been underway throughout the entirety of the 20th century, and the current conceptualisation – and also pathologisation – of grief is both a product of pivotal tendencies within grief research and in contradiction with – for example – Sigmund Freud's groundbreaking work (Granek 2010:66). Hence, the conception of grief as a form of psychological problem that is to be treated and studied is a relatively recent invention. One might even suggest (echoing Michel Foucault's work on sexuality) that we have gradually but relentlessly moved from an ancient *ars lugendi* (the art of grieving) to a more recent and modern *scientia luctus* (the scientific study and scrutiny of bereavement).

One part of this shift stems – as Granek also notices – from what might be called the inherent rationalising tendency of modernity. In his thought-provoking book on the social and cultural importance of death, Zygmunt Bauman directed attention to this rationalising tendency in our relationship to death and how this has given death its own sequestered position in society (Bauman 1992:152). In his historical testimony of changes in 'death mentalities' in the

Western world, Philippe Ariès (1974) pointed out how death had been increasingly professionalised throughout the past century and stated that 'the manipulation of the dead became a profession' (Ariès 1974:97). This development was also detailed in Brian Parsons's (2018) recent research on the transition of the funeral trade from 'undertakers' to 'funeral directors'. A similar development has happened to the management of grief and it has also been given its own specialists and experts that can help alleviate the pain of loss and help individuals to cope with it. The so-called 'doctors of grief' that Ariès (1974:99) mentioned many years ago have now grown in numbers. As pointed out in the Introduction to this book, one of the facets of the age of spectacular death is that the sequestration of death – and, by extension, also of grief – has changed. This means that the movement of grief into the realm of psychiatry and psychology makes grief something to be viewed within a scientific and treatment-based context and as something increasingly to be handled by professionals. It is no longer an emotion that is to be dealt with, alleviated or handled by an individual's family or close relations – instead it is to be managed by people with formal educational credentials obtained through professional training programs. In a Danish context this development can be seen in the growing amount of grief support groups that exist all over the country, that all have different forms of organisation and which are led by volunteers with either personal experience, people with different forms of grief education and sometimes also psychologists. For example, a quick look at the Danish *Sorgvejviser* (*Grief Guide*) shows that there are now around 500 groups registered on this webpage alone (Sorgvejviser 2017). Concurrently with this, the amount of different grief education programmes in Denmark has also grown substantially during recent years and it is now possible to attend classes, courses and diploma programmes in which you learn how to handle or take care of bereaved individuals. What is interesting in this trend is of course the sheer amount of different educational programs, but also what they offer, how they offer it, the 'ideology of grief' on which they rest and not least the financial aspect involved in the different programs.

As noted, grief (not as a normal human response to loss, but as a potential psychological disorder) has now entered the world of psychiatry, and the ICD-11 contains the diagnostic classification of *Prolonged Grief Disorder* (World Health Organization 2018). In Denmark, as well as elsewhere, this means that national clinical guidelines must be developed and implemented as well. However, before this has even been completed, many of the aforementioned grief educations are already focusing on how to differentiate between what they call 'natural grief' and 'complicated grief' reactions. This means that a market has been created to teach everything from nurses and medical doctors to morticians, psychologists, social workers and anyone else with a professional (and/or personal) interest in grief about how to simultaneously help people who have lost a loved one and to be attentive to whether they are suffering from a disorder that has not yet been fully implemented. This market situation means that different (and often competing and conflicting) conceptualisations of grief now exist in Denmark and that there are substantial financial factors at play when it comes to defining what a pathological or a normal grief reaction consists of, what types of research initiatives to support and how to treat pathological grief. The consequence of this is that grief counselling is now a costly affair for individuals and the advertising for different educations promises everything from knowledge about the diagnosis of Prolonged Grief Disorder (PGD) to making the participants better equipped to handle life with grief. This again leads to a myriad of different – and competing – ways of conceptualising, diagnosing and treating grief. Why is this important? Well, since there is still debate as to which form of pathological grief is actually real or supported by evidence (Brinkmann 2017), i.e. what is the best way to define certain aspects of bereavement as pathological, there are also different conceptions of how to treat, help and handle bereaved individuals among the different forms of education programs. And these differences are competing for the right to define what is normal and what is pathological grief, what nomenclature to use and how to measure it most precisely (see, e.g. Larsen, Lauritzen and O'Connor 2018; Maciejewski et al. 2016; Maciejewski and Prigerson 2017). We would argue that this could be seen as what Peter Conrad (2005, 2007) has called 'an engine of medicalisation' – the drive towards seeing ever more parts of human life as treatable medical problems. These different ways of understanding grief could, over time, chip away at the diversity of grief reactions and deem an increasing number of otherwise unproblematic grief reactions unhealthy or abnormal. As Kurt Danziger (2003) has pointed out, the new inventions and changing conceptions of different psychiatric categories is not so much a tale of scientific progress as it is a less progressive story of social interests and everyday practices. This is why these differing views on grief are all competing for the definitional rights to grief – the one who gets to decide what is abnormal and pathological also gets to decide how to treat it and what not to treat.

This professionalisation and medicalisation of grief (as two intimately intertwined processes) has also been analysed by Julia Bandini (2015) in her discussion of the bereavement exclusion (BE) in the DSM-5, and she points to three possible consequences: overdiagnosis and overtreatment, an expanding market for pharmaceutical companies to advertise and sell to, and a more general loss of traditional and cultural ways of grieving. While the diagnosis has not yet been formally implemented in Denmark, we may still discuss some of these aspects regarding the professionalisation and medicalisation and concomitant commercialisation of grief. It is not difficult to imagine that the number of people who will be diagnosed with some sort of grief disorder will see a massive rise when the PGD is finally implemented, simply because there is no certainty as to how many may in fact suffer from it. Thus, the assumed percentage varies considerably and the most recent systematic review and meta-analysis finds that around 10% of all bereaved may fit the diagnostic classification (Lundorff et al. 2017). Moreover, the results from this review point to the large degree of heterogeneity in the samples and the poor representativeness of the collected research, so the results must necessarily be taken with caution. This means that we have no 'real' sense of how many individuals may suffer and the way in which the diagnosis is implemented will then have massive implications concerning the number of individuals who will end up being diagnosed. Overmedicalisation and over-treatment then becomes a real problem. Secondly, while there – at the time of writing this – is still no available drug-treatment for PGD, in time there may be. Nonetheless, though there is no specific drug-treatment, there could be many different forms of therapeutic treatment and which one is the most beneficial is currently being researched (see, e.g. Bryant et al. 2014; Jordan and Litz 2014; Maccallum and Bryant 2013; Rosner et al. 2014; Wittouck et al. 2011). This is also turning into a competition, an engine driving this process of professionalisa-tion, since what is at stake here is the power to define how to treat the proposed 10% of bereaved individuals and 'sell' these treatments to a substantial market. Lastly, there can be little surprise as to how this diagnosis has major implications concerning our traditional and cultural ways of grieving. It may be seen as a form of disciplining of individuals who do not fall in line with normative standards of either society at large or within familial contexts (Walter 2005) or it may be understood as a process that has changed our way of talking about and under-standing human suffering (Brinkmann 2014). One consequence of implement-ing a diagnosis that has been discussed by Ester Holte Kofod (2015) is that it may come to constitute a normative ideal for individuals, meaning that the diagnosis becomes a sort of benchmark for how much you loved someone – the notion here being that if you do not become 'sick from grief', this must mean that you did not love the deceased enough.

The contemporary professionalisation and commercialisation of grief is also recognisable in other areas of society that go beyond the specific education of individuals who work with the bereaved. This part of what we would like to call 'spectacular grief' refers to what Geoffrey Gorer (1955) more than half a century ago brought attention to when he described the so-called 'pornography of death'. It was Gorer's contention that when death and grief with the advent of modern society increasingly had become privatised experiences, the phenomenon of grief has become equivalent to something like masturbation in earlier society – death and sex had changed places and thus grief was now something one did alone and almost shamefully. This repression of death and grief has, however, not removed the need for or interest in either – instead these topics have now become porno-graphic. This means that in the age of spectacular death, the old saying that 'sex sells' has now been supplemented by the notion that 'grief sells'. It now seems that everywhere one looks there exists an acute interest in grief and that this interest can be capitalised upon. In this way, grief is nowadays increasingly com-mercialised and commodified (Walter 2020:52–66). The aforementioned grief counsellor/grief supervisor programmes are but one example of this. They are educational programmes that compete with each other for participants and the price of admission can be steep. Simultaneously, there is a constant production of documentaries, autobiographical books, movies, theatre productions, music and so forth that all – directly or indirectly – deal with topic of grief. This is, at first glance, not a problematic development, but there are certain aspects of this trend that requires sociological inquiry and critique. It is surely beneficial (not least for the grieving) that grief and death break free from their previous status as taboo subjects and can now be discussed more openly. However, this transformation has seemingly not made individual or personal grief any easier, as has also been discussed elsewhere (Jacobsen 2016). If one looks at Denmark, the availability of infotainment/entertainment-based outlets for grief has not necessarily made death and grief any easier to cope with – people still struggle with their grief and a quick look at the current debate also reveals this (see e.g. Kamp 2018; Knudsen 2016; Sørensen 2017). The notion that grief sells may prove accurate, because we are so interested in seeing the spectacular or even singular grief of others, not least since we seem to lack the sense of, and experience with, how to deal with our own grief. This commercialisation of grief thus offers an outlet for something we lack in our everyday lives and thereby we come to experience grief as a vicarious emotion (Stearns 1994), since there is no other place for us to properly engage with grief. As Norbert Elias (1985/2001) pointed out in his important work on death in modern society, it is a lonely endeavour precisely because we lack the language and an emotional repertoire to engage with the dying. Perhaps we also lack the language and cultural norms to handle grief. This is what enables and provides an engine for a market for grief to be sold as a commodity where individuals – from a safe distance – can experience, vicariously, the grief of others.

The memorialisation and mediatisation of grief

Grief has not only been individualised/singularised and professionalised/commercialised with the coming of the age of 'spectacular grief'. There is also no doubt that the sight of death that was all-too-familiar to our ancestors as a first-hand experience has now increasingly become something primarily to be observed from afar through the screens of televisions, computers and mobile phones. In many ways, we have lost touch with death – and with it, perhaps also with grief. Simultaneously, modern society was bent on doing away with many of the (mostly religious) traditions and rituals associated with death and grief as part of its 'de-traditionalisation' of society (Giddens 1991). Although it seems as if this strategy was successful for some time, a new demand for the memorialisation of death and grief has risen in recent decades and traditions, rituals and practices that were seemingly dead and buried are now reappearing alongside new inventions as means to help people deal more meaningfully with death and grief. In this section, we will briefly look into how grief in contemporary society is becoming memorialised and mediatised and some examples will illustrate these tendencies.

Throughout human history, and across cultural boundaries, the living have always ritualised, mourned and celebrated their dead. Some of the reasons for such ritualisations have been a need to express intense feelings of sorrow, shock, sadness and loss, or desires to making the life that disappeared meaningful and memorable, whereas other reasons stem from a sense of guilt or shame, and yet others from a fear that the dead might return and haunt the living. No matter the specific reason, ritualisations, commemorations and celebrations of the dead is a constitutional part of all known cultures. The ways we memorialise our dead, however, do not stand still, but change throughout time. Looking at how our ancestors mourned their dead, it was in many ways quite similar to, but also different from, the way we do it nowadays. As C. Wright Mills (1940:910) once observed, our so-called 'vocabularies of motive' (the purpose and meaning with which we imbue our actions) have in modern society to a large degree changed from religious motivation to a much more rational and secular sort of motivation. This also means that our emotional and practical orientation changes. As Reinhart Koselleck (2002) has also shown, we have witnessed a secularisation of memorial practice throughout modern times from religiously to increasingly politically instigated and inspired memorials. Even though (or perhaps even because) the 20th century seemingly attempted to reduce the sting of death and grief on social life, a new tendency during the latter part of the 20th and the early 21st century has seen the light of day: a wish for retrieving the time-honoured rituals and practices that were abandoned throughout the 20th century and to invent new and more personally meaningful ways of dealing with death and grief. As mentioned, mankind has always needed to commemorate the dead, and death rituals are one of the key ways in which human beings seek to remember the dead and make sense of things after a death. Even though our present-day society is often described as de-ritualised and purged of tradition, there is much to suggest that the rituals are far from dying out. Rituals associated with death and grief not only remain significant and meaningful today, they are also continually reinvented and readjusted to fit the current age. In fact, there are those who claim that our present-day society is very much engaged in inventing and creating a wide range of new commemorative rituals that also touch upon and affect the overall memorial tradition. This is what Erika Doss (2010) has dubbed 'memorial mania' – the demand for new collective rites, ceremonies and memorials to make death and tragedy meaningful. There have been many different reasons for the recent rise in this memorial mania: terrorist attacks, school shootings, natural disasters and so on. So besides the more official ways of memorialising the dead – as those conducted by the state, church or other official agencies – there has been a keen interest in more unofficial and less 'top-bottom' types of memorialisation often described with notions such as: 'home-grown rituals', 'emerging rituals', 'secular rituals', 'do-it-yourself rituals', 'nascent rituals' or 'organic rituals' (see, e.g. Grimes 1982; Moore and Myerhoff 1977; Jacobsen 2015). What is the purpose of these new forms of memorialisation? In many ways, they serve the same function as earlier forms, but now under new social conditions – for example, described above by the processes of individualisation/singularisation and professionalisation/commercialisation. They want to make death personally meaningful to the individual but themselves also, in time, often end up becoming engines for more formalised and commercialised forms of expression.

For centuries, the public display of collective mourning was almost exclusively reserved for royalties and national heroes – for those who had served the public in one way or the other, either as part of the power elite or through deeds that would make the public forever indebted to their memory. Hence kings, queens, the nobility, war heroes, scribes and others from the top layers of society would be first in line to have permanent memorials erected in their honour or to have processions and marches held in their memory, thereby imbuing their lives with some sort of collective remembrance and symbolic immortality. Today, we are experiencing a sort of democratisation of this privilege, even though it is still primarily reserved for royalties, celebrities or the uber-wealthy to have their names mentioned in the history books, on street signs or as beneficiary names for sports stadiums, airports, shopping malls, hospitals and the like. Despite this, we have seen the rise of a seemingly new type of memorials and memorialisation that celebrate or mourn not only the lives of the rich and famous, but also the lives and deaths of ordinary people. This new type of mourning and memorial practice is often described as 'spontaneous memorialisation' and its concomitant physical gatherings of various memorial artefacts as 'spontaneous shrines'. One of the first scholars to take an explicit interest in the phenomenon of spontaneous memorialisation in a more substantial sociological or folkloric context was Konrad Köstlin (1992), who specifically described those memorials to the dead (*Totengedenken*) that might occasionally be observed in connections with deaths on German roads: small gathering of objects infused with an almost sanctified expression – candles, crucifixes etc. – demonstrating that a person had lost his or her life on the road here. Spontaneous memorialisation/memorials have also since been captured by differing word use: 'impromptu memorials', 'roadside memorials', 'temporary memorials', 'public memorials', 'grassroots memorials', 'folk memorials' and so on (with the suffix or extension of '-isation' in order to capture the commemorative and ritual activities surrounding the memorials, which are, as mentioned, at times also referred to as 'shrines') (see, e.g. Doss 2008; Margry and Sánchez-Carretero 2011; Reid 2003; Santino 2006, 2019).

It is difficult to provide any exact date for the rise of spontaneous memorials – perhaps they have been there for a long time, and some even date them back to ancient practices of tying snippets of coloured ribbon on a tree branch or placing flowers at the roadside where someone had been killed. However, there is an impression among many scholars (not least evident in the increasing number of published studies) that spontaneous memorialisation has become a much more visible phenomenon throughout many parts of the world, particularly during the past few decades. The mourning after the Hillsborough tragedy in 1989 when Liverpool supporters were trampled to death is sometimes regarded as one of the first major incidents (not least because of live television coverage) sparking widespread public participation. Others mention the extensive mourning proceedings after Princess Diana's death in a car crash in Paris in 1997 as the time when the practices of placing thousands of flower bouquets, lighting candles, strangers meeting for commemorative ceremonies and extensive media coverage of the grief following the dramatic death of a celebrity reached its epitome. Prior to Princess Diana's death and the Hillsborough tragedy, however, there were similar kinds of collective rites of mourning as when the deaths of John F. Kennedy, Elvis, John Lennon and Olof Palme were mourned, and later we have seen similar expressions of almost global proportions with the premature deaths of Michael Jackson, George Michael, David Bowie and Prince.

Leaving aside the specific dating of the rise of such memorial practices, spontaneous memorialisation is today part of the way in which death is mourned and the way in which grief is displayed. This is particularly the case when members of the 'media class' such as performers, sports players and public figures die (and especially if they die young, unexpectedly or under tragic circumstances), but it is also the case when ordinary people are murdered in public spaces, when terrorist attacks result in fatalities, when natural disasters strike or when someone dies from an accident. Were these practices only reserved for those already widely known to the public, there would be nothing new to report. The interesting thing, however, is that we may also – and much more frequently – see this practice (obviously at a significantly smaller scale) when quite ordinary people die, for example, in traffic accidents or fall victim to indiscriminate street violence. Such events – disasters, assaults and accidents causing death to individuals or groups – seem to warrant collective attempts to find meaning and to express grief in public (see, e.g. Brennan 2008). There are many different dimensions of, and variations within, the phenomenon of spontaneous memorialisation – too many to mention here – but a common thread seems to be that grief is not reserved for the family and friends of the deceased and that there is a certain ritual inventiveness involved (see, e.g. Haney, Leimer and Lowery 1997).[3] There are many different reasons why people come together and engage in spontaneous memorialisation, such as meaning-making, memory preservation, emotional sharing or moral indignation and political protest (Senie 2006) that constitute some of the main reason why people who are mostly strangers come together and collectively mourn the death of someone often unknown to them. This is no longer a private event only for the immediate family of the deceased, but an open community that takes its memorial practices into the public realm. The mourning of death that was previously removed to those 'other places', which Michel Foucault (1986) memorably called 'heterotopias', such as the cemetery, are now being performed in public. Spontaneous memorialisation/shrines at times seem to become less spontaneous and more planned and choreographed. Today, what was previously a relatively seldom sight has become convention. Take as an example how football players now show a minute of silence prior to many games throughout the season in order to commemorate someone recently deceased or the victim(s) of tragic events, even when the death(s) mourned have nothing to do with the game of football as such.[4] Moreover, just as official memorials such as the Memorial to the Murdered Jews of Europe located in Berlin or the Ground Zero memorial in Manhattan (Brescó and Wagoner 2019), spontaneous and temporary memorials may also in time come to serve as more permanent sites for collective remembering and mourning, for example, when memorial plaques are placed or permanent instalments are erected at the site of what was first merely a spontaneous shrine. The initially ephemeral becomes permanent and the spontaneous becomes solidified in memorial installations (on this so-called 'heritagisation', see Milosevic 2018).

Two recent Danish cases may serve to illustrate how spontaneous memori-alisation has nowadays become an almost expected response to unimaginable or unexpected death, particularly whenever someone known to the general pub-lic – often referred to as a 'celebrity' – dies and leaves an emotional void not only for their families and friends, but also for their fans. Denmark lost two significant public figures in the autumn of 2018 and the spring of 2019 – Kim Larsen and Morten Lindberg (a.k.a. Master Fatman). Kim Larsen, former front-man of the Danish rock band Gasolin from the 1970s and often described as a 'national troubadour', passed away on 30 September 2018 at the age of 72 after a short battle with prostatic cancer. His last public performance was at the Skanderborg Festival six weeks prior to his death. Morten Lindberg, popularly known as Master Fatman (due to his impressive weight), died suddenly of cardiac arrest on 26 March 2019 at the age of 53. Master Fatman was widely known in Denmark for his 'cosmic love' philosophy, and was a regular radio host, televi-sion celebrity, film maker, DJ and singer. Without any comparison between Kim Larsen and Master Fatman – the former had, after all, been around for a life-time and had produced the soundtrack to many people's lives (songs for student parties, weddings, anniversaries and funerals) – their deaths were subsequently marked by widespread public mourning and memorialisation. In both cases, col-lective rituals were performed bearing witness to the spectacularity of publicly expressed grief in contemporary society. The mourning practices were extensive and elaborate. In the case of Kim Larsen, a memorial walk was organised with approximately 30,000 participants singing his famous songs and carrying torches throughout the streets of Copenhagen, spontaneous memorials were constructed at Christiania (the experimental 'self-governing quarter' of Copenhagen) as well as outside his local bar in Odense, a memorial concert at the central square of the capital city was held, etc. In the case of Master Fatman, there was a memorial march with samba music, colourful costumes, dancing, happenings and a bicycle hearse took his coffin through the most iconic street of Strøget in the centre of Copenhagen. In both cases, in the days following the deaths of Kim Larsen and Master Fatman, thousands of lamenting comments and RIPs were posted on various social media sites and the media covered their deaths with commemora-tive programs, reruns of old television shows and live reportage from the memo-rial walks and the memorial concerts.

The memorialisation of the deaths of Kim Larsen and Master Fatman (but also the spontaneous memorialisation in connection to the unknown victims of accidents and violent crime, as well as people who have died more expectedly and peacefully) thus bears witness to how spectacular grief is today also closely connected to mediatisation – the fact that our experience of death and grief is now increasingly mediated and mediatised (Jacobsen 2016). There are many different 'deathscapes' (Maddrell and Sidaway 2010) in our society – places devoted to the commemoration, worshipping, remembrance and mourning of death and the dead. Some of these places/spaces are relatively fixed and solid, such as the cemetery with its gravestones or official monuments and memorials, whereas others are more fluctuating and less permanent, such as the spontaneous memorial sites or the mourning practices and grief displays on the internet. Within the past two–three decades, the media/social media have become new places of mourning that supplement and at times even replace the more conventional face-to-face types of ritual, gesture and conversation known in previous times. On the internet, one will find new ways of expressing grief and compassion, of creating virtual memorials and of sharing the often difficult emotions involved in the loss of loved ones (see, e.g. Döveling and Giaxoglou 2018; Kakar and Oberoi 2016; Sumiala 2014). This goes for mourning the deaths of, and providing condolences to, family and friends, but it is also evident in the mediatisation of celebrity and public deaths (see, e.g. Burgess, Mitchell and Münch 2018). In this way, the mediatisation of mourning rituals and memorial practices in contemporary society makes it pertinent that the thesis of forbidden, privatised and individualised grief so prominent among scholars writing throughout the 20th century needs updating and re-focusing in order to capture the situation in the 21st century. These practices of spontaneous memorialisation – either in public places or on the internet – fit well with what Zygmunt Bauman (2000) has termed 'liquid modernity', in which the solid, stable, static and stationary has gradually given way to the liquid, unstable, changing and fluid. However, the practices – even though they are at times customised and personalised to fit individual needs and demands – seem to be at odds with the individualisation that Bauman saw as a sign of the times and instead they inaugurate a new search for community in death and grief.

Conclusion

In this chapter, we have tried to present some contours of what has been described as 'spectacular grief'. Obviously, the contemporary culture of grief (just like its companion culture of death) is much more complex and multi-faceted than can be captured by one simple catchy phrase. There are indeed many criss-crossings, zig-zaggings, trans-versings and counter-currents that make it difficult to definitively assign one all-encompassing, or in and of itself adequate, label to our current conceptualisation of, and relationship to, grief.

Having said that, however, this chapter has provided a delineation and discussion of three main trends in the way in which contemporary society deals with death and grief. Before we ventured into this, we sought to describe how grief is an historically and culturally contingent phenomenon. Though we may not know if, or to what degree, the individual emotional experience of grief has changed through time, we can – with a large degree of certainty – say that the ways in which grief is expressed, controlled and culturally mediated have changed. Then we turned to the three main trends. Firstly, we directed focus on the fact that one aspect of these changes has been the individualisation of grief and its annexation by psychiatric logic. Looking at these developments through the theoretical lens of Andreas Reckwitz's perspective, we exemplified how things like grief tattoos and grief literature can be seen as manifestations of the social logic of singularisation. These unique experiences are valorised precisely because they are singular, exceptional or deeply personal. Secondly, we discussed how this individualisation and singularisation of grief has occurred simultaneously with an increasing professionalisation and commercialisation of grief. We showed how, since grief is increasingly regarded as an individual matter, it is also a matter that is aided by a rising number of grief professionals. These professionals participate in the growing industry of grief education and are all fighting for both their own share of the market and the right to define what is 'normal' and 'abnormal' grief and how to treat them both. This professionalisation is intertwined with commercialisation since both the educational and entertainment aspects of grief are now for sale; grief sells, as we put it. Finally, we examined how memorialisation has been transformed from something reserved for royalty and national heroes into something we also practice for ordinary individuals – in this way, our lives and deaths are increasingly regarded as something unique. This development is closely connected to the individualisation and commercialisation of grief, since secular individuals attempt to make death and grief meaningful, but unwittingly become part of the industry of grief. As highlighted, we have seen a rise in what are called 'spontaneous memorials' and exemplified this – and also the rising mediatisation of grief – by looking at the deaths of Kim Larsen and Master Fatman and the public reaction and by seeing them as manifestations of spectacular grief.

Through the description, illustration and discussion of these three trends, the chapter has provided parts of a much more comprehensive and complex roadmap by showing some of the main routes through which our understanding and practice of grief has moved in recent decades. Obviously, the chapter has not provided a full roadmap of the myriad of minor and winding roads, shortcuts or detours that are also available and at times even used, but it has attempted to show that grief – like any other human emotion – is not immune to the pushes and pulls from social and cultural forces that make grief so much more than merely the private emotional property of the individual.

Notes

1 In all fairness, David Huron does mention the possibility that grief can be a cultural phenomenon (Huron 2018:63). However, in the vast majority of the article, he argues in favour of perceiving grief as an individual feeling with individual symptoms.

2 What Andreas Reckwitz describes does not only cover the duty of the individual to be singular, but also how this goes for cities, companies, societies etc.
3 There is now an attempt to document and collect the many different forms and practices associated with spontaneous memorials/memorialization; see, for example: http://www.spontaneousmemorials.org/.
4 An emerging memorial practice that can also be seen as an expression of 'spectacular grief' is how football fans request to have their ashes scattered across playing fields or to have their mortal remains placed in columbaria in stadiums (Vaczi 2014).

References

Ariès, Philippe (1974): *Western Attitudes Toward Death: From the Middle Ages to the Present.* Baltimore, MD: Johns Hopkins University Press.
Ariès, Philippe (1981): *The Hour of Our Death.* London: Allen Lane.
Bandini, Julia (2015): 'The Medicalization of Bereavement: (Ab)Normal Grief in the DSM-5'. *Death Studies*, 39(6):347–352.
Bauman, Zygmunt (1992): *Mortality, Immortality and Other Life Strategies.* Cambridge: Polity Press.
Bauman, Zygmunt (2000): *Liquid Modernity.* Cambridge: Polity Press.
Bauman, Zygmunt (2001): *The Individualized Society.* Cambridge: Polity Press.
Beck, Ulrich and Elisabeth Beck-Gernsheim (2002): *Individualization.* London: Sage Publications.
Brennan, Michael (2008): *Mourning and Disaster: Finding Meaning in the Mourning for Hillsborough and Diana.* Newcastle: Cambridge Scholars Publishing.
Brescó, Ignacio and Brady Wagoner (2019): 'Memory, Mourning and Memorials'. In: Kyoko Murakami et al. (eds.). *The Ethos of Theorizing.* Concord, CA: Captus Press, pp. 222–233.
Brinkmann, Svend (2014): 'Languages of Suffering'. *Theory and Psychology*, 24(5):630–648.
Brinkmann, Svend (2017): 'Could Grief Be a Mental Disorder?' *Nordic Psychology*, 70(2):146–159.
Bryant, Richard A. et al. (2014): 'Treating Prolonged Grief Disorder a Randomized Clinical Trial'. *JAMA Psychiatry*, 71(12):1332–1339.
Burgess, Jean, Peta Mitchell and Felix Münch (2018): 'Social Media Rituals: The Uses of Celebrity Death in Digital Culture'. In: Zizi Papacharissi (ed.). *A Networked Self: Birth, Life and Death.* London: Taylor & Francis, pp. 224–239.
Carleheden, Mikael and Anders Petersen (2019): 'Introduktion til den danske udgave'. In: Andreas Reckwitz (ed.). *Sigulariteternes samfund.* Copenhagen: Hans Reitzels Forlag, pp. 11–18.
Conrad, Peter (2005): 'The Shifting Engines of Medicalization'. *Journal of Health and Social Behavior*, 46(1):3–14.
Conrad, Peter (2007): *The Medicalization of Society : On the Transformation of Human Conditions into Treatable Disorders* (1st edition). Baltimore, MD: Johns Hopkins University Press.
Danziger, Kurt (2003): 'Where History, Theory and Philosophy Meet'. In: Michael J. Kral and Darryl B. Hill (eds.). *About Psychology: Essays at the Crossroads of History, Theory and Philosophy.* New York: New York Press, pp. 19–34.
Doss, Erika (2008): *The Emotional Life of Contemporary Public Memorials: Towards a Theory of Temporary Memorials.* Amsterdam: Amsterdam University Press.
Doss, Erika (2010): *Memorial Mania: Public Feeling in America.* Chicago, IL: University of Chicago Press.

Döveling, Katrin and Korina Giaxoglou (2018): 'Mediatization of Emotion on Social Media: Forms and Norms in Digital Mourning'. *New Media and Society*, 4(1):1–4.

Elias, Norbert (1985/2001): *The Loneliness of the Dying*. London: Continuum International Publishing Group Inc.

Elias, Norbert (1991): *The Society of Individuals*. Oxford: Blackwell.

Foucault, Michel (1986): 'Of Other Spaces'. *Diacritics*, 16(1):22–27.

Giddens, Anthony (1991): *Modernity and Self-Identity – Self and Society in the Late Modern Age*. Cambridge: Polity Press.

Gorer, Geoffrey (1955): 'The Pornography of Death'. *Encounter*, October, pp. 49–52.

Gorer, Geoffrey (1965): *Death, Grief and Mourning*. Garden City, NY: Doubleday.

Granek, Leeat (2010): 'Grief as Pathology: The Evolution of Grief Theory in Psychology From Freud to the Present'. *History of Psychology*, 13(1):46–73.

Grimes, Ronald L. (1982): 'Defining Nascent Ritual'. *Journal of the American Academy of Religion*, 50(4):539–555.

Haney, Allen, Christina Leimer and Juliann Lowery (1997): 'Spontaneous Memorialization: Violent Death and Emerging Mourning Ritual'. *Omega: Journal of Death and Dying*, 35(2):159–171.

Huron, David (2018): 'On the Functions of Sadness and Grief'. In: Heather C. Lench (ed.). *The Functions of Emotions: Why and When Emotions Help Us*. Cham: Springer, pp. 59–91.

Jacobsen, Michael Hviid (2015): 'Spontaneous Memorialisation and Spontaneous Shrines as "Organic Ritualisation"'. In: Power, Memory, People – Memorials of Today. Køge: Køge Kunstmuseum, pp. 208–215.

Jacobsen, Michael Hviid (2016): '"Spectacular Death" – Proposing a New Fifth Phase to Philippe Ariès's Admirable History of Death'. *Humanities*, 5(19):1–20.

Jacobsen, Michael Hviid and Anders Petersen (eds.) (2020a): *Exploring Grief – Towards a Sociology of Sorrow*. London: Routledge.

Jacobsen, Michael Hviid and Anders Petersen (2020b): 'Introduction: Towards a Sociology of Grief – Historical, Cultural and Social Explorations of Grief as an Emotion'. In: Michael Hviid Jacobsen and Anders Petersen (eds.). *Exploring Grief – Towards a Sociology of Sorrow*. London: Routledge, pp. 1–18.

Jacobsen, Michael Hviid and Anders Petersen (2020c): 'Grief in an Individualized Society: A Critical Corrective to the Advancement of Diagnostic Culture'. In: Michael Hviid Jacobsen and Anders Petersen (eds.). *Exploring Grief – Towards a Sociology of Sorrow*. London: Routledge, pp. 205–224.

Jakoby, Nina R. (2012): 'Grief as a Social Emotion: Theoretical Perspectives'. *Death Studies*, 36(8):679–711.

Jalland, Patricia (2012): *Death in War and Peace: A History of Loss and Grief in England, 1914–1970*. Oxford: Oxford University Press.

Jensen, Anne K. G. (2015): 'Tatoveringer hjælper forældre i Sorgen over deres døde barn'. *Kristeligt Dagblad*, August 25.

Jordan, Alexander H. and Brett T. Litz (2014): 'Prolonged Grief Disorder: Diagnostic, Assessment and Treatment Considerations'. *Professional Psychology: Research and Practice*, 45(3):180–187.

Kakar, Vani and Nanki Oberoi (2016): 'Mourning with Social Media: Rewiring Grief'. *Indian Journal of Positive Psychology*, 7(3):371–375.

Kamp, Simone (2018): 'Hun filmede det urørlige: Hvorfor helvede har ingen lært os, Hvordan vi taler om Sorgen?' *Politiken.dk*, March 25.

Kellehear, Allan (2007): *The Social History of Dying*. Cambridge: Cambridge University Press.

Kerrigan, Michael (2007): *The History of Death: Burial Customs and Funeral Rites from the Ancient World to Modern Times*. Guilford: The Lyons Press.

Knudsen, Søren Egemar (2016): 'Vi Mangler et Sprog Til at Tale Ordentligt Om Døden'. *Politiken.dk*, January 26.

Kofod, Ester Holte (2015): 'Grief as a Border Diagnosis'. *Ethical Human Psychology and Psychiatry*, 17(2):109–124.

Koselleck, Reinhart (2002): *The Practice of Conceptual History: Timing History and Spacing Concepts*. Stanford, CA: Stanford University Press.

Köstlin, Konrad (1992): 'Totengedenken am Strassenrand: Projektstrategie und Forschungsdesign'. *Österreichische Zeitschrift für Volkskunde*, 95:305–320.

Larsen, Lene, Line Rettig Lauritzen and Maja O'Connor (2018): 'Kompliceret sorg og vedvarende sorglidelse – Begrebsmæssig adskillelse og sammenhæng'. *Psyke und Logos*, 39(1):15–36.

Lundorff, Marie et al. (2017): 'Prevalence of Prolonged Grief Disorder in Adult Bereavement: A Systematic Review and Meta-Analysis'. *Journal of Affective Disorders*, 212:138–149.

Maccallum, Fiona and Richard A. Bryant (2013): 'A Cognitive Attachment Model of Prolonged Grief: Integrating Attachments, Memory and Identity'. *Clinical Psychology Review*, 33(6):713–727.

Maciejewski, Paul K., Andreas Maercker, Paul A. Boelen and Holly G. Prigerson (2016): "Prolonged Grief Disorder' and 'Persistent Complex Bereavement Disorder', but Not 'Complicated Grief', Are One and the Same Diagnostic Entity: An Analysis of Data from the Yale Bereavement Study'. *World Psychiatry*, 15(3):266–275.

Maciejewski, Paul K. and Holly G. Prigerson (2017): 'Prolonged, but Not Complicated, Grief Is a Mental Disorder'. *British Journal of Psychiatry: The Journal of Mental Science*, 211(4):189–191.

Maddrell, Avril and James D. Sidaway (eds.) (2010): *Deathscapes – Spaces for Death, Dying, Mourning and Remembrance*. London: Ashgate Publishing.

Margry, Peter Jan and Cristina Sánchez-Carretero (eds.) (2011): *GrassRoots Memorials: The Politics of Memorializing Traumatic Death*. Oxford: Berghahn Books.

Mills, C. Wright (1940): 'Situated Actions and Vocabularies of Motive'. *American Sociological Review*, 5(6):904–913.

Milosevic, Ana (2018): 'Historicizing the Present: Brussels Attacks and Heritagization of Spontaneous Memorials'. *International Journal of Heritage Studies*, 24(1):53–65.

Moore, Sally F. and Barbara G. Myerhoff (eds.) (1977): *Secular Ritual*. Amsterdam: Van Gorcum.

Parsons, Brian (2018): *The Evolution of the British Funeral Industry in the 20th Century: From Undertaker to Funeral Director*. Bingley: Emerald Publishing.

Pearce, Caroline (2019): *The Public and Private Management of Grief – Recovering Normal*. London: Palgrave/Macmillan.

Petersen, Anders and Michael Hviid Jacobsen (2018): 'Grief – The Painfulness of Permanent Human Absence'. In: Michael Hviid Jacobsen (ed.). *Emotions, Everyday Life and Sociology*. London: Routledge, pp. 191–208.

Reckwitz, Andreas (2020): *The Society of Singularities*. Cambridge: Polity Press.

Reid, Jon K. (2003): 'Impromptu Memorials to the Dead'. In: Clifton D. Bryant (ed.). *Handbook of Death and Dying, Volume Two: The Response to Death*. Thousand Oaks, CA: Sage Publications, pp. 712–720.

Rosenblatt, Paul C. (2004): 'Grieving While Driving'. *Death Studies*, 28(7):679–686.

Rosner, Rita, Gabriele Pfoh, Michaela Kotoučová and Maria Hagl (2014): 'Efficacy of an Outpatient Treatment for Prolonged Grief Disorder: A Randomized Controlled Clinical Trial'. *Journal of Affective Disorders*, 167:56–63.

Santino, Jack (ed.) (2006): *Spontaneous Shrines and the Public Memorialization of Death*. London: Palgrave/Macmillan.

Santino, Jack (2019): 'Public Mourning – Displays of Grief and Grievance'. In: Michael Hviid Jacobsen and Anders Petersen (eds.). *Exploring Grief – Towards a Sociology of Sorrow*. London: Routledge, pp. 140–152.

Seebach, Sophie and Rane Willerslev (eds.) (2018): *Mirrors of Passing: Unlocking the Mysteries of Death, Materiality and Time*. Oxford: Berghahn Books.

Senie, Harriet F. (2006): 'Mourning in Protest: Spontaneous Memorials and the Sacralization of Public Space'. In: Jack Santino (ed.). *Spontaneous Shrines and the Public Memorialization of Death*. London: Palgrave/Macmillan, pp. 41–56.

Sorgvejviser (2017): 'Sorgvejviser'. Copenhagen: Det Nationale Sorgcenter'. Available online at: https://www.sorgvejviser.dk/sorgtilbud/.

Spellman, W. M. (2015): *A Brief History of Death*. London: Reaktion Books.

Stearns, Peter N. (1994): *American Cool: Constructing a Twentieth-Century Emotional Style*. New York: NYU Press.

Stearns, Peter N. (2007): *Revolutions in Sorrow*. New York: Routledge.

Stearns, Peter N. (2019): 'Grief in Modern History – An Ongoing Evolution'. In: Michael Hviid Jacobsen and Anders Petersen (eds.). *Exploring Grief – Towards a Sociology of Sorrow*. London: Routledge, pp. 21–36.

Sumiala, Johanna (2014): 'Mediatization of Public Death'. In: Knut Lundby (ed.). *Mediatization of Communication*. Berlin: De Gruyter, pp. 681–702.

Sørensen, Sofie (2017): 'Vi befinder os i sorgens århundrede'. *Politiken.dk*, April 14.

Teodorescu, Adriana and Michael Hviid Jacobsen (eds.) (2020): *Death in Contemporary Popular Culture*. London: Routledge.

Vaczi, Mariann (2014): 'Death in the Cathedral: Mortuary Practices in Sport Stadiums'. *Journal of the Royal Anthropological Institute*, 20(4):635–652.

Wagner, Peter (2018): 'Singularity: A New Key for the Sociological Diagnosis of the Present Time? – Andreas Reckwitz: *Die Gesellschaft Der Singularitäten: Zum Strukturwandel Der Moderne*'. *Archives Européennes de Sociologie*, 59(3):524–532.

Walter, Tony (1999): *On Bereavement: The Culture of Grief*. Buckingham: Open University Press.

Walter, Tony (2005): 'What Is Complicated Grief? A Social Constructionist Perspective'. *Omega: Journal of Death and Dying*, 52(1):71–79.

Walter, Tony (2020): *Death in the Modern World*. London: Sage Publications.

Wittouck, Ciska et al. (2011): 'The Prevention and Treatment of Complicated Grief: A Meta-Analysis'. *Clinical Psychology Review*, 31(1):69–78.

World Health Organization (2018): *International Statistical Classification of Diseases and Related Health Problems* (11th Revision). Bern: World Health Organization.

10

FREEDOM AND UNAVAILABILITY

The art of dying in the age of spectacular death

Carlo Leget

Introduction

On 11 August 2016, death presented itself as it had never before. That summer I had been writing an English monograph on the contemporary art of dying. Staying at my partner's house in Erlangen, Bavaria, I worked on the manuscript with a dedication and concentration that would never have been possible at my university in Utrecht, the Netherlands. When my brother-in-law had called me on 4 August, telling me that they had returned from their holidays and my eldest sister had immediately been admitted to the hospital because she had not been feeling well, I imagined it was just thoughtful of him to inform me. I was not worried, since my sister had been in good health for many years. A week later, however, my sister was dead, 50 years old and still looking as healthy as anyone who had just enjoyed a three-week vacation in Italy. She had died in a week, from an abnormal life-threatening cellular process that is generally known by the metaphor 'cancer'.

The difference between writing about a contemporary art of dying and sitting at the deathbed of my sister was like the difference between walking around a frozen lake and falling through the ice of the same lake. One is submerged into another relationship with the world. In the liminal space that is opened when one is confronted with the death of someone close, everything changes and normal life is suspended. The time one can stay in this liminal space, however, is limited. One cannot live in frozen water and the hole in the ice freezes again. Time takes away not only those we love and the memories we have of them, but also a direct access to the lived experience of existential phenomena like the birth of one's child or the death of a loved one. The experience of being confronted with death is characterised by what we might call an 'existential unavailability'.

In this chapter, I will depart from Danish sociologist Michael Hviid Jacobsen's proposition that we live in an age of spectacular death. The question I want to reflect upon in this contribution is what living in an age of spectacular death means for the way people make sense of their own death and the deaths of those who are dear to them. Reflecting upon the sociological analysis of our contemporary attitude towards death and dying, it is important to realise the qualitative difference between speaking and writing about the death from a third-person perspective on the one hand, and from a first- or second-person perspective on the other. As Vladimir Jankélévitch explains in his phenomenological analysis of death, the second-person perspective is an important access to the phenomenon of death, being a privileged middle position between what he calls the tragic subjectivity of the first-person perspective and the anonymity of the third-person perspective (Jankélévitch 1977:29). Sociology writes from the third-person perspective, death's existential unavailability imposes itself in a confrontation with death from a first- and second-person perspective.

I will start this chapter with an analysis of the five characteristics of the age of spectacular death against the background of modernity. In this analysis, it will become clear that the way we deal with death and dying in our culture comprises a number of paradoxes. Underlying all these paradoxes is the basic tension between human freedom and the existential unavailability of death and dying. North Atlantic culture hardly has tools to deal with these tensions and paradoxes at a personal level, unlike previous centuries in which people could fall back upon what was then called an 'art of dying'. Therefore, in the second part of this contribution I will ask myself what such a contemporary art of dying might look like, and how such an art of dying might deal with the basic tension between freedom and unavailability in a fruitful way. In the third part of this chapter, I will return to the five characteristics of the age of spectacular death and reflect on the question of how a contemporary art of dying is both supported and complicated by societal developments around death and dying in the country I live in.

Spectacular death and the paradoxes of modernity

Few works on the history of death and dying in Western Europe have been so influential in shaping our understanding of previous centuries as the work of Philippe Ariès. In his later work, he describes the attitude towards death through the ages, distinguishing between four phases in history, and ending with what he calls a 'forbidden death'. According to his view, we have arrived in a death-denying era, reigned over by medicine that considers death as a defeat (Ariès 1974).

Although the work of Ariès has been heavily criticised, his books remain very influential. Whether one agrees with his characterisation of four phases or not, it is clear that his depiction of the 'forbidden' death fails to take account of the developments that have been taking place in the last five decades. Since the 1970s, a number of societal developments seem to have changed our attitude towards death. According to Michael Hviid Jacobsen, our attitude towards death and dying at the beginning of the 21st century can be characterised as a 'spectacular death'. In his view, this new phase after the four phases Ariès distinguished, has, at least, five characteristics (Jacobsen 2016).

The first characteristic of the 'spectacular death' is the fact that for most people death has disappeared from our direct and daily experience even more than Ariès noticed, having developed into something we become more and more familiar with as spectators, filtered through media screens. Secondly, as is the fate of many aspects of life being put under a neoliberal regime since the 1980s, death has become commercialised and different aspects of our confrontation with death and dying have been turned into marketable commodities. Thirdly, in the wake of the efforts to consider death, dying and grief no longer as taboos, and trying to find meaning in dying and commemorating the dead, we have witnessed a re-ritualisation of death, accompanied with a decrease in the role of traditional religions. Fourthly, a transition has been made from death as the subject of the medical profession towards dealing with death and dying as an interdisciplinary approach in which many professions are involved: the palliative care revolution. As the fifth characteristic, death has become the subject of an increasing number of scientific disciplines, ranging from the humanities and social science to natural science. Jacobsen calls this the 'specialisation of death'.

If we reflect upon Jacobsen's idea of the age of 'spectacular death' against the background of modernity, we can see how these five characteristics of our attitude towards death all express a similar paradox. In order to grasp these paradoxes, it is helpful to follow the analysis of the German sociologist Hartmut Rosa on the way modernity has changed our relationship to the world (Rosa 2019). According to Rosa, the primary goal of the project of modernity was to enlarge our freedom as human beings by making the world 'available'. Countless scientific and technological developments have enabled us to make the world visible, accessible, controllable and usable (Rosa 2019:21).

Modernity has brought many blessings: by making the world available we have been able to extend the human life span, combat diseases and raise the average life standard in many parts of the world to a degree that was the privilege of few people in former centuries. But we have also paid a price. By making the world available, an instrumental rationality has become dominant and our relationship to the world has become one of reification. Combined with an economic system that is built on an imperative of escalation of growth, we are caught up in a process of continuous acceleration. Because of this acceleration, the world we live in has increasingly become 'mute': things do not speak to us anymore, but are reduced to raw material that can be used to produce feelings of happiness. Our efforts to make the world available have resulted in a state of alienation.

Looking at the five characteristics of the age of spectacular death, we may recognise the tension between availability and alienation in different forms. The new *mediation/mediatisation* of death and dying increases the availability and accessibility of depictions of death and dying, but simultaneously increases the distance to the direct confrontation with the phenomenon of death. The direct experience is replaced by the illusion of a direct experience, stripped of all existential and sensory dimensions and unpredicted effects. The *commercialisation* of death and the desire to present death as a marketable commodity increases the illusion of freedom of choice around death, and simultaneously covers up the fact that the phenomenon itself is a radical limit to human freedom, taking away the choosing subject itself. The *re-ritualisation* of death contributes to taking away the social taboo around death and dying, and increases an illusion of meaning production. What is covered up is the fact that meaning (just like understanding) cannot be produced like good client experiences can be produced, at least not on an existential level. The *palliative care revolution* paradoxically transforms the medicalisation of death from a monodisciplinary into a multidisciplinary illusion of control and mastery; by the increase of professional perspectives involved, the illusion of a controllable good death increases. Again, although there are many aspects in the process of dying that can be controlled, death as an event is marked by an existential unavailability, which is beyond any control. The *specialisation* of death, lastly, also fosters the illusion of making the world more visible, accessible, controllable and usable. All scientific knowledge, however, is third-person knowledge: not helpful for discovering meaning when one is confronted with the impending death of oneself or someone dear.

If we come back to the main question of our contribution, we now see the core of the problem raised by the age of spectacular death: according to the analyses from a third-person perspective, the developments in our contemporary culture give us the illusion that death has become more available; at the same time, however, they make it more difficult to existentially engage with death and dying from a first- and second-person perspective. The existential unavailability that was already characteristic for the first- and second-person perspective, is becoming more complex by the paradox of a 'cultural (un)availability' installed by the age of spectacular death. How then to deal with this double unavailability from a first- and second-person perspective?

In his most recent work, Hartmut Rosa has developed a theory on what is needed to address the process of alienation. For this, he introduces the concept of 'resonance', which is a kind of relationship to the world in which the world is experienced as 'speaking to us' (Rosa 2019). According to Rosa, resonance has four constituting elements: firstly, one should be touched, affected, letting the world come in and speak to us; secondly, there should be a response in the form of an emotion, feeling, thought or any other human reaction; thirdly, both that which speaks to us and we ourselves are transformed because of this resonance; and fourthly, all of this has an aspect of constitutive inaccessibility or unavailability (*Unverfügbarkeit*).

Rosa's idea of resonance is helpful for carefully thinking about both the existential and the cultural unavailability of death. The problem with the five paradoxes of the age of spectacular death is that these five cultural developments strengthen an illusion of mastery and control, but are not really helpful at a personal level because they do not address the balance between the availability and the unavailability of death in the right way. For this we need a more personal way of dealing with death and dying, something we could call an 'art of dying' that manages to avoid both the Scylla of making death available and the Charybdis of re-mystifying death. How would such an art of dying look like in an age of spectacular death?

Freedom and unavailability: Towards a contemporary art of dying

When I started doing empirical research in Dutch nursing homes in the late 1990s, one of the things that struck me was the great gap between a rhetoric of a free and self-chosen death in societal discussions on the one hand, and the questions around inner freedom of the people who made these choices in nursing homes on the other. Freedom of choice was defined as negative freedom: absence of constraints for people who were considered to be mentally competent. In other words: those patients that were not showing signs that their ability to make rational choices was compromised, were supposed to be eligible for euthanasia or physician-assisted dying, if also other legal requirements were fulfilled.

Completely lacking in these nursing homes were tools that helped patients, firstly, to develop their positive freedom, and secondly, to reflect critically on the implicit or hidden societal factors that compromised their freedom. Positive freedom can be defined as the ability to make choices that are connected with a fulfilled and authentic life. Being trained as a theologian who had just completed a dissertation on life and death in the theology of Thomas Aquinas, I started looking to history to find out whether previous centuries had a tool to help people prepare for a good death.

I discovered the 15th-century block books that had been developed after the great epidemics of what was later coined as the Black Death (Girard-Augry 1986; Bayard 1999). In this *ars moriendi*, the struggle to discern between right and wrong and make the right decisions preparing for a good death were depicted as a fivefold struggle between angels and devils. The *ars moriendi* tradition survived for centuries, inspiring millions of people preparing for a good death.

Looking at the late medieval block books from a late-modern perspective, it was clear that although they were attractive because of their simplicity and clarity, they would no longer be helpful for the majority of people living in our contemporary world. They were too much focused on life after death, too dichotomous, too exclusively spiritual and had too much moralising for the people I encountered in the nursing homes I did my research in. And yet they fascinated me and continued to do so, because they seemed to express practical wisdom that had been tested and confirmed for many centuries.

In the past 20 years, I have been working on developing a contemporary version of the late medieval *ars moriendi*, apt to help people find orientation in their attitude towards death and dying, without being confined to a specific religious tradition or philosophy of life (Leget 2017a). The project has resulted in a conversation and reflection tool that is being used in many healthcare settings in both the Netherlands and Belgium, and still the subject of ongoing empirical and philosophical research.

One of the first problems I had to solve in order to develop a contemporary art of dying tradition, was a new central goal. In its medieval version, the art of dying was aimed at preparing to enter eternal life or heaven. In order to enter heaven, one had to resist five temptations presented by demonic forces, and follow the good advice of angels and saints who helped the moribund to hold on to faith, hope and love of God. My experience in the nursing home was that the majority of patients had little to no hope for an afterlife, or sometimes even contradictory ideas about life after death. I would need to make a thorough revision of the medieval tradition, beginning with a new central goal. But also, the idea of devils and angels would need some revision.

Central to the new art of dying is the idea of inner freedom, framed in the metaphor of 'inner space' (Leget 2017a:59–78). Inner space is deliberately framed as a metaphor, in order to use a word that is not exclusively tied to one specific spiritual or religious tradition or philosophy of life. Characteristic of inner space is the ability to respond to a situation with a certain amount of inner freedom, which allows one to be aware of inner thoughts, emotions, tensions, polyphony inside oneself. Inner space is something we can experience physically, emotionally, cognitively, socially, and it also can be felt in our relation with non-human beings. It is the starting point of the art of dying, the seed of inner freedom, but as it grows, it may also be the goal of the art of dying, the fruit of freedom. It is something we all can find in ourselves if we are healthy, and if inner space is shared, it is something that helps people to feel secure, open up, connect and develop each other.

Inner space is not the same as positive freedom – the latter also requires a training of character – but rather a state or quality of one's inner life that is helpful for developing one's character and making deliberate choices. Inner space is also a concept that helps with dealing with the existential unavailability of death, because it enables one to live with tensions, unresolved questions or even a mystery that is beyond concepts or words (Jankélévitch 1977). This ability to live with a mystery helps in dealing with the existential unavailability of death. Death resists all ambitions of the project of modernity, and continues to do so, even when we live in a culture that is deeply marked by these ambitions.

In order to look how inner space may contribute to the development of positive freedom with regard to death and dying from a first- and second-person perspective, I reinterpreted the five medieval temptations and reformulated them into five existential questions at the end of life: who am I and what do I really want? How do I deal with suffering? How do I say goodbye? How do I look back on my life? What can I hope for? In 'living these questions', as the poet Rainer Maria Rilke has coined it, people who are dying can try to find their way in as moral actors, taking responsibility for their way of living and dying. These individual processes take place against the background of broader cultural developments that have an impact on what people consider to be normal and natural. In order to see how cultural developments and tendencies have an impact on individual processes, it may be helpful to simplify them a bit and present them as taking place on a continuum constituted by two poles.

Who am I and what do I really want?

Patient autonomy is a big thing in North Atlantic culture. Freedom of choice of patients has been endlessly debated in bioethics and put down in all kinds of laws and legislation. In the last decades we have seen a wide range of variations on the idea of 'patient-centred care'. At first sight it seems clear what is meant: the big questions about one's identity and freedom of choice as a human being can only be answered by patients themselves, not by their family, nor by their physicians or other care-givers. On the continuum between being connected with myself versus being connected with the others in my life, it seems clear that patient autonomy is about the first pole. Moreover, the idea of human beings as self-made independent individuals and the importance of autonomy interpreted as self-determination have been promoted by the rise of neoliberalism that has marked our culture from the 1980s (Brown 2003).

From a more philosophical perspective, however, what the human self is is not so clear as it might seem at first sight, nor are the existential choices that people make. What we call the human 'self' is a mystery constituted by a dialectical relationship between myself and the others who co-define my identity (Ricoeur 1990). The human self is not fully self-made, nor exclusively the result of external factors or causalities. Human identity is only directly accessible via the detour of storytelling and the traces of one's actions. And free will shares in this existential unavailability: we discover what we really want by discerning between the things we are in resonance with. Things we do not know, or that do not touch us, can never be something we might discover as wanting or desiring. This means that human autonomy and self-determination are rooted in a receptivity and passivity. Autonomous and authentic choices are answers to what resonates in our inner selves.

The problem of human autonomy in the face of death and dying can be framed as follows. In terms of negative freedom, the only thing that matters is to maximise the impact of the individual and minimise the input from others. For developing the positive freedom that is needed to find one's own individual and unique way of death and dying, however, this dichotomy between 'myself' and 'the others' is not very helpful since both are interrelated and integrated; there is no self without the others that co-constitute it (van Nistelrooij et al. 2017). From this perspective, inner space is of great importance: only by becoming aware of one's inner polyphony that reflects the many voices, perspectives and values that make up the human self, may our choices gain the quality of existential choices.

How do I deal with suffering?

This brings us to the second tension, which is in regard to human action and the way we respond to the situation we are in. Central to the project of modernity is the ambition to make the world available, we said earlier, in order to increase freedom and well-being and to decrease human suffering. Looking at the developments in medicine in the past century, we have been very successful in extending the human life-span for most people in the North Atlantic world and realise a better overall quality of life in terms of fighting disease and postponing death. It seems self-evident to fight diseases and reduce suffering, whether from a physician, patient or family perspective. Contemporary medicine is highly specialised and interventionist, and palliative medicine has the tendency to develop in the same direction.

From a more philosophical perspective, however, there seems to be a certain one-sidedness in the way we are inclined to react to suffering on the continuum between doing (*action*) and undergoing (*passio*). I deliberately add the Latin words here, because the word *passio* connects undergoing, suffering and being a patient. Our late-modern mindset has difficulties accepting the fact that sometimes the world cannot be made available, and things cannot be controlled. This is not to say that we should indulge in perverse idealisations of suffering. On the contrary: suffering asks for a human response. The point is, however, that responses of unlimited interventionist action and therapeutic obstinacy can become sources of human suffering themselves.

The problem with developing the positive freedom to deal with suffering is that we often lack the resources to reflect on our inclination to act at any cost and 'do something!', whatever it may take. It takes courage and inner space to take a step back from cultural expectations, and admit the existential unavailability of both living and dying. Human action is a phenomenon broader than interventions based on rational decisions. Human action is a far richer phenomenon in which doing (*actio*) and undergoing (*passio*) are in a dialectical relation, as are our conscious and our subconscious dimensions, and people who have learned to find their way living with chronic pain report how active acceptance or undergoing of pain may be a key to dealing with what cannot be controlled and is not available.

How do I say goodbye?

Neoliberalism has turned the North Atlantic world in a society of well-preserved consumers. We manage to look young and fit up to an undefined age, because ageism is a 'no go'. We are trained to pursue the things that we find attractive as consumers, hold on to them and allow them to define our identities, and replace or throw away what is not useful anymore. Because of the ever-increasing speed of the economic mills that support our life standards, throwing things away has become a skill of major importance. And although we seem to have reached the limits of sustaining this lifestyle, given the ecological problems we are facing, our skills of holding on and throwing away have been so deeply rooted in our lifestyle that they also seem to have an impact on our attitude towards death and dying. In many countries in the North Atlantic world, discussions about physician-assisted dying have come up, expressing a desire to live life as long as it is experienced as valuable, and getting rid of it as soon as it becomes unbearable or one fears that it might develop in this direction. Given the ideal of modernity that everything in life should be made available or under control, it is not a big surprise that also death is put under this regime.

From a more philosophical view, the tension between holding on and throwing away can be situated on a continuum between holding on and letting go. Both holding on and letting go can become visible in many different ways. Holding on to life without any inner space may have the character of desperately clinging to the last straw of hope, against all odds. But holding on to life may also have the character of slowly growing to surrendering life with much inner space, ready to let go of life whenever the time has come. In the same way, letting go may have many manifestations, and throwing away is just one of them. Throwing life away – often in the form of a flight forwards in order to avoid further suffering or the fear for suffering – can be contrasted with letting go of life as an authentic expression of gratitude towards, e.g. a loving God.

The point of a contemporary art of dying is not to judge or disqualify some ways of dying rather than other ways. The contemporary art of dying is meant to help people develop positive freedom in the face of death. This positive freedom requires a broader framework and mindset than the one offered to us by neoliberalism or modernity. It also asks for developing inner space in confrontation with a phenomenon that is existentially not controllable or available. How to say goodbye well is related to both one's way of doing and undergoing, holding on and letting go. It is also related to one's relationship with the past. That brings us to the fourth question.

How do I look back on my life?

In the last 50 years in many countries in the North Atlantic world, public morality has changed deeply. From traditional moral authorities like the Church, a new moral compass has been sought by anti-authoritarian and democratic movements. Instead of the external authority, people began to look for a moral compass inside of themselves, their feelings, their authenticity (Taylor 1991). Looking back on one's life, the big question is no longer 'Did I live according to what was expected of me?' or 'How will I be judged?', but rather questions like 'Did I get out of life what was in it for me?'. According to Bronnie Ware's bestseller on the top five regrets of the dying (Ware 2011), the biggest regrets are not about what went wrong, but what was left unexplored or what was not done.

One's relationship with the past can be situated on a continuum between remembering and forgetting. Remembering the past can be a great source of gratitude and satisfaction, helping one to let go of life, but it can also be a prison out of which one seemingly cannot escape. Forgetting about the past can be either a perfectly healthy way of adapting to a new situation, or a deliberate avoidance of one's personal responsibility towards the mess that one has made of one's life. Both poles of the continuum can be lived with or without inner space.

Reflecting on positive freedom with regard to looking back on one's life, and taking responsibility, North Atlantic culture seems to oscillate between either too much or too little responsibility. Too much responsibility is assigned to dying people when the idea of availability is projected on one's life; a self-made man is responsible for everything he did and he did not do. There is no possible escape here. There is no such thing as bad luck, only chances that have not been created and opportunities that have not been grasped. Too little responsibility is at stake when everything in one's past life is only considered in the light of necessary steps of self-development. There are no mistakes, let alone sins: things that went wrong have made me to the person I have become. In this scenario, every possible form of moral self-evaluation evaporates to the benefit of self-centred complacency.

This inability of modernity to deal with the unavailable is well-illustrated by the way guilt and forgiveness are dealt with in palliative care research literature. In line with trend-setting psychological research on forgiveness, unforgiveness is seen as stressful (Worthington and Scherer 2004). Because stress affects health, forgiveness is presented as a better coping mechanism that should be preferred above unforgiveness. Thus, forgiveness is relocated from the realm of morality to the realm of health. From a more philosophical perspective, however, such a relocation is highly problematic. From an ethical perspective, forgiveness seems to have a core of unavailability or grace that completely disappears from the psychological accounts of forgiveness. Real forgiveness cannot be equated or reduced to understanding, loving or forgetting; it is a creative act that transcends and transforms an economy of justice (Flaßpöhler 2016). Forgiveness is beyond the dichotomy of doing and undergoing, holding on and letting go, forgiving and forgetting.

What can I hope for?

Modernity has highly impacted our relationship with the world, as we learned from Hartmut Rosa and many others. Our attempts and increasing successes of making the world available have promoted the dominance of an instrumental rationality by which the world is reduced to what is visible, accessible, controllable and usable. Gradually the world has stopped 'speaking to us' and we have lost resonance with other sources of knowing than our rationality. In late-modern North Atlantic culture this is reflected in a decrease of the impact of traditional religious institutions on the one hand, and a rise of free and individually shaped forms of spirituality on the other. The question 'What can I hope for?' has been transposed from a collective religious key to an individual privatised spiritual question.

From a more philosophical perspective, the different ways in which people look for answers to the question of whether there is anything beyond death, can be situated on a continuum between knowing and believing. Again, the pole of knowing may present itself in different forms, such as the radical empiricist position that what cannot be measured cannot be said to exist, to the inner security of people who report having had a near-death experience and say they 'know' they have been there. Also, the pole of believing may have many appearances, from the firm testimony of fundamentalists that have banned any doubt, to the deep confidence and faith of those who trust in God's incomprehensible ways. Inner space (or the absence of it) is always colouring the many positions on this continuum.

At the core of one's position on the continuum between knowing and believing, again we find an unavailability that is hard to deal with from the perspective of modernity; we ourselves are not the ones who decide about how to situate ourselves on this continuum. What's more, many of us will discover an inner polyphony here, e.g. simultaneously denying something as traditional as heaven on the one hand, and hoping to meet a deceased daughter again in the afterlife on the other. Inner space is needed to become aware of this inner polyphony and the existential unavailability of one's own position, in order to develop positive freedom to deal with the question 'What can I hope for?'

Now we have sketched the five tensions of the contemporary art of dying and the impact of the cultural context, it is easy to see the importance of such a contemporary art of dying for the first- and second-person perspective. Contemporary North Atlantic culture has developed in such a way that not only the existential unavailability of death is obscured, but the development of the positive freedom needed to deal with our own deaths is complicated as well. In the last part of this contribution I will go back to the characterisation of our time as the age of spectacular death. How do all five characteristics of a spectacular death relate to the contemporary art of dying, and how do they impact the efforts of people who try to make sense of death and dying from a first- or second-person perspective?

The art of dying in the age of 'spectacular death'

The label 'age of spectacular death' is an abstraction based on shared developments across countries and continents, influencing our attitude towards death and dying. At the same time, there are many differences in the way people in separate – sometimes even neighbouring – countries discuss death and dying, based on differences in history, culture and mentality and often maintained by something as seemingly trivial as language and media boundaries. Therefore, in the last part of this contribution I will focus on the way the five characteristics of a spectacular death seem to be at work in my own country, the Netherlands, and how they have an impact on developing a contemporary art of dying.

Let me start by saying that I can recognise all five characteristics of a 'spectacular death' in Dutch society. I also think that their relationship to a contemporary art of dying in which positive freedom is fostered is highly ambivalent. Let us discuss the five characteristics separately, displaying their ambivalence in this respect.

Reflecting on the way death and dying are *mediated* by the media, there is no doubt that death has become a topic that has had a lot of media attention in the last decade. In the Netherlands I see two trends. Firstly, there have been television programmes like *Over My Dead Body* (*Over mijn lijk*), in which young people with a terminal disease are interviewed and filmed until their death. People with terminal illnesses and their family members write blogs on the internet, physicians working with patients in the palliative phase do the same, and there are multi-media campaigns by the government to raise awareness of speaking about one's own death. All this perfectly fits in a long Dutch tradition of fighting taboos in general, among which death continues to be a major one (Kennedy 2002).

Secondly, a lot of media attention and impact has been generated by the evaluations and discussions around the five-yearly evaluations of the Euthanasia Law, initiatives of the Dutch Right to Die Society (*NVVE: Nederlandse Vereniging voor Vrijwillig Levenseinde*) and the *Expertise Centrum Euthanasie* (the former 'Euthanasia Clinic') in order to extend the euthanasia law and a big societal discussion about elder people who are tired of life, who according to some should have the right to a physician-assisted death. This second trend fits into a long Dutch tradition of debate around active life termination that has been going on from the early 1970s.

Despite the differences between the two trends in implicit or explicit goals, what is striking is that the attitude of the general public is influenced by a mix of information and emotion. By looking at dying people, listening to experiences of family members or hearing viewpoints of stakeholders, death as a social taboo is broken. At the same time, death as a psychological taboo or the confrontation with the existential unavailability of death and dying from a first- or second-person perspective remains perfectly intact. What's more, because the pro-euthanasia message perfectly fits into the ideals of modernity (making the world visible, accessible, controllable and usable), a direct relation between the problem of suffering and the solution of physician-assisted dying is corroborated, fuelled by emotional factors like fear, compassion, sympathy and courage.

Also, the role of *science* is highly ambivalent. The Netherlands is a highly developed and relatively small country (around 17 million inhabitants) that values transparency, equality and control. From the 1980s when the societal debates around euthanasia had reached the stage in which preparations were made to change the law, big national surveys have been done to research the practice and views of both physicians and the general public. These surveys have played an important role in the development of healthcare policy and legislation based on empirical research. In the light of developing a contemporary art of dying and developing positive freedom, however, some critical questions can be raised about these surveys and their side-effects.

In the first place, scientific research is never as morally neutral as it presents itself. Research not only has the image of objectivity, telling the people how the world is, but it also contributes to creating a picture of what seems to be normal. This normalisation has two dimensions. By presenting what generally speaking is the case (normality), a standard is set with new norms (normativity). From an ethical point of view, there is a big gap between 'is' and 'ought', and ethicists who move from a description of reality to normative conclusions know that they commit a fallacious argument. From a political point of view, however, scientific research can be a useful instrument for removing the ethical dimension from a societal discussion. When research has made visible that certain developments take place and all stakeholders seem to be happy about it, why then engage further in ethical discussions? This is exactly what has happened in the Netherlands, a country inclined to solve moral problems with pragmatic consensus-based regulations (Kennedy 2002).

In the second place, reading the five-yearly scientific reports in which the euthanasia law is evaluated, it is interesting that the procedure always seems to function pretty well. Although one could come to critical conclusions based on the analyses of the data presented (e.g. with regard to the expertise of Dutch physicians in the field of palliative care; an expertise needed to be able to fulfil the legal requirement of 'no reasonable alternative options'), the reports never come to critical conclusions or recommendations.

In the third place, it is interesting that in the last 30 years the evaluations of the euthanasia law have been performed by the same universities. Even if there might be something to the argument that perhaps they have the best experience, expertise and network to do the job, from a scientific point of view this seems a suboptimal way to aim for objective and independent results.

Research on end of life issues in the Netherlands has contributed to the illusion in the general public that they have sufficient knowledge about death and dying, and know what to do when they are diagnosed with a life-threatening illness: think about euthanasia. This, of course, seems to be one-sided and ambivalent development that does not foster positive freedom. Originally intended as a last resort for physicians who were confronted with the conflict between the duty to relieve suffering and the prohibition to kill a patient, euthanasia has developed into the best researched and discussed way of dying, wrongfully considered to be a right by a great number of Dutch citizens.

What then about the development that Michael Hviid Jacobsen has called the *palliative care* revolution? Can this approach be a fruitful context for developing a contemporary art of dying in which positive freedom with regard to death and dying is promoted? Palliative care has been developed since the 1990s in the Netherlands, partly as an answer to the international criticisms on the Dutch euthanasia debates. In the last 25 years, palliative care has been developed up to a relatively high level of availability and expertise in the Netherlands. Nevertheless, the message of palliative care is far more difficult to get across to the general public than that of euthanasia. In practice we see that the great majority of physicians have integrated both palliative care and euthanasia in their practice, although according to international definitions, both are irreconcilable.

For developing a contemporary art of dying, palliative care in the Netherlands has been a very fruitful interdisciplinary context, since the palliative care approach has explicit room for addressing the psycho-social and spiritual dimension of suffering (van de Geer and Leget 2012; Leget 2017b). The *ars moriendi* or 'diamond' model (the latter name because of its visual shape) has been used in many palliative care contexts in the Netherlands in the last 15 years. It has proven to be a workable alternative for sustaining people in developing their positive freedom in a culture as highly secularised as that of the Netherlands.

Similar to the palliative care revolution, the phenomenon of *re-ritualisation* also seems to be a recent development, with possibilities for fostering a new attitude towards death and dying. In the last decade a new profession has come up in the Netherlands: that of ritual counsellor, united in a professional organisation. Ritual counsellors assist people in funerals, the last phase of life, marriage, baptism, to welcome newborns to life, or at other special occasions in life. They are a new phenomenon, filling the gap that the churches have been leaving more and more in the last decades. Because most of the ritual counsellors work as independent ritual providers, their profession is related to the last characteristic of the age of spectacular death: *commercialisation*. In this case, the rituals around death and dying especially are sold as products, commodities, cooperating and/ or competing with traditional stakeholders as funeral homes.

Conclusion

In this chapter, we have asked ourselves what living in the age of 'spectacular death' means for making sense of one's own death, and that of one's loved ones. We discovered a number of paradoxes and ambivalences in the five characteristics of the age of spectacular death. These paradoxes are all rooted in the ideal of modernity to make the world 'available' to us. We have seen that the apparent 'availability' of death, as is believed in the age of spectacular death, proves to be a misguided thought from the moment death really enters our life by experiencing the loss of a dear person, or receiving the diagnosis of a life-limiting illness.

Because of the existential unavailability of death, we have sought for a contemporary art of dying that helps develop positive freedom with regard to our encounter with death. We discussed a contemporary art of dying centred around the metaphor of inner space, and containing five existential questions that can be 'lived' in order to find authentic and personal answers around death and dying. We have seen how each of these questions confronts us with tensions produced by our contemporary culture that is so deeply marked by the ideals of modernity.

In the last part of this contribution, we have returned to the five characteristics of the age of spectacular death as they are visible in the Netherlands. We have seen that all five characteristics have an impact on the way death and dying are perceived by the Dutch general public. We have also seen that they contribute to the illusion that we have death 'in control' and made available to us. How fragile this illusion is, however, only becomes clear in the real confrontation with the phenomena of death and dying.

A contemporary art of dying could be a helpful way of developing positive freedom towards death and dying, without losing sight of the existential unavailability of death. Promoting such an art of dying, however, one cannot step out of the late-modern context of spectacular death. In order to develop positive freedom in the age of spectacular death, one will have to take seriously each one of its characteristics. With that in mind, the palliative care revolution is perhaps the best point of departure and context for finding the right balance between positive freedom and the existential unavailability of death.

References

Ariès, Philippe (1974): *Western Attitudes Toward Death from the Middle Ages to the Present.* Baltimore, MD: Johns Hopkins University Press.

Bayard, Florence (1999): *L'art du bien mourir au XVe siècle.* Paris: Presses de l'Université Paris-Sorbonne.

Brown, Wendy (2003): 'Neoliberalism and the End of Liberal Democracy'. *Theory & Event,* 7(1).

Flaßpöhler, Svenja (2016): *Verzeihen: Vom Umgang mit Schuld.* München: Pantheon.

Girard-Augry, Pierre (1986): *Ars moriendi (1492) ou L'art de bien mourir.* Paris: Dervy.

Jacobsen, Michael Hviid (2016): '"Spectacular Death" – Proposing a New Fifth Phase to Philippe Ariès's Admirable History of Death'. *Humanities,* 5(19):1–20.

Jankélévitch, Vladimir (1977): *La Mort.* Paris: Flammarion.

Kennedy, James (2002): *Een weloverwogen dood: Euthanasie in Nederland.* Amsterdam: Bert Bakker.

Leget, Carlo (2017a): *Art of Living, Art of Dying: Spiritual Care for a Good Death.* London/ Philadelphia, PA: Jessica Kingsley Publishers.

Leget, Carlo (2017b): 'The Relation between Cultural Values, Euthanasia and Spiritual Care in the Netherlands'. *Polish Archives of Internal Medicine,* 127(4):261–266.

Ricoeur, Paul (1990): *Soi-même comme un autre.* Paris: Seuil.

Rosa, Hartmut (2019): *Resonance: A Sociology of Our Relationship to the World.* Cambridge: Polity Press.

Taylor, Charles (1991): *The Ethics of Authenticity.* Harvard, MA: Cambridge University Press.

van de Geer, Joep and Carlo Leget (2012): 'How Spirituality is Integrated System-Wide in the Netherlands Palliative Care National Programme'. *Progress in Palliative Care,* 20(2):98–105.

van Nistelrooij, Inge, Merel Visse, Ankana Spekkink and Jasmijn de Lange (2017): 'How Shared is Shared Decision-Making? A Care-Ethical View on the Role of Partner and Family'. *Journal of Medical Ethics,* 43(9):637–644.

Ware, Bronnie (2011): *The Top Five Regrets of the Dying: A Life Transformed by the Dearly Departing.* Carlsbad, CA: Hay House.

Worthington, Everett L. and Michael Scherer (2004): 'Forgiveness is an Emotion-Focused Coping Strategy that Can Reduce Health Risks and Promote Health Resilience: Theory, Review and Hypotheses'. *Psychology & Health,* 19(3):385–405.

POSTSCRIPT

The age of 'spectacular death' revisited

Michael Hviid Jacobsen

Digesting death

The topic of death (in theory as well as in reality) is an awfully big, dense and almost indigestible mouthful to chew – in fact, no book will ever be able to capture or cover all the different angles, facets, depths, blindspots, curves, layers, dimensions and detours associated with our human desire to understand or solve the conundrum of death. In this way, there is no one single book about our relationship to death that may explain it all, just as we do not have a TOE (a theory of everything) about life. At the end of the day, our system of knowledge is necessarily too compartmentalised and neatly divided into disciplines such as theology, philosophy, physics, sociology, biology, anthropology and so on, which means that our perspective on the world and thus also on the topic of death will always be sliced into pieces fitting for the respective system of knowledge we are working within. Moreover, death is a difficult topic to pin down – and it is perhaps today downright impossible to say anything original about death that was not already stated by the ancient scribes and philosophers or which cannot be read on the back of a cereal box. Despite many hopeful contenders, there is therefore no *the* Book of Death around, because our knowledge will always be selective, fragmented and incomplete, because all attempts – however comprehensive and deep – to capture death will always stop short of getting to the core of our innermost fears and thoughts, and because death in many ways defies meaningful discourse.

Leaving such shortcomings and the necessary incompleteness of our knowledge about and understanding of death aside, there is good reason to suspect that we may in fact be capable of at least catching some glimpses of the way in which we live with, and live towards, death and that we may, based on available historical sources, be able to compare this to past practices and attitudes, thereby understanding the basic universality of death as well as its time-specific and culture-specific manifestations. This, I believe, has been – and continues to be – one of the main driving forces or ambitions of all those involved in so-called 'death studies' or 'death research' – to understand death as a cultural universal, but also a cultural construction. These scholars have a genuine interest in trying to decipher the way we 'do death', as it were, now as well as previously, and often based on theoretical insights, detailed empirical studies or a combination of these sources. I think there is great potential in such endeavours. When we undertake studies of death and dying (and for that matter, closely associated phenomena such as grief and ideas of immortality), we get to the heart not only of what death is all about (or at least about how we deal with the inevitability of death), but also of what human life is all about: how it is lived, why it is lived the way it is and how this relates to the status and role of death in society. Thus, when we study death, we often do so not in order to say so much about 'death in itself' (for what is 'death in itself' really besides emptiness, negation, absence and nothingness), but rather in order to try to understand how our collective and individual practices, beliefs, attitudes, rituals and emotional responses reflect the way we live in a given time and age. We want, in short, to understand death as an inseparable part of life.

To humans, death is and remains an enigma, a conundrum, a puzzle – something they find utterly impossible to comprehend or imagine. The contributions included in this volume have all provided important pieces of the comprehensive and perplexing puzzle of death and in this way, also to the understanding of the way we now – in the first decades of the 21st century in the Western world – live with, and live our lives towards, death. In the remainder of this postscript I will provide some scattered reflections based on my reading of the book's contributions and how they each in their way engage with the notion of 'spectacular death'. Moreover, as a last-minute addition during the preparation of the book, I have included some considerations on how the current coronavirus crisis might possibly affect our understanding of, and consciousness of, death and how it in many ways seems to support and exemplify the proposed notion of 'spectacular death'.

On the conception of 'spectacular death'

This book has been wrapped around what has been called 'spectacular death'. Obviously, this is only one among many other available inroads to interpreting the course of contemporary developments within what – with a term borrowed from Philippe Ariès (1981) – we might call the 'domain of death'. In many ways, the notion of 'spectacular death' can be described as an analytical tool, as either an 'ideal type' (in Max Weber's use of this term) – a purposively exaggerated and purified intellectual/theoretical construct – against which we can measure and compare empirical reality, or as a so-called 'sensitising concept' (in Herbert Blumer's memorable words) that suggests something that playfully triggers our imagination into thinking about what the real world actually looks like. Sensitising concepts thus provide us with a way to organise our experience and verbalise our understanding of a given phenomenon. I believe that 'spectacular death' can serve as an ideal type as well as a sensitising concept that makes it possible for other researchers to compare their own findings against what I have been proposing, and that they may develop and refine their own ideas and hypotheses from, or in opposition to, this concept if they find it useful. I hope that 'spectacular death' will prove useful to think with as well as to think against. At the same time, it is my hope that 'spectacular death' will neither become what Eva Illouz called a 'bulldozer concept' that completely flattens everything that comes in its way nor develops into what Ulrich Beck once termed a 'zombie category' that continues to haunt the minds of the living even though that to which it refers has been dead and buried for a long time.

My own first specific, but admittedly not very elaborate, use of the notion of 'spectacular death' – having previously preferred the concept of 'paradoxical death' – in fact dates back two decades to 2001 when I in my first published book *Dødens mosaik* (*The Mosaic of Death*) toyed with the idea – obviously inspired by Guy Debord (1967/1970) – that death in our time was fast turning into a spectacle (Jacobsen 2001). Later, I developed the notion of 'spectacular death' even further when in a Swedish anthology, I attempted to propose a sketchy update of Ariès's magisterial history of death from the Middle Ages to the present day (Jacobsen 2009). Even though my attempt was then as tentative and inadequate as it was undoubtedly bold, it nevertheless provided me with a platform for a continued aspiration to try to think more systematically about how we might conceptualise our contemporary relationship with death and dying. This led me – after a more scrutinous effort – to suggest the notion 'spectacular death' in an international publication some seven years later (Jacobsen 2016). Here I tried to outline, as we saw in the Introduction earlier in this book, a number of dominant features of 'spectacular death' such as: 'the mediation/mediatisation of death', 'the commercialisation of death', 'the re-ritualisation of death' and two aspects of the professionalisation of death under the headings of 'the palliative care revolution' and 'the specialisation of death'. Even though this listing was, and remains, far from exhaustive of all that is currently going on in our relationship with, and attitudes towards, death and dying, they nevertheless seem to capture at least some identifiable and recognisable features of how we as individuals and as a culture meet and deal with death in contemporary society. They seem to point to certain processes that reflect not only how we relate to death and dying, but also to life in general, i.e. that fact that our access to the world and many of our relationships are nowadays facilitated and filtered through technological screens; that many facets of life in contemporary consumer society are increasingly commercialised and commoditised; that a relentless individualisation, de-traditionalisation and secularisation has created a loss of meaning, a confusion of direction and a need for new types of collective, civic and communal support; and that large parts of life (including death and dying) are now left to anonymous professionals and equally anonymous systems (such as the medical profession and the healthcare system in particular).

Obviously, much more theoretical refining and in-depth empirical detail could, and indeed should, be provided in order to make the proposed idea of 'spectacular death' more convincing and substantiated. Being myself nowadays more of an 'armchair sociologist' than one, in Chicago sociologist Robert E. Park's memorable words, who gets the seat of his pants dirty by doing 'real research' (meaning empirical studies), my aspiration so far has admittedly been more conceptual and theoretical than data-driven. Therefore, it has been thrilling to see how all the contributors to this volume have provided flesh and blood to the dry bones and unanimated skeleton of 'spectacular death'. It has also been interesting to observe how a volume was published just a few years after my own first use of the notion of 'spectacular death' (Connolly 2011), albeit with a somewhat different understanding than the one pursued in my own writings. It is my contention that the notion of 'spectacular death' first of all has potential, but also that it needs and deserves much more elaboration and exemplification than what has so far been provided – not least if the notion intends to capture many more intensive and extensive dimensions of the collective 'death mentality' in the Western world in the early 21st century as Ariès did with his useful notions and illustrations of 'tamed death', 'death of the self', 'death of the other' and 'forbidden death' for the preceding one thousand years.

On the complexities of 'spectacular death'

Unless it is just going to end up as yet another addition to our ever-expanding arsenal of redundant academic jargon, any kind of conceptual invention should always be subjected to criteria of appropriateness, adequacy and usefulness. Thus, some qualifications and reservations are obviously called for when invoking such a pretentious notion as that of 'spectacular death' and especially when boldly trying to place it in the direct lineage of the historical phases proposed in the work of Philippe Ariès.

Firstly, it is important to emphasise that not all deaths are necessarily spectacular in the age of 'spectacular death'. Some deaths are much more spectacular than others (take as an example hereof the tragic death of American basketball legend Kobe Bryant whose helicopter crash was reported when these lines were written). Simultaneously, some deaths are much more unspectacular than others. In my own country of Denmark, we have approximately 150 deaths per day – of these very few, if any, are spectacular in any sense of the term. They are painful and mournful for the family and friends, but for society as such they leave little to no mark. It has always been like this. The deaths of royalty have always attracted attention, just as the deaths of the scribes or political or religious leaders have always impacted public life, whereas the deaths of peasants or workers remained culturally unrecognised. The death of celebrities has always attracted more attention than that of ordinary 'unknown' people, and this is particularly the case – as chapters in this volume by Ruth Penfold-Mounce and Rosie Smith, as well as Jacque Lynn Foltyn have demonstrated – in a society of the spectacle like ours that treats its celebrities as royalty and its royalty as celebrities. Having said that, however, in the age of 'spectacular death', even seemingly unspectacular deaths can – under the right circumstances – become spectacular, as when news reports discuss the dead body of a refugee boy being washed up on the shore, causing international outrage, when a teenager's suicide video goes viral, when an otherwise anonymous person is attacked and murdered in a public place or when unnamed individuals die from famines or disasters. Due to the worldwide accessibility of technology, this almost instantaneously stirs public outrage, creates headlines and calls for action. The unspectacular suddenly becomes spectacular, especially if it seems tragic, meaningless or could have been prevented. We also need to remember that in Ariès's work, not all deaths during 'tame death' were equally tame, and in 'forbidden death', not all deaths were equally forbidden. The same obviously goes for 'spectacular death'. As we saw in Chapter 8 by Arnar Árnarson, even two seemingly not that different cases of youth death from Iceland were mourned and memorialised in completely different ways, not least due to the different social and ethnic backgrounds of the deceased and the frames these deaths were interpreted in by the public. The notion of 'spectacular death' thus more captures potentiality and dramatic effect rather than it pointing out that all deaths are necessarily, in and of themselves, spectacular.

Secondly, following this, we need to admit that 'spectacular death' does not capture everything related to death in the real world or mirror every possible instance of death and dying that takes place. It is a catch-all phrase used more to sensitise our way of seeing and interpreting than to embody everything about mortality in a given historical epoch. It is for all practical intents and purposes an academic construct invented behind a desk by someone whose access to the bountifulness of the real world is as limited as anyone else's. As Zygmunt Bauman once admitted in his own book on death and immortality about the relationship between the abstract terminology that we as researchers (sociologists, for example) employ in order to capture the world and the world as it is lived in, uninterpreted and pristine, by people:

> We do not live, after all, once in a pre-modern, once in a modern, once in a postmodern world. All three 'worlds' are but abstract idealizations of mutually incoherent aspects of the single life-process which we all try our best to make as coherent as we can manage. Idealizations are no more (but no less either) than sediments, and also indispensable tools, of those efforts.
>
> *(Bauman 1992:11)*

This insight also applies to attempts at capturing – reducing and distilling – the specific death mentality of a given time and age such as 'tame death', 'death of the self', 'death of the other', 'forbidden death', 'spectacular death' and so on. We do not live in one age and then suddenly, as if by a snap of the fingers, in the next. These are all intellectual abstractions and idealisations concocted in the mind of the researcher who by inventing and applying such labels can create a sense of order where no order, or perhaps even disorder, prevails and who can propose clear-cut sequences, when there are in fact recurrences, overlaps, relapses, blurred lines of division and so on. Such notions are in the end nothing but constructs conceived by social scientists – they are figments of their imagination, as it were – when trying to make sense of the world as it is seen from their immediate vantage points.

Thirdly, we need to recognise that scientific terminology can be seductive, sometimes even leading its users astray. It would be against its intention if the notion of 'spectacular death' obscured more than it clarified. It would be unfortunate if it makes us look for the spectacular, even when it is perhaps nowhere in sight. It would be misleading if it makes us think that the age of 'spectacular death' inaugurates a time when all deaths are suddenly spectacular. As mentioned above, this is not the case. Nowadays, our relationship to life – and to death – is as complex and multi-faceted as ever before. Moreover, our relationship to the real world of real death is never clear-cut or one-dimensional, but there are always hidden layers, whimsical ambivalences and distant cavities that await our ability to discover and excavate them. Although the notion of 'spectacular death' has perhaps not yet persuaded many colleagues (for some recent exceptions, please see Kirshner 2018; Stone 2018; Vdovychenko 2018), there is, however, no doubt that it will eventually begin to catch on, acquire a life of its own and will be used as a scale with which to measure and compare other conceptual developments within 'death studies'. This is how it should always be – our conceptual efforts are for a large part always until further notice. They have a birth, a life and, in due time, a death of their own.

Fourthly, we need to understand that it is difficult to test and validate scientific terminology and this also applies to 'spectacular death'. It needs to be stressed that the concept is intended to be inspirational rather than verifiable. This is also why it was earlier stated that the notion of 'spectacular death' was more akin to an ideal type or a sensitising concept than something that should be tested or proven. The purpose of the concept of 'spectacular death' is thus primarily to sharpen our sociological imagination and to direct our attention to the fact that something new is currently happening within the realm of death and dying that requires the development of adequate tools with which to capture it.

Based on these qualifications and reservations (and many others could undoubtedly be invoked), it is – as always – recommended to use scientific terminology with a pinch of salt and with due caution whenever interpreting the world through the lens of intellectually invented catchphrases. It has been my hope and aspiration that the idea of 'spectacular death' might shed more light than it leaves darkness. In my view, the way we understand and interpret contemporary death culture requires an update and a refreshing look at what is going on right now, which no longer can be deciphered solely by drawing on Ariès's important ideas from the 1970s and 1980s of 'forbidden death' or 'hidden death'

(Ariès 1974, 1981). Obviously, we did not, as mentioned above, *once* live in an age of 'forbidden death', and then *suddenly* in an age of 'spectacular death'. The world of academic representation and the world of lived reality is not necessarily the same – the apparent smoothness of social transformation is in reality often a rather messy matter. When I first came up with the idea of 'spectacular death', by now more than a decade ago, I was far from sure that this was in fact the most appropriate or accurate descriptive term with which to describe our contemporary death culture. However, concepts seem to develop a life of their own. The more I contemplated and nurtured the idea of 'spectacular death' and compared it with the world I witnessed – the emerging ritual practices, the popular cultural manifestations of death, dying and grief, the media representations of death, the academic intensity surrounding the topic of death and so on – the more convinced I became that there was a new spectacularity to death that we did not see when Ariès wrote about his phases of 'death mentality' in the 1970s and 1980s. Moreover, changes within culture in general, and death culture perhaps in particular, are indeed slow and not sharply distinguishable from what went before. Thus, in the age of 'spectacular death' there are still remnants of 'forbidden death' (as well as signs of some of the other preceding phases). It is indeed difficult to understand exactly the very time and age in which we ourselves live – history is always easier understood in hindsight. As G.W.F. Hegel once insisted, the owl of Minerva does not spread its wings and fly until the falling of the dusk, meaning that it is only at the end of the day that we with some certainty may say what really went on. This goes for studying life as well as studying death. If the present is difficult to understand, the future is even more so. In a time and age when ideas of 'future research' or 'futurology' seem to be gaining increasing recognition, we must keep in mind that the future – of life as well as of death – is for all practical intents and purposes unknowable. Glimpses may be caught, tendencies may be teased out, trends may be detected, but the future as future is, and remains, an unknown territory for us. Perhaps it thus only makes sense to evaluate if our current phase of historical development deserves the notion of 'spectacular death' when we (or more likely, our successors) look back at it from a point in time in the future, but I do still believe that we may be able to say that this was indeed a time of 'spectacular death'.

On the consequences of 'spectacular death'

The chapters in this book have each in their own way shown that there are indeed significant and documentable movements and changes in our attitudes towards death in contemporary society. Although the authors are not all necessarily convinced that 'spectacular death' is perhaps the most catching or accurate umbrellalogical notion with which to capture all these different – at times mutually supportive, at other times seemingly unrelated – movements and changes, they recognise the way in which death, especially through the media, is nowadays more publicly accessible and observable than was the case just a few decades ago. Most of the contributors also express some concern that one of the main consequences of 'spectacular death' is the fact that we remain as alienated from human mortality as ever before, because we now primarily witness and know death from afar and through different types of mediation.

Several of the book's chapters deal with technology's increasingly important role in shaping and mediating our meeting with death and dying. For example, Chapter 1 by Elaine Kasket, Chapter 5 by Daniel William Mackenzie Wright and Chapter 7 by Tal Morse all illustrate how technology nowadays becomes one of the main gateways to our knowledge and observation of death. Whereas prehistoric man witnessed, touched and smelled death, we look intensely at it only momentarily and zap away again when it becomes too uncomfortable. Secularisation and the rise of the technological society – as is indeed one of the preconditions for 'spectacular death' – is also that we now seem to owe our death to another party than prehistoric man. Whereas Prince Henry in William Shakespeare's play *Henry IV* had to Falstaff insisted that 'thou owest God a death', and Sigmund Freud during World War I claimed that 'everyone owes nature a death', nowadays, it seems as if we all owe the media/social media a death. Only the death that is publicly recognised and mourned seems to really matter. Obviously, this is not entirely true. But with the number of 'Likes', 'Retweets' or posted 'RIPs' being increasingly a sign (also posthumous) of popularity and social capital, perhaps there is something to this after all. To die without being publicly missed and mourned on the internet is almost akin to not having lived or mattered at all.

Previously, our encounter with and experience of death was mostly unmediated and, as it were, 'in your face' – there was nothing standing between death and us (besides what was made available of warnings, premonitions and comforting symbolism in church iconography and the scriptures and in the rituals performed). Today, we increasingly see how our access to death is mediated and/ or ritualised through technology, but also through commodities. This is also the reason why several authors in the book have been concerned with the processes of commodification and commercialisation of death as a sign of the times. Chapter 4 by Michael C. Kearl and Chapter 6 by Dina Khapaeva both dealt with how death is nowadays being increasingly commercialised either through specific artefacts (such as the craniums adorning clothing brands and other consumer items) or through the spooky imagery that is fostered and proliferates through film productions and popular culture. This also means that death is often being used to market and sell things, and the danger thus lurks that this will lead to a trivialisation of death that takes the all-important and death-defining sting out of it. Death *is* real, and no matter how many layers of fiction or commercial glitter paper we try to wrap around it, death does happen to real people on a daily basis. In a world of fictionalised and commercialised death, death ends up becoming empty entertainment – something that does not really differ from many other experiences of life. Moreover, in such a world, nobody dies for real or for long, but they are resurrected in the next episode or re-appear in a new box office hit.

Commercialised and fictionalised death is used to evoke emotional responses in viewers, readers and buyers, but also to make these responses less painful and less lasting that those associated with real death. In what Croatian-American sociologist Stjepan G. Meštrović (1997) once called 'the postemotional society', dead feelings constantly need to be reawakened and reanimated in order to make our lives interesting and energised. One of the consequences is that death itself has become trivial and tedious. Meštrović thus observed how 'death has been made ordinary, pedestrian, the stuff of everyday experience, devoid of the rituals and collective effervescence that used to keep it sacred' (Meštrović 1997:128). Because of the loss of the sacredness of death, of its secretive and divine power, we now desperately try to make it ever more spectacular, but it seems that this spectacularisation only leads to new forms of alienation from death at the individual and cultural levels. Finally, the theme of individualisation has also surfaced in several of the book's chapters. For example, Chapter 9 by Michael Hviid Jacobsen, Peter Clement Lund and Anders Petersen insisted that 'spectacular death' breeds 'spectacular grief' which again influences our burial, mourning and memorialisation practices and impacts grieving patterns and processes. The authors showed how the rise of a professionalised diagnostic culture of grief within psychology and psychiatry underpinned this process of individualisation, thus making grief something that pertains to the individual instead of regarding grief as a social and cultural phenomenon. In Chapter 10, Carlo Leget also discussed how the process of individualisation so characteristic of 'spectacular death' has meant that dying people now lack something to fall back upon when nearing death, and that the art of dying known to our ancestors needs to be re-established if people are to find some meaning and comfort towards the end of life. This aligns with what was recently noted by Irish medical doctor Seamus O'Mahony in his insightful book *The Way We Die Now*: 'In our atomized world, death is far more shocking for us because we cannot imagine anything beyond this self, this life' (O'Mahony 2016:60). This is perhaps the price paid for commercialisation, individualisation and secularisation – that we are now left alone with death and that we are unable to accept that life eventually will and must go on without us.

But what about the future of death then? What is to come after the age of 'spectacular death'? As mentioned earlier, the future is, and remains, unknowable until we arrive safely at it. We can therefore only speculate if the future inaugurates a return to the old ways of 'tamed death', 'death of the self', 'death of the other' or 'forbidden death', or if something entirely new may be in the offing. However, we are obviously allowed to speculate freely about what may perhaps become part of the landscape of death sometime in the future, for example: will we see 'death drones' as new ways of getting rid of the remains of the deceased or as a means for scattering the ashes; will we witness a revival of ancient Viking rituals of sailing the corpse to sea in a burning boat; will we begin to transport our dead to other planets for their final rest; will we Westerners be inspired by other ethnic groups, belief systems and religions when it comes to understanding the meaning of death and immortality and how to secure the passage to the latter safely; will the intensified quest for a more climate-friendly way of life also inspire new and more climate-friendly ways of performing burials; will the demand for the self-oriented and individualistic cult of personalised funerals continue to grow, or will we begin to think more traditionally or collectively; will the funeral industry retain its privileged position in the planning and execution of the final farewell or will other types of more family-based or communal initiatives begin to challenge its monopoly etc.? The questions are many and the answers few. Whatever is going to happen, a few things remain certain. First of all, there is a guarantee that new inventions will come along the way that we never even imagined were possible – this is, and has always been, part of the technological push forward. Secondly, people will every now and then feel a sense of loss and nostalgia for the old ways, and thus try to revive or reconstruct them under new circumstances in order to create meaning. Finally, death as such will continue to be a part of human life. There is little if any evidence anywhere to suggest that we should be able to annihilate or nullify death. If we were to do so, then the meaning not only of death would change beyond recognition, but so would our understanding of what life means.

The chapters in this book have provided us with many new insights and refreshing interpretations relating to the proposed notion of 'spectacular death'. Some authors have found this concept illuminating and useful for their own way of framing their research experiences, others have been more reluctant to adopt the specific terminology, and yet others have proposed that we may already have passed the age of 'spectacular death' and moved into the age of 'immersive death' (according to Daniel William Mackenzie Wright in Chapter 5). No matter whether the concept of 'spectacular death' has been embraced or analytically has been kept at arm's length, there is no doubt that it may provide us with a searchlight with which to capture parts of the landscape of death that would otherwise have been shrouded in darkness. This, I believe, is what most concepts may hope and aspire to do – they do not tell us the whole truth and nothing but the truth about the real world, but they allow us to understand parts of it. Moreover, concepts are not in themselves the end goal of scientific investigation – they are merely intended to serve as stepping-stones in the process of exploring, theorising, explaining, and not least, understanding. Canadian sociologist Erving Goffman (1959:246) once labelled his own expansive and imaginative dramaturgical metaphor merely as a scaffold that should be dismantled again once its potential had been exhausted and its initial uses were served. Obviously, the same goes for the notion of 'spectacular death'. Concepts should never become ends in themselves, but should only serve as a means for enhancing and enriching understanding.

The Coronavirus and 'spectacular death'

In 1915 during the first months of World War I, Sigmund Freud wrote the essay 'Thoughts for the Times on War and Death' (1915/1957) dealing with how death was now suddenly making itself visible to modern civilized man [sic] in an unexpected and, to Freud's contemporaries, unprecedented manner. The essay is, in fact, a twin essay, in which the first section is devoted to describing the growing disillusion with the collapse of the *Pax Britannica* and the peaceful relationship between the imperial powers of Europe. At that time, European states had co-existed in relative peace for an unparalleled period. It is, however, in the second part of the essay that Freud more detailed dealt with the changing relationship to death in the wake of the outbreak of the Great War. It was his contention that with the coming of a world war, whose human casualties and suffering he could not have predicted when he was writing his piece, the bulwark of modern society against death would collapse and expose death in a new and disturbing manner to an utterly unprepared generation – a generation that in a historical perspective had gradually grown accustomed to witnessing very few deaths. In Freud's view, this meant that 'in the unconscious, every one of us is convinced of his own immortality' (Freud 1915/1957:289). However, with the outbreak of World War I, people's ingrained belief that they were, in their unconscious, immortal would be shattered by the omnipresence of death. Freud thus insisted that exposure to death would inaugurate a rupture in our comprehension of and approach to death in modern society.

More than one hundred years after its initial publication, Freud's essay has suddenly acquired a new topicality, this time not due to a devastating world war, but rather due to the arrival of an invisible but very deadly virus. While this book was being prepared, the world started waging an all-out war on the Covid-19 pandemic killing, by the time of writing these lines, more than 300.000 people worldwide – and still counting. Just a few months into the year 2020, everything was seemingly optimistic and calm, the world economy was booming, world leaders were primarily concerned with a climate crisis and very few anticipated an almost instantaneous break-down of the economy, of healthcare systems, of global traveling patterns, of everyday routines and our very sense of security. In an almost Biblical allegory, the Angel of Death suddenly started knocking on our doors.

We thus currently live in a global culture of fear that is fast spreading like ripples in water. The current Coronavirus crisis is very much about death – it is about how many people will die before we can control the pandemic and develop a vaccine or provide an effective cure. Until then, nobody is safe. It is also about how we can take care of the dying and dispose of all those already dead in a dignified and respectful manner despite the extreme pressures on our healthcare systems and public services. Each day has its new death toll, nationally and globally. We compare numbers of death by the nation to see if we are doing 'better' than the rest, we are told how many are currently affected by the virus, how many are hospitalised in intensive care units and how many have seemingly – stressing this continuous uncertainty – recovered from the disease. The sudden outbreak of the Coronavirus, as with the outbreak of World War I mentioned above, has testified to our new exposure to invisible sources of death and also revealed our vulnerability – as individuals and collectivities – to the panic that follows in its wake.

I contend that the arrival and handling of the Coronavirus as well as the public and private communication about it have in many ways exemplified the thesis on 'the spectacular death' as developed throughout this book. In these days, weeks and months, it seems as if death is potentially everywhere but in fact, we do not really see it. True, we now on breaking news programs – but from the safety of our living room chairs – witness how Italian military convoys remove the coffins containing the Corona dead in the dead of night, we see numerous caskets lined up in a Spanish church prepared for a mass funeral ceremony and we see mass graves on an island close to New York City filling up with the corpses of those who need to be buried quickly and who cannot afford other burial options. We are daily shown statistics, graphs and tables counting the dead, the infected and the seriously ill requiring intensive care. We are told to avoid contact with others, cough into the crook of our elbows, and continuously wash and rub our hands with hand sanitizers if we want to stay safe. The potential for death is now something children in kindergartens and schools learn about, and they are advised – by their parents and well-meaning pedagogues – to keep a safe distance to their friends and playmates. The Coronavirus crisis now suddenly shows us death on a scale far exceeding that of the terrorist attack on 9/11 2001 but contrary to this event there is not identifiable and guilty party to blame and hunt down. The culprit is invisible and, in many ways, so is death. Death has been reduced to numbers, models and precautionary measures that in many ways make real death and dying – as it is felt, experienced and mourned – disappear. Sure, we do get our daily dose of death, but it is – as always in the age of spectacular death – death diluted, death distorted, death distanced.

Due to the Coronavirus outbreaks, death has suddenly returned to us in an almost unparalleled manner whose impact we need to go back many decades to match and it has done so in a way that perfectly reflects our age of spectacular death. Mostly, Corona death is something we hear about in the news, read about on the internet or contemplate with worry within our inner citadels, while the real dying and the real dead are removed from sight and are buried in urgency and privacy. For all practical intents and purposes, for most of us there is no death, and our lives will in all likelihood go on – when the governments eventually re-open our societies – as if nothing of consequence really happened. During the Corona crisis, we hardly see any dead people although death tolls keep rising by the day. To most of us – as Jean Baudrillard (1991/1995) once famously said of the Gulf War – it is as if the Corona crisis did not cause any casualties and thus as if the pandemic never really happened. Death is now spectacular through its absent presence.

References

Ariès, Philippe (1974): *Western Attitudes Toward Death from the Middle Ages to the Present.* Baltimore: Johns Hopkins University Press.
Ariès, Philippe (1981): *The Hour of Our Death.* London: Allen Lane.

Baudrillard, Jean (1991/1995): *The Gulf Did Not Take Place*. Bloomington: Indiana University Press.

Bauman, Zygmunt (1992): *Mortality, Immortality and Other Life Strategies*. Cambridge: Polity Press.

Connolly, Tristanne (ed.) (2011): *Spectacular Death: Interdisciplinary Perspectives on Mortality and (Un)Representability*. Chicago, IL: University of Chicago Press.

Debord, Guy (1967/1970): *Society of the Spectacle*. Detroit: Black & Red.

Goffman, Erving (1959): *The Presentation of Self in Everyday Life*. Harmondsworth: Penguin Books.

Freud, Sigmund (1915/1957): 'Thoughts for the Times on War and Death', in James Strachey (ed.): *The Standard Edition of the Complete Psychological Works of Sigmund Freud (Volume 14)*. London: Hogarth Press, pp. 275–300.

Jacobsen, Michael Hviid (2001): *Dødens mosaik – en sociologi om det unævnelige [The Mosaic of Death – A Sociology of the Unmentionable]*. Copenhagen: Gyldendal.

Jacobsen, Michael Hviid (2009): 'Den femte fase – Med Philippe Ariès ind i det 21. århundrede' [The Fifth Phase – Taking Philippe Ariès into the 21st Century]. In: Anders Gustavsson (ed.). *Döden speglad i aktuell kulturforskning*. Uppsala: Gustav Adolf Akademien, pp. 15–40.

Jacobsen, Michael Hviid (2016): '"Spectacular Death" – Proposing a New Fifth Phase to Philippe Ariès's Admirable History of Death'. *Humanities*, 5(19):1–20.

Kirshner, Ghyli (2018): '*Grey's Anatomy* and Spectacular Death'. *Diggit Magazine*. Available online at: https://www.diggitmagazine.com/timeline-item/greys-anatomy -and-spectacular-death.

Meštrović, Stjepan G. (1997). *Postemotional Society*. London: Sage Publications.

O'Mahony, Seamus (2016): *The Way We Die Now*. London: Head of Zeus Ltd.

Stone, Philip R. (2018): 'Dark Tourism in an Age of "Spectacular Death"'. In: Philip R. Stone et al. (eds.). *The Palgrave Handbook of Dark Tourism Studies*. London: Palgrave/ Macmillan, pp. 189–210.

Vdovychenko, Nataliia (2018): 'Michael Jackson's Spectacular Death'. *Diggit Magazine*. Available online at: https://www.diggitmagazine.com/timeline-item/michael-ja cksons-spectacular-death.

Walter, Tony (2020): *Death in the Modern World*. London: Sage Publications.

INDEX

Ingram Content Group UK Ltd.
Milton Keynes UK
UKHW020834250623
423921UK00024B/256

9 780367 368272